Adultery

Adultery

Infidelity and the Law

Deborah L. Rhode

Harvard University Press

Cambridge, Massachusetts
London, England
2016

First printing

Library of Congress Cataloging-in-Publication Data
Rhode, Deborah L., author.
Adultery : infidelity and the law / Deborah L. Rhode.
pages   cm
Includes bibliographical references and index.
ISBN 978-0-674-65955-I (alk. paper)
I. Adultery—Law and legislation—United States—Criminal provisions.
2. Adultery—Law and legislation—United States.   3. Adultery—Social
aspects—United States.   I. Title.
KF9435.R48 2016
345.73'0253—dc23   2015031476

For Lawrence Friedman

Contents

Adultery

1

Introduction

Adultery, said Anthony Burgess, "is the most creative of sins."[1] Perhaps that is why it so frequently figures in novels and popular media. Paradoxically, however, although affairs are a major theme in literature and a major focus of gossip among the public, their scholarly treatment has been far less extensive.[2] That is particularly true in law, which is one of the best arenas in which to study the evolution of moral norms. This book aims to help fill the gap. It provides the first comprehensive account of adultery and its legal consequences in the United States, with some attention to international comparisons. The aim is to enhance our understanding of the evolution of the legal standards and social attitudes concerning adultery and to develop more informed public policies.

In essence, the book argues that the United States should repeal its civil and criminal penalties for adultery. These penalties are now infrequently and inconsistently enforced, and they ill serve societal values. Such sanctions remain on the books because American attitudes reflect a fundamental ambivalence. Disapproval of marital infidelity has increased at the same time that support for criminal prohibitions on adultery has declined. Yet intermittent enforcement of those prohibitions is out of step with international trends. And too many talented leaders have paid an undue price for conduct that bears no relationship to their job performance. Marriage as an institution is worthy of public respect, but criminalizing extramarital affairs is not the best way of supporting it.

For many Americans, the lingering role of legal prohibitions on infidelity will come as a surprise. "You've got to be kidding me," said a sixty-one-year-old man sued for adultery by an aggrieved Chicago husband in 2004. "Is this thing for real?" The answer was yes. Illinois is one of the few states that retains a civil damages action for "alienation of affection." "They say you can't buy love," noted the *Chicago Tribune*, "but one Chicago man is trying to make somebody pay for it."[3] The case arose when Stephen Cyl learned that his wife of fifteen years had met a neighbor in a local bar, and had begun an affair. Incensed, he sued. "I want them to admit what they did to me," Cyl told reporters. He sought unspecified damages for "great mental suffering and anguish." Cases like Cyl's offer a window on American attitudes toward adultery, and their relation to legal standards. Adultery remains illegal in twenty-one states, and this book explores the way that such legal prohibitions are out of sync with social practices.

Overview of the Argument

This opening chapter portrays the social context of adultery in America. An understanding of its frequency, causes, and consequences is essential for evaluating the laws that attempt to regulate it. According to conventional usage and legal definitions, *adultery* refers to sexual relations between a married person and someone who is not his or her spouse. By that definition, estimates suggest that somewhere between 19 and 23 percent of men and 14 to 19 percent of women report committing adultery, although most experts believe that the actual incidence of infidelity is greater. The causes are varied, as are the consequences. Values, opportunities, and the quality of the marital relationship all affect the incidence of adultery.[4] Some affairs are a response to problems in the adulterer's marriage or personal life, while others provide benefits such as adventure, romance, and sexual variety. Although many individuals report satisfaction from affairs at least in the short term, experts believe that "for most people and most marriages, infidelity is dangerous."[5] Adultery is a leading cause of divorce and domestic violence, and children often bear some of the costs.

Chapter 2 explores the historical roots of current prohibitions. It begins by reviewing English common law, which provided the foundations for American legal regulations. Analysis focuses on the double standard, which made enforcement more stringent for women than men, and on the difficulties of divorce, which encouraged extramarital affairs. American law largely tracked English common law on adultery, but it made the penalties stiffer. Enforcement of adultery laws became less common in the late eighteenth and nineteenth centuries. With the separation of church and state following the American Revolution and the decline in the power of religious authorities, moral offenses became a less central concern. By the late nineteenth century, the most significant legal deterrent to adultery was no longer criminal prohibitions, but rather a fault-based divorce system that punished an adulterous spouse through financial penalties and denial of child custody. Adultery was also a factor in civil damage actions for alienation of affection, and in employment and immigration contexts where good moral character was a required qualification. A final legal context in which adultery mattered was in homicide cases. If a man killed his wife's lover, juries simply did not convict, and this unwritten law was common until the mid-twentieth century.

Chapter 3 surveys contemporary American legal standards. It begins with the story of a sixty-six-year-old attorney who pled guilty to adultery in 2004 and lost his job as a consequence. This was an unusual case, but similar prosecutions are possible in any of the twenty-one states that still criminalize adultery. Infidelity can also carry workplace penalties or provide a basis for damages in cases alleging alienation of affection, and serve as a factor in allocating property and custody in divorce cases. The chapter argues that intermittent idiosyncratic invocations of adultery prohibitions do little to enforce marital vows or reinforce confidence in the rule of law. There are better ways to signal respect for the institution of marriage and better uses of law enforcement resources than policing private, consensual sexual activity.

Chapter 4 explores adultery in military contexts, the arena in which prohibitions are most frequently enforced. The discussion begins with the case of Lieutenant Kelly Flinn. She was the first woman to pilot a B-52 bomber, and was discharged from the U.S. Air Force in 1997 while facing charges stemming from adultery. Flinn was not alone. In the five years preceding her discharge, the military court-martialed nearly 900 individuals on charges that included adultery. Many more cases were handled administratively. At the same time that civilian adultery prosecutions have declined, military prosecutions have escalated, partly as a result of the increase of women in the armed forces. The chapter critically examines those prosecutions in the context of some celebrated cases. One involved four-star general David Petraeus, who resigned as director of the Central Intelligence Agency after disclosure of his extramarital affair. The case brought military prohibitions into public focus. Sixty-two percent of Americans believed that adultery should not be a military crime. This chapter supports that position and argues for the removal of adultery as a basis for military discipline.

Chapter 5 explores alternative lifestyles that frequently involve adultery. Estimates of the number of Americans in consensual multiple-partner relationships generally range from 0.5 million to 9.8 million. These relationships encompass a wide variety of practices including everything from polygamy to "swinging," in which married or committed couples exchange partners for casual sex. The chapter argues that such alternative lifestyles should receive greater social and legal tolerance. Some of these relationships have benefits that include the sharing of resources and a greater fulfillment of physical, emotional, and social needs than is often found in monogamous relationships. The chapter argues for decriminalizing polygamous cohabitation but not permitting multiple marriage licenses. This approach would remove the sanctions that have forced polygamy into isolated, rural communities, while restricting access to the benefits associated with marriage. At the same time, further efforts should be made to address the abuses sometimes accompanying polygamy, such as underage marriage, tax fraud, and domestic violence. This strategy would respect the individual privacy and religious liberty of adults who have freely chosen an alternative lifestyle while mitigating its harms.

Chapter 6 explores adultery in political contexts. Among presidents alone, seventeen have had known sexual affairs, most of which involved adultery. The chapter raises several questions. What makes politicians willing to risk so much for sex? What does it say about their fitness for public office? Why are so few female politicians involved in sexual scandals? When and why does private conduct become a matter of public concern? The discussion addresses these questions in the context of America's best-known examples of politicians' adultery, such as Franklin D. Roosevelt, John F. Kennedy, Bill Clinton, Eliot Spitzer, John Edwards, and Mark Sanford. According to popular opinion polls, most Americans think that such private conduct is relevant for public leadership positions and should be disclosed. However, Chapter 6 argues that infidelity is not an accurate predictor of ethics or effectiveness in political office. A further problem with drawing adverse inferences from personal conduct is that it encourages the media to pander to our worst instincts and diverts attention from substantive issues. Peephole journalism is corrosive not only for politicians but also for the public.

The point is not that voters should entirely disregard sexual conduct when evaluating qualifications for leadership. Rather, it is that context matters. The nature and consequences of the conduct are relevant, as are the other issues at stake. Did the affair involve illegal conduct, financial improprieties, or unduly reckless behavior? Is moral leadership a crucial aspect of the position? What policy concerns will be implicated if the politician is forced out of office?

Chapter 7 explores adultery from an international perspective. The discussion highlights the enormous variation in cultural attitudes. In France, the mistress of a former prime minister can stand alongside the wife in a state funeral; in Muslim countries, parties guilty of infidelity can be stoned, flogged, or hanged, and three-quarters of surveyed Muslims approve of the penalty. In developed countries, the trend is to decriminalize adultery and to reduce its significance in other legal contexts such as divorce and child custody proceedings. By contrast, in Islamic nations, adultery is a serious crime and enforcement is targeted overwhelmingly at women and girls. Some countries even treat rape and out-of-wedlock pregnancy as evidence of adultery. Honor killings to avenge infidelity often go unpunished. The chapter argues for decriminalizing adultery and viewing these honor killings as serious human rights abuses.

A concluding chapter draws together the themes of the book and their implications for public policy. The discussion reviews the unbecoming history of laws governing adultery—their intrusive inquiries, inconsistent application, and gender bias. With our increasing respect for individual privacy and increasing tolerance for alternative lifestyles, legal penalties for adultery seem increasingly anachronistic. Adultery should not be a basis for criminal or civil liability, employment decisions, or custody and alimony awards. Fidelity is a value, but not one that the state should police.

The Frequency of Adultery

"Life is short. Have an affair," suggests Ashley Madison, an Internet site for those interested in discreet extramarital relationships. As that tagline suggests, although adultery is as old as marriage, it has gotten easier. According to the president of the American Academy of Matrimonial Lawyers, "If there's dissatisfaction in the existing relationship, the Internet is an easy way for people to scratch the itch."[6] Adultery has also become easier as men and women work together in increasing numbers, and they can often disappear for a few hours in crowded, anonymous cities or travel quickly to other places. Contraception and abortion limit the possibility of complications. The increasing availability of pornography also has raised expectations of how "good sex should be." Greater sexual expectations have fed desires for experimentation: sexual boredom is considered unacceptable, the sign of a failing relationship, and extramarital relationships are an obvious solution.[7] On the other hand, a number of factors have curbed the rise of infidelity. The increasing accessibility of divorce has made adultery less necessary. And, as subsequent discussion notes, public disapproval of extramarital affairs has increased in recent years.

Just how often adultery occurs and how it has changed over time is difficult to pin down. The data available only involve heterosexual relationships because same-sex marriage is a recent and relatively unstudied phenomenon. The first major survey concerning adultery in the United States was by Alfred Kinsey in the 1950s. It reported that about half of all married men and a quarter of married women had sexual intercourse with someone other than their spouse.[8] One of the most reliable recent studies is the General Social Survey sponsored by the National Science Foundation. In 2010, 19 percent of men and 14 percent of women said that they had been unfaithful at some point during their marriage.[9] A 2011 survey cosponsored by the Kinsey Institute found slightly higher rates: 23 percent of men and 19 percent of women reported extramarital affairs, and those figures were comparable to those of another national survey.[10] However, such statistics are not entirely reliable.[11] Most researchers believe that self-reports understate the actual numbers.[12] As one expert put it, "People lie on surveys. People lie to present an idealized vision of themselves."[13] According to Frank Pittman, an Atlanta psychiatrist who studies adultery, "You have to realize that if someone is going to lie to their husband or wife, they sure as hell are going to lie to a polltaker. You're asking them to expose the worst thing they ever did."[14]

Studies popularized in the media have errors running in the opposite direction: these studies grossly overstate rates of infidelity due to nonrandom self-selected samples. According to one expert, there may be more worthless "facts" on adultery than on almost any other aspect of human behavior.[15] For example, a *New Woman* survey found that 41 percent of responding wives had cheated on their husbands.[16] Shere Hite claimed that 70 percent of women married five years or more were having sex outside of their marriage; Joyce Brothers claimed 50 percent.[17] Books aimed at popular audiences report rates ranging from 20 to 70 percent of women and 30 to 80 percent of men.[18] Such reports have influenced popular perceptions. Most Americans significantly overestimate the frequency of infidelity. In one 1997 Gallup poll, 60 percent of Americans thought that half or more of married women had committed adultery, and 79 percent thought half or more of married men had done so.[19]

One other weakness of the empirical literature on adultery is its failure to differentiate among various forms. We know nothing systematic about the frequency of occasional one-night stands, habitual philandering, or long-term, committed extramarital relationships.[20] But while these limitations counsel caution, the information available is sufficient to draw certain broad conclusions.

The demographics of adultery paint an interesting picture. Infidelity does not consistently correlate with religion or education, although some studies find that those who attend religious services frequently are less likely to have extramarital affairs.[21] Adultery does correlate with age, class, and gender. A woman's chance of having an affair used to be practically nil after she reached her fifties, but recent evidence suggests a significant uptick, partly due to the availability of new treatment to maintain female health and sex drive.[22] Those who commit adultery are more likely to be middle or upper class than in poverty and more likely to be employed than unemployed.[23] Separated and divorced individuals are more likely to have an affair with a married partner than are married individuals.[24] Men are more likely to have affairs than women, have a greater number of partners, and have a lower likelihood of being in long-term relationships.[25] However, most evidence suggests that the gender gap in adultery rates has narrowed as women have more workplace opportunities for travel and interaction with men, and the feminist movement has made a double standard less acceptable.[26] For example, women seem to be more likely to have one-night stands, and men less likely, than in prior eras.[27] Also, as no-fault divorce has replaced punitive laws, and women have grown more economically self-sufficient following marital dissolutions, they are less vulnerable if an affair ends their marriage and may be more willing to risk infidelity.[28] Still, as one expert notes, philandering is primarily a male activity, and when women attempt to follow suit, they often "mess it up by falling in love."[29] It is instructive that the 2015 hacking of Ashley Madison data revealed that of the site's roughly 34 million users, only 15 percent were female and only a small number of those profiles were active.[30]

Causes of Adultery

In *Heartburn*, Nora Ephron's searing autobiographical movie, the heroine tearfully tells her father about her husband's infidelity, only to be advised, "You want monogamy? Marry a swan."[31] But it now appears that not even swans are monogamous.[32] Evolutionary psychologists see sociobiological reasons for the frequency of nonmonogamous sex among humans as well as animals. For men, infidelity is rooted in the desire to mate with as many women as possible to ensure that their bloodline survives. For women, infidelity may ensure extra resources from an additional partner and a kind of "mate insurance" if their primary partner dies or deserts them. Also, women who have sex with different men can produce more genetically diverse children, which allows for adaptation to a changing environment.[33] Recent research also suggests that some individuals may be genetically predisposed to infidelity.[34]

Adultery in contemporary societies reflects multiple factors, including values, opportunities, and the quality of the marital relationship.[35] Causes vary depending on the nature of the affair—is it a one-night stand, a long-term relationship, or part of a pattern of philandering? Some infidelity is a response to problems in marriage or one's personal life; it arises out of boredom, loneliness, depression, insecurity, anger, or revenge.[36] Affairs can give people a sense of achievement, adventure, romance, intimacy, and sexual variety.[37] Part of their appeal is that they take place in settings removed from the repetitive routines of daily existence.[38] Adulterers have opportunities to reinvent themselves and their lives.[39] As one woman explained, "I was curious about other men. I was curious about who I had become. And I was angry with [my husband] and I'm afraid there was a certain revenge to this." A desire for growth and self-fulfillment can also encourage adultery. Another woman noted, "I was breaking out of years of being the Brownie Scout mother and the cookie baker and the Sunday School teacher."[40] Status also plays a role. For some individuals, self-esteem is tied to attracting members of the other sex.[41] In subcultures such as those involving professional athletes, being seen with a groupie is a measure of achievement.[42] Some individuals also use affairs as a way to get out of a marriage; others use them as a catalyst to change the marriage or to satisfy needs while keeping the marriage intact, despite its limitations.[43] Adultery is associated with more sexually permissive attitudes, but the causal direction is unclear. We don't know whether more accepting attitudes are responsible for an increased likelihood of extramarital relationships, or whether affairs result in greater acceptance of such relationships.[44]

The most obvious reason for adultery among married individuals is dissatisfaction with the marital relationship.[45] In one large national survey, participants who reported that they were "not too happy" with their marriage were almost four times more likely to report extramarital affairs than those participants who responded that they were "very happy" in their marriages.[46] Emotional disconnection is one of the most commonly cited causes of infidelity.[47] Another is a decline in frequency of sexual activity, especially for men.[48] Many therapists view adultery as a symptom of a troubled relationship, not its source.[49] Rather than work through their problems, parties seek escape from them.

However, not all infidelity is related to marital unhappiness; it sometimes reflects opportunity structures and is more the cause of marital difficulties than the effect.[50] In one survey, over half of the men and a third of the women engaged in extramarital affairs rated their marriage as happy or very happy.[51] In a famous scene from the 1989 film *When Harry Met Sally*, Harry tells his best friend, Jess, that his wife has just left him for a tax attorney. Jess responds, "Marriages don't break up on account of infidelity. It's just a symptom that something else is wrong." Harry responds, "Oh really? Well that 'symptom' is fucking my wife."[52]

Even strong relationships can experience infidelity if the right opportunities come along. For example, individuals who engage in sex with coworkers or one-night stands while traveling are not necessarily dissatisfied with their marriages.[53] As one man explained, "I really don't see what's so bad about having a few affairs every now and then. . . . I just do it for the fun of it. . . . It doesn't mean I don't love [my wife] anymore, because I do."[54] Another husband in his forties described entering into an affair with a coworker as almost involuntary. "I actually really enjoyed just kind of talking with her. I didn't really want the relationship to move beyond where it was." He didn't envision his weekly lunches with the woman evolving into "this sexual thing."[55]

Most evidence suggests gender differences in the motivations for adultery. For example, in one study, 56 percent of men who entered into affairs said they had happy or very happy marriages, compared with 30 percent of women.[56] Men's dominant explanation for sexual affairs was that they developed through sexual attraction that was relatively independent of the marriage. For many, sexual engagement with another person did not reduce their love for or emotional attachment to their wives.[57] For men, the strongest predictor for having an affair was their attitude toward monogamy. For women, it was marital unhappiness.[58] When one survey asked what would justify affairs, women were more likely to list emotional factors, such as love, intimacy, sharing, and companionship. They "want to be wanted," as the adulterous heroine in the 2015 novel *Hausfrau* put it.[59] By contrast, surveyed men were more likely to cite sexual justifications, such as novelty, change, experimentation, and curiosity.[60] In another study, over half of women, but only about a quarter of men, were in love with their extramarital partner.[61] For some men, the "other woman" functions as a "trophy."[62] Such reasons are less common for women. On average, women characterized their affairs as more emotional than sexual, and men characterized their affairs as more sexual than emotional.[63] In one survey, twice as many women cited romance as their reason for having an affair as those who cited sex.[64] In another study, men's most common reason for an affair was sexual fulfillment; women gave equal emphasis to friendship and a feeling of being loved.[65] Women see affairs as a path to independence more often than men do. As one woman put it, "This is the one thing I know I am not doing for anyone else. I am not taking care of anyone, this is for me."[66] Although, as noted earlier, gender differences are decreasing when it comes to sex without emotional involvement, a gap still remains. Men are more open to short-term sexual affairs than women and more often attribute their involvement to a need for sexual variety.

Although most research focuses on what drives married individuals to seek affairs, some studies focus on what motivates single individuals to participate in them. Laurel Richardson's study, presented in *The New Other Woman*, found that a few women deliberately looked for married men. As one explained, "I get a relationship in which I can feel special to someone without having to make a commitment."[67] Another woman felt that she was "not taken for granted as you are when you become a wife." A third woman was blunter: "I frankly don't want a lot of the crap that goes with marriage. I like having my independence." In the first episode of the British television series *Mistresses*, one woman who was having an affair with a married colleague explained to her friends that husbands were desirable because they were already "bedroom trained. They're low maintenance and you have a ready exit strategy. No mess, no fuss." However, most women in Richardson's study did not intentionally choose a married man; they happened into their relationships by accident. As women age, the pool of available single men becomes smaller and smaller, and many of those men prefer younger partners.[68]

What was in it for the other woman? For some in low-paying jobs, "involvement with a married man [was] an integral part of an economic survival strategy." For others, it was the sex. As one woman put it, "Why bother being with a man unless the sex is good? There is no other point. Women are nicer people. They're better friends, more loyal, warm and they have much more empathy than men. So the only point in having a relationship with a man is good sex." But for many couples, it was not the "sexual aspect" that kept them together.[69] It was emotional intimacy. In one study of some 250 women who had affairs, when asked what they considered to be the most important aspect of their relationship, the response was not sex but communication. One woman explained, "I needed companionship and someone to make me feel special. The sex was just thrown in."[70]

Consequences

The consequences of infidelity vary widely. Many adulterers report considerable satisfaction, at least in the short term. In one study, 80 percent felt some or a lot of happiness. Affairs offer a sense of validation and "being alive" that is missing in some marriages.[71] As one woman explained, "My husband was pompous, heavily involved in his career [and] didn't think a wife had a life beyond the Hoover. So this affair . . . was a boost to my ego and appearance."[72] Another woman, also the wife of a workaholic uninterested in sex, regained a sense of herself as someone others might desire. Her lover made her "feel pretty and wanted again."[73] Some evidence suggests that long-term adulterous relationships are, on average, more psychologically fulfilling than marriage. With none of the social and legal supports that buttress marriage, adulterous relationships that endure do so because they are right for the couple.[74] There is also pressure on participants to be on their "best behavior." Forty-two percent of women report better sex in extramarital affairs; men engage in more extensive courting.[75] The other woman often "bends over backwards trying to please." As she reasons, "no man would want to leave his wife for yet another 'nag.' "[76] She may also be particularly conscious of the need to accommodate her partner's sexual needs. As one study noted, "If the other woman won't allow him to be sexually adventurous, then what the hell does he need her for? He can be bored at home."[77]

For a small percentage of couples, affairs also strengthen their marital relationship.[78] Henry Gauthier Villars, a nineteenth-century Parisian rake, explained in a famous quip, "Adultery is the foundation of society, because in making marriage tolerable, it assures the perpetuation of the family."[79] Sometimes the "escape valve of a little romping is all that one of the pair needs to shake them back into the sanity of reality and what they could lose in the way of history, family, friends, and financial well being." An affair can also be a catalyst for necessary change. One wife viewed the day she found out about her husband's infidelity as "the best and worst day of my life." Some couples find that their relationships are "stronger now than a lot of other marriages that haven't been tested in this way."[80] Marriage therapists agree. Somewhat surprisingly, many do not view infidelity as one of the worst things that can happen to a relationship. In one survey, therapists ranked having an affair only ninth in terms of damage done to a marriage, after issues like poor communication and unrealistic expectations.[81] If a couple decides to stay together, honest dialogue about the affair makes their relationship more likely to last.[82] If they decide to separate, their next relationships may have a greater chance of survival because of what they have learned about themselves and their behavior in their previous relationship.[83]

For most couples, however, outcomes are less positive.[84] Pamela Druckerman's cross-cultural study of adultery found that "when Americans do cheat, it gets very messy. . . . Adultery crises in America last longer, cost more and seem to inflict more emotional torture than they do in anyplace else I visited."[85] Infidelity diverts time and energy away from the marital relationship and often causes considerable guilt and anxiety among straying spouses. Some studies find that in about two-thirds of cases, the innocent spouse finds out about the affair.[86] The results can be devastating. Wives of philanders frequently suffer post-traumatic stress disorder.[87] For many spouses, adultery undermines self-esteem and trust. As one woman put it, "The hardest part to deal with was not the infidelity itself but the fact that he had lied to me for two years. I still cannot forget this. . . . Since that day I have loved my husband a little less."[88] Obsession with the affair can leave spouses "bitter and often alone. Some become lifelong victims."[89]

Many spouses experience "inner mortification and social ridicule."[90] Such humiliation can be compounded by a sense that their competitor is inadequate. As one husband put it, "I wouldn't mind so much but he seemed so dull and stupid. Why did she have to choose him, for God's sake?"[91]

Some spouses respond by being hypervigilant, monitoring their partner's every move. For one wife, "The worst aspect of the whole experience was becoming a suspicious person. I hated the woman I had become, going through the rubbish, the computer, his mobile phone."[92] To be on the receiving end of such suspicion can be even worse. One woman described the aftermath of her affair as "suburban purdah." Her husband checked her phone bills, searched her purse, and installed a tape recorder in her car.[93] Some vestiges of the traditional double standard still linger, and they influence both cultural and legal reactions to infidelity. Women caught having an affair suffer more guilt and more damage to their reputations than men.[94]

Because betrayal is "threatening, psychologically and financially, . . . some spouses turn a blind eye"; the result is a "complex dance of deceit and denial by both partners." Wronged spouses may "refuse to join up the dots because they are afraid of what they might see. Once the secret is out, they cannot avoid dealing with the consequences: confrontation, possible separation, [and] public shame." Family and friends often assist in the process by remaining willfully ignorant themselves. They don't want to get "drawn into the drama, be forced to take sides, appear the sanctimonious prig or the bearer of bad news."[95]

When spouses acknowledge affairs, their relationship may never recover. Adultery is the strongest predictor of divorce.[96] In some studies, infidelity increases the likelihood of divorce approximately two to three times. In one survey, more than half of individuals who engaged in extramarital affairs divorced or separated from their spouse.[97] After the discovery of adultery, men are more likely to divorce their wives than wives are to divorce their husbands.[98] Of course, it is important not to confuse correlation with causation. As noted earlier, adultery is often more a symptom than a source of marital difficulties. But in many cases, it may be the final straw that terminates a troubled relationship. And when the affairs don't work out, the adulterous spouse is left alone, as in *Hausfrau*, with what was simply a "mistake masquerading as love."[99]

Moreover, divorce is not the worst outcome of adultery. Adultery or suspicion of adultery is a frequent cause of domestic violence and the principle motivating factor in a majority of cases of homicide of wives by husbands.[100] Men are more jealous than women and more likely to respond with violence.[101] Women retaliate in other ways. One wife packed her husband's belongings into crates and had them delivered to his office with the word "adulterer" scrawled across the top.[102] Women's jealousy is greater when their rivals are more physically attractive; men's jealousy is greater when their rivals are higher in social status and resources. Evolutionary psychologists have suggested that men are more concerned with sexual infidelity than women because it jeopardizes their reproductive success. Women are more concerned with emotional infidelity and the risk of having to share their partner's resources with another woman. Many studies have found that jealous men focus more on the sexual aspects of their spouse's affairs and that jealous women focus more on the emotional aspects.[103] As one woman put it, "I don't mind if he fucks them as long as he doesn't talk to them."[104]

Innocent spouses are not the only casualties of adultery. Children also suffer. Of all the lies associated with affairs, the lies that parents tell themselves about children are among the most disturbing. In one study, only about a quarter of the parents said that their decision to start the affair had been inhibited by the possibility of hurting their children should something go wrong. Even fewer said that such worries had influenced their decision to continue the affair once it had started.[105] Parents want to believe that their children are "too young to understand what is happening." A common assumption is that "they cannot see what is going on" or "it doesn't concern them." The facts suggest otherwise. Parental infidelity can have a profound impact on children. When an affair is discovered, "the emotional explosion ripples through the house. Both parents are likely to be preoccupied, . . . and have limited resources for dealing with yet more stress from their children who are likely to be more demanding than usual." Children's reactions vary with age. Young children need more time and attention, so they are particularly vulnerable to neglect. Older children are more likely to learn about the affair and to be forced to take sides or be drawn into parental conflicts.[106] A child who carries a secret can "blackmail the unfaithful parent," which, experts note, is "an extremely destructive way for a child to learn about power."[107] Even adult children may find it difficult to trust and respect parents who lied to them about affairs.[108]

The other woman may fare no better. Some research finds that fewer than a quarter of adulterers leave their marriage for their lover, and those new relationships are unlikely to endure.[109] In one study, over a third of single women involved in affairs reported that they were "sad and lonely." Many worried that their relationships were "going nowhere" or felt shortchanged by how things turned out.[110] As one woman noted, "I was fooling myself. I thought he could be depended upon for the big things—that he would be there if I really needed him. He wasn't." For some women, the comparison to their lovers' wives was a source of discontent. As one woman candidly acknowledged, "I wanted so desperately to be a wife. His wife. God, anybody's wife. I began to feel ashamed and useless and used. Damn it, *used.*" Many women rejected the idea of having another affair. One woman put it bluntly: "Too much denial. Too much repression. Too much pitying yourself."[111] In *Never Satisfied: How and Why Men Cheat,* Michael Baisden's advice to the other woman is to "pack her emotional and sexual suitcase and find a man of her own. . . . In the ruthless game of cheating, there are no romantic conclusions or happy endings, only rude awakenings and hard lessons."[112]

Although some women didn't like the feeling of being in competition with another woman, most managed not to think about it or feel guilt about their relationship. The dominant attitude was that the wife "was his problem. If he wanted to lie, that was on his conscience." These other women tried to avoid feeling jealous. "I know he sleeps with her," explained one, "but it doesn't mean anything. It's a habit like brushing your teeth." One woman even made it a point "not to know [the wife's] first name. I didn't want it to become that personal." But much as they tried to distance themselves from the wives, many single women faced the stigma of being labeled as "home wreckers" even though their male partners were the ones who were cheating on their spouses.[113]

Public Opinion

Popular opinion polls on adultery show a striking consensus: over 90 percent of Americans consider it wrong.[114] At the same time that disapproval of premarital sex and gay sex has diminished, disapproval of infidelity has increased.[115] Eighty percent of Americans say adultery is "always wrong," compared with 70 percent in 1970.[116] Among college-educated individuals, the rate of disapproval has grown from half in the mid-1970s to three-quarters in 2010.[117] Some commentators believe that as divorce has become easier and more acceptable, the justification for adultery has weakened.[118] Ninety-nine percent of married Americans say that they expect sexual exclusivity from their spouse.[119] Close to half of individuals say that they would leave their spouses if they committed adultery.[120]

Some, but not all, surveys suggest that the double standard has largely vanished. About the same percentage who say that marital cheating by men is morally wrong say the same about cheating by women.[121] Other polls find a slight gender gap in attitudes. At the time of their first marriage, 94 percent of women and 84 percent of men believe they should be faithful.[122] Slightly more women than men (72 percent versus 66 percent) view it as a "very serious moral problem" if a wife cheats on her husband. When the adulterer is male, even more women (77 percent) than men (66 percent) think that it is an extremely or very serious moral issue. About two-thirds of Americans know someone who has committed adultery, and men and women evaluate that behavior differently.[123] Men tend to view adultery by either sex the same; 43 percent said that adultery hadn't lowered their opinion of the straying husbands and 41 percent said it hadn't lowered their opinion of straying wives. Women, by contrast, were much harder on men than on their own sex. Thirty-nine percent said adultery hadn't affected their opinion of unfaithful wives, compared with only 27 percent who said it hadn't affected their opinion of wandering husbands—70 percent had lowered their opinion of the men in question. As one expert explained, more women than men assume that women who cheat must have been provoked.[124]

Political ideology affects responses: 2 percent of Republicans, 5 percent of Independents, and 10 percent of Democrats said they were willing to accept adulterous relationships.[125] Republicans (84 percent) are more likely to think of the adultery as a serious moral issue than Democrats (74 percent) or Independents (66 percent).[126]

A clear and commanding majority of Americans also view adultery as one of the most serious moral offenses. In a Pew Research Center poll, adultery was ranked as worse than cheating on taxes, alcoholism, and smoking pot.[127] In a *TIME* / CNN poll, it ranked worse than prostitution.[128] An Angus Reid Public Opinion poll found only pedophilia to be more widely condemned.[129] When asked if adultery is an unavoidable part of married life, 72 percent said no.[130] In a survey of twenty-four countries, disapproval of adultery was stronger in the United States than anywhere else except Ireland and the Philippines.[131] Despite this strong condemnation, most Americans, typically between two-thirds and three-quarters, agree that adultery should not be a crime.[132]

When asked if adultery should disqualify a person from certain positions, Americans are divided. In 2009, respondents to a CNN poll were almost exactly split on whether adulterers lacked the "personal character and integrity" to hold a political office.[133] In a 2007 *Newsweek* poll, 43 percent of Americans said they wouldn't vote for a candidate who had an extramarital affair.[134] Forty-six percent of those surveyed in another 2007 poll would not mind much if a presidential candidate was known to have had an affair.[135] However, in the face of a concrete case, the public is less divided. In 1999, in the wake of President Clinton's adulterous affair with White House intern Monica Lewinsky, almost three-quarters of Americans (72 percent) said that adultery should not disqualify a person from the presidency.[136] As Chapter 6 notes, after the House of Representatives voted to impeach him, Clinton's national approval rating jumped 10 points to 73 percent, one of the highest levels ever.[137]

As to other positions, respondents said that adultery should not disqualify a person from being a CEO (72 percent), congressperson (66 percent), schoolteacher (59 percent), or military general (64 percent), but that it should disqualify an individual from being a member of the clergy (67 percent).[138] When asked if adultery should be grounds for dismissal from positions involving unequal power relationships, a majority of Americans said yes for a professor whose affair was with a student (73 percent), a military officer whose affair was with someone of lower rank (55 percent), and a boss whose affair was with an employee (55 percent).[139] The majority of Americans did not think that adultery should be grounds for dismissal in the case of a married military member whose affair was with a civilian (63 percent) or where two coworkers were involved (61 percent).

Implications

When told that I was working on a book on adultery, colleagues' first question was most often, "What is your take?" My response was, "I'm against it, but I am also against making it illegal or a factor in employment, military, custody, immigration, and related contexts." To understand why, the chapters that follow begin with a discussion of the evolution of laws governing adultery and then examine their current application.

2

Legal History

With marriage came adultery, along with social and legal condemnations of the practice. One of the best ways to understand the evolution of moral norms and practices governing infidelity is through a legal lens. The law governing extramarital relationships has given meaning to sexual norms and has reinforced sexual inequality. Legal doctrine has functioned as a form of moral theater, in which judges and juries have sought to reconcile competing desires for sexual fulfillment and family stability.[1] This historical backdrop sheds light on the current role of adultery law, in which formal sanctions remain but are inconsistently and infrequently enforced.

Prohibitions on adultery figure in virtually all ancient codes. Because extramarital sex could "adulterate" the bloodline of a family, the traditional focus was on infidelity involving a married woman. A married man's infidelity with a single woman was often seen as a lesser offense, and sexual double standards that disadvantaged women were persistent and pervasive. Prohibitions date from around 2250 BCE. The

Code of Hammurabi, which governed the tribes in Babylonia, specified death as the punishment.[2] The Assyrian code also prescribed death for the adulterous couple, and gave a man who caught his wife in the act the right to kill her immediately.[3] Egyptian law prohibited infidelity by both the husband and the wife, but unfaithful wives were punished more severely.[4] The Hindustani Laws of Manu, promulgated at least 200 years before the birth of Christ, were particularly severe; for a woman, the punishments included being devoured by dogs in a public place.[5] The Bible's Ten Commandments included a prohibition on adultery, as did Roman law, which punished wives more severely than husbands.[6] Against this backdrop, English common law developed detailed civil and criminal standards governing adultery, which provided the foundations for American law.

English Legal Prohibitions

English common law followed Biblical definitions of adultery and prohibited sexual intercourse by a married woman with a man other than her husband. The marital status of the man was irrelevant. Sexual intercourse between a married man and an unmarried woman constituted the lesser offense of fornication.[7] However, except during a brief period under the rule of Oliver Cromwell, when adultery was a capital offense, the common law treated adultery as a crime only if it was open and notorious, and therefore a public nuisance.[8]

Other forms of adultery were only considered a private wrong, the tort of criminal conversation. The tort was oddly named; it involved neither a crime nor conversation. That doctrine permitted a husband to sue his wife's lover in civil courts for damages. In order to come within civil courts' jurisdiction, which was initially limited to property loss, the crime was originally described as damaging a husband's property interest in his wife's services.[9] The higher the husband's social status, the greater the monetary penalty. Wives had no corresponding rights. Under the common-law doctrine of coverture, a woman lost all legal rights upon marriage, when her identity merged with that of her husband. Accordingly, in criminal conversation cases, wives could not sue for damages for adultery by their husband; nor could they testify in suits against them, even though it was their reputation that was at risk.[10] Although women in these cases were faulted for having "lept the Fence of Virtue and Chastity," they were often presented as passive victims who had fallen prey to the "crafty snares of the Defendant."[11]

English ecclesiastical courts defined adultery more broadly than did the common law. For those courts, the evil of extramarital sex was not so much the chance of spurious offspring as the breach of marital vows. Accordingly, the law was gender neutral; married persons, male or female, were guilty of adultery if they had sex with someone other than their spouse.[12] An unmarried person who had sex with a married man or woman was guilty only of fornication. A charge brought in 1723 conveys the nature of the crime: Thomas Aleway, "not having God before his eyes, but moved and seduced by the instigation of the devil . . . wickedly, impurely, flagitiously and diabolically tempted, incited and solicited one Anne, then and still being the wife of . . . Owen Blower . . . to fly from . . . Owen and to commit adultery with the aforesaid Thomas Aleway. . . . And that the same Thomas Aleway . . . in adultery lived; to the great displeasure of Almighty God . . . and to the evil example of all others in like case transgressing."[13] History does not record the sentence.

The most severe penalty for adultery in the ecclesiastical courts was excommunication, but the more standard sanction was public penance.

The adulterer, clad in a white sheet, would make a confession of the crime in the church or marketplace.[14] Difficulties of proof were overcome through presumptions. Suspicious circumstances, public notoriety, and the character and reputation of the accused were all relevant. A woman and man being alone in a "suspected place kissing and embracing each other in a very immodest posture" was sufficient to raise "vehement suspicion." Allegations in adultery suits included references to "indecent behavior," "extraordinary familiarities," and "scandalous conversation."[15]

As a means of controlling infidelity, the system left much to be desired. Procedures were cumbersome, and a guilty party could avoid penance by payment of a fine or bribe.[16] By the late seventeenth century, jurisdiction over sexual misconduct was transferred to the local courts, and by the mid-eighteenth century, prosecutions for adultery had become increasingly rare.[17]

Actions for criminal conversation were more common and sometimes subject to abuse. Until the action was abolished in 1857, there were cases of connivance in which husbands and wives conspired together to trap a wealthy man in the act of seduction and sue him for damages. The notoriety that accompanied criminal conversation trials provided the public with a ready store of titillating gossip, and the threat of a suit was an incentive for blackmail. A pamphlet reporting on a prominent criminal conversation trial in 1692 set the tone for future publications by including a maidservant's detailed description of the accused practicing coitus interruptus with the Duchess of Norfolk. In 1782, publicity for such pamphlets promised that they had "all the interesting scenes fully, minutely and circumstantially displayed" and were "teeming with such extraordinary incidents as to awake the curiosity of the most incurious reader."[18]

English Divorce and the Double Standard

The difficulty of divorce under English law made adultery more common. Until the mid-nineteenth century, divorce with the possibility of remarriage was available only by act of Parliament. In theory, it was available for husbands whose wives committed adultery, but in practice it was limited to the very wealthy. Before the law was changed in 1858, there were fewer than 300 divorces, and only four granted to women.[19] Other individuals could sue in the ecclesiastical courts for a separation from bed and board, which was available in cases of adultery or life-threatening cruelty.[20] Many of those who separated from their spouses lived with new partners in a state of open adultery. Some remarried because bigamy, although punishable as a felony, was infrequently prosecuted and sanctions were mild in the absence of fraud.[21] As one judge put it, couples who had "hurt no one" should be "free from the vexatious interference of the law."[22]

Social conventions treated women's and men's infidelity very differently. A single act of adultery by a wife was an unpardonable breach because it introduced the possibility of spurious offspring. A mother found guilty of adultery was by definition considered unfit to have custody of her children. By contrast, as historian Lawrence Stone puts it, adultery by the husband was regarded as a "regrettable but understandable foible, rather than a serious threat to a marriage, and therefore was something best ignored by a prudent wife."[23] Given their legal and economic disabilities, many women had little choice but to tolerate infidelity.[24] Studies of church records in early London found that women were much less likely than men to cite adultery as a cause for divorce. The reason was not that husbands were more faithful, but rather that male sexual sins were not of themselves considered sufficient cause to grant a divorce.[25]

The double standard was grounded in public attitudes and social practices. Royalty set an example. From the middle ages until the late nineteenth century, kings of England and Europe commonly took at least one mistress, and these women frequently received titles and social prominence.[26] Edward VII invited several of his mistresses to his coronation. They were seated in what was known at the time as the "king's loose box." Another mistress was allowed to be present at the king's deathbed. In the colonies, British husbands often took local mistresses and kept their wives and families at homes in Great Britain. The diaries of the eighteenth-century lawyer and writer James Boswell offer an illuminating portrait of sexual mores among the prosperous classes in that period. In addition to patronizing brothels, Boswell had at least six mistresses, who produced at least two illegitimate children. He died of venereal disease and the mercury pills he took to combat it.[27]

The class system compounded the injustice of the double standard. For the aristocracy, in an era of marriages dictated by concerns of wealth and social standing, the availability of a mistress provided rich men companionship of their own choosing. Lower-class women who worked in factories and domestic service were prey to unwelcome advances by supervisors and masters. Refusals could result in dismissals, but so could pregnancy, which left poor women in a no-win position.[28]

The double standard was grounded not only in concerns about illegitimacy, but also in women's traditional common-law status as the property of husbands and in their presumed natural tendency toward greater virtue and delicacy than men.[29] For a husband, to be a cuckold meant ridicule and disrespect: he was viewed as unable to control his own household.[30] The Matrimonial Causes Act of 1857 codified the double standard. It gave husbands grounds for divorce based on a wife's single act of adultery; wives only had grounds in cases of aggravated adultery (adultery coupled with cruelty, rape, sodomy, bigamy, or unwarranted desertion). Supporters of this approach argued that it would be too harsh to punish husbands who were merely "a little profligate."[31]

The unfairness of the double standard came to public attention with the struggles of Caroline Sheridan Norton, whose husband sued Prime Minister Lord Melbourne in 1836 for having an adulterous relationship with her. Norton's husband also barred her from their home and from seeing their children. Norton was not able to divorce her husband nor to testify in her own defense in the adultery case. Neither was she entitled to support while they were separated. In a series of widely circulated pamphlets, Norton assailed the injustice of the law that enabled an adulterous wife to be discarded, but not an adulterous husband.[32] However, it was not until 1923 that English law abolished the double standard and gave wives the same right as husbands to sue for divorce on grounds of simple adultery.[33]

With the erosion of the double standard in matrimonial proceedings came the rise of collusive divorces and fabricated adultery. In the typical case, a woman was hired for a trip to a seaside hotel with no obligations except to be seen by an obliging chambermaid while in bed with the husband before breakfast.[34]

But the double standard continued to flourish in other contexts. It had long been established as a defense for murder in situations in which the husband encountered another man making love to his wife. The assumption was that, in the heat of passion, the husband could justifiably lose self-control and kill his wife's lover, and therefore he deserved a lesser penalty such as manslaughter or no penalty at all.[35] Juries typically refused to convict in such cases, a practice that became known as the "unwritten law."

The press delighted in such adultery proceedings, and coverage was so explicit that Queen Victoria inquired of her lord chancellor whether steps could be taken to prevent such publicity. In her view, the details were of "so scandalous a character that it makes it almost impossible for a paper to be trusted in the hands of a young lady. . . . None of the worst French novels can be as bad as what is daily brought and laid upon the breakfast table of every educated family in England, and its effect must be most pernicious to the public morals of the century."[36] Defenders of such coverage, for their part, attempted to reclaim the moral high ground and presented publications as "Antidotes against Debauchery."[37] If cases were not fully reported, it would remove "that check upon the violation of the marriage vows that the fear of publicity now supplied."[38] Indeed, some coverage in periodicals presented adultery not just as an opportunity for titillation, but as a serious social problem. They offered stories of issues that arose because of gaps in the laws—men who took mistresses because divorces were so hard to get, or deserted wives who began extramarital unions of out of economic necessity.[39] Yet it was not until the twentieth century that these accounts compelled enough public attention to reform divorce laws.

American Criminal Prohibitions

When the Puritans imported English prohibitions on adultery into the colonies, they treated it as a criminal, and sometimes capital, offense.[40] In the colonial system of justice, sins were crimes; an offense against God threatened the social order.[41] In Puritan theology, the entire community had responsibility for upholding morality, for, as Puritan minister Cotton Mather warned, "heinous breaches of the Seventh Commandment" could bring the judgment of Sodom upon all of New England. Accordingly, community members had a stake in exposing infidelity, and in close-knit New England communities, moral monitoring was pervasive. Clement Codom of Gloucester, Massachusetts, "heaved the door off the hinges" to see what his neighbor John Pearce was doing with the widow Stannard. Inquisitive neighbors witnessed Susan Attcheson, a married woman, having her hand in the breeches of John Nevill, while his hand was in the slit in her skirt. The court fined Nevill and ordered Attcheson whipped. In 1732, a New England woman testified to having "look'ed in at a hole" in her neighbor's house, where she saw his wife and another man "on the bed in the act of Adultery." In the fishing town of Marblehead, Massachusetts, neighbors wielding clubs attacked the home of William Beale, whose wife, Martha, was suspect for having a prior marriage annulled and maintaining an intimate relationship with a servant. "Come out, you cuckholly cur," they called to William. "We are come to beat thee. Thou livest in adultery."[42]

Community scorn and ostracism were part of the punishments for adultery, but there were legal sanctions as well. Adultery was a capital offense in most colonies.[43] Although death sentences were seldom imposed, there were unlucky exceptions. In 1634, Mary Latham and James Britton were hanged for their affair in Massachusetts; Mary had betrayed her elderly husband and boasted of it publicly.[44] However, juries were reluctant to convict in capital cases, so, after the middle of the seventeenth century, executions for adultery ceased.[45] Some accused adulterers were acquitted, even in the face of irrefutable evidence of marital misconduct, such as the birth of a child that the woman's husband could not have fathered. Sometimes charges against alleged adulterers were reduced to "suspicious company keeping." Occasionally the court only ordered symbolic hanging: the couple had to sit on the gallows for an hour with ropes around their necks.[46]

Definitions of adultery varied across jurisdictions and remained, as one commentator put it, "deplorably disharmonious."[47] Although the laws universally condemned a married woman who had sex with a man other than her husband, they differed on whether adultery was committed by an unmarried paramour or by a husband who had sex with a single woman.[48] In effect, the laws codified a double standard. A married woman was liable regardless of the marital status of her partner; a married man was liable for fornication, a less serious crime, if his partner was unmarried. As the law evolved, a majority of states defined the crime of adultery to require only a single act of extramarital sexual intercourse. However, some jurisdictions reflected English common-law requirements that adultery be open and notorious; others demanded cohabitation.[49] Some statutes barred adulterers from ever marrying their paramours, or from doing so while the wronged spouse was still alive.[50] The theory was that the remarriage added insult to injury, and that this rule might dissuade individuals from seeking a divorce or committing adultery in the first instance.[51]

Common punishments for extramarital sex were fines, banishment, and whipping, with the last being more common for women than for men, because women had no independent resources from which they could pay a financial penalty.[52] In 1736, Thomas Clarke of Dorchester, Massachusetts, had to choose between a five-pound fine and ten stripes for having "in a wanton and Lascivious Manner had the use and Carnal Knowledge of the Body of Susannah the Wife of Joseph Browne."[53] A hefty bond might also be required to prevent an adulterous couple from seeing each other. Such bonds doubtless caused friction in marriages because the husband had to advance the sum, even when his wife was at fault. Some offenders also were required to wear the letters *AD* on a garment or have them burned on their forehead.[54] Nathaniel Hawthorne's celebrated novel *The Scarlet Letter* was grounded in fact: In 1639, Mary Mendam was convicted of adultery in Plymouth Colony for "committing the act of uncleannesse" with an Indian. Compounding her crime was the fact that it "arose through [her] allurement and inticement." She was sentenced to be publicly whipped and to wear a badge on her left sleeve containing the letters *AD* for the rest of her life, and, if found without it, she was to have the letters burned on her face.[55]

Prohibitions on adultery were less frequently enforced in the South than in New England. Dispersed farms and plantations made it difficult to monitor neighbors' personal lives, and in some backcountry areas, where clergy were in short supply, people accepted extramarital unions. Some courts also ignored the crime. When Richard Owens sold the contract for his servant Anne Gould to Joseph Wicks, he first "did make use of her body" and infected her with venereal disease. The court ignored Owens's sexual crime, found him guilty only of fraud, and merely ordered him to provide a new servant.[56] Many other cases of adultery never reached the courts. Aggrieved parties often had no interest in airing their troubles. Wives had no independent means of livelihood if the marriage broke down, and husbands often preferred to avoid public humiliation. For example, when Mary Taylor of Maryland admitted that George Catchmey was the father of her child, her husband and her paramour discussed their options. Catchmey warned Taylor that if he sought their prosecution for adultery, the court would "record him Cuckhold" and give custody to Catchmey. The men agreed instead that Catchmey would provide payment to Taylor in tobacco and Taylor would care for the child. The arrangement came to light only because Mary had exchanged insults with the midwife to whom she had confessed, and the midwife took the story to Maryland authorities. They, however, declined to proceed because the adultery had been committed in Virginia.[57]

Enforcement of adultery laws throughout the nation became less common in the late eighteenth and nineteenth centuries. With the separation of church and state following the American Revolution, and the decline in the power of religious authorities, moral offenses became a less central concern. Prosecutions for adultery and fornication often functioned less to "make sinners squirm" than to compel child support from men who fathered bastards.[58] In one Virginia county between 1801 and 1810, there were no indictments for fornication or adultery.[59] In an Indiana county between 1823 and 1860, sexual offenses (mainly fornication and adultery) accounted for only 2 percent of the prosecutions.[60] In 1875, in the Ohio Courts of Common Pleas, there were twenty-eight indictments for adultery in a population of almost three million. Only six people in the state went to jail. Yet, in the same year, 304 divorces were granted on grounds of adultery. In 1880, of some 58,000 prisoners in prisons and local jails in the United States, only 161 were there for adultery.[61]

Nineteenth-century enforcement patterns reflected what legal historian Lawrence Friedman has labeled the "Victorian compromise." The view, rarely made explicit, was that vice was inevitable; men's sexual energies had to find some outlet. But "it was crucially important to build dams and containments; structures of justice and social order that encouraged self-control, enthroned models of right behavior, and punished *extreme* deviance."[62] In many jurisdictions, adultery was prosecuted only when it was open and notorious.[63] This practice sharply broke with colonial traditions, which made no distinction between open and clandestine sin; if anything, Puritans hated concealed sin more. They wanted "exposure, confession and contrition." By the nineteenth century, as Friedman puts it, vice "won a certain grudging degree of toleration... so long as it remained in the shadows."[64] Open defiance of conventional morality was another matter. In 1848, Alabama convicted a married man of "living in adultery" with Polly Williams. For some seven months, the defendant, Collins, spent one night a week at Williams's home. In holding Collins liable, the judge reasoned that although an occasional act of intimacy was not a crime, Collins and Williams were pursuing a course of conduct that was notorious, and they were thus committing an "outrage upon decency and morality."[65] In Alameda County, California, between 1880 and 1900, the only prosecution for adultery involved a married woman who ran a boardinghouse and moved in with a former lodger. The enraged husband filed a complaint. The lodger was sentenced to two months in the county jail; the wife went free.[66]

Such a gender pattern was unusual. As previously mentioned, in most cases, churches, society, and the law dealt more harshly with women who engaged in extramarital sexuality than with male offenders.[67] In 1831, William Corbett, in *Advice to Young Men*, offers the conventional explanations for the double standard:

> But, bad as is conjugal infidelity in the husband, it is much worse in the wife: a proposition that it is necessary to maintain by the force of reason, because the women, as a sisterhood are prone to deny the truth of it. They say that adultery is adultery, in men as well as in them; and that therefore the offense is as great in the one case as in the other. As a crime, abstractly considered, it certainly is; but as to the consequences, there is a wide difference. . . . The husband by the breach of that vow, only brings shame upon his wife and family; whereas the wife, by a breach of her vow, may bring the husband a spurious offspring to maintain, and may bring that spurious offspring to rob of their fortunes, and in some cases of their bread, her legitimate children. . . . And why is the disgrace deeper? . . . Women should be, and they are, except in a few instances, far more reserved and more delicate than

men; nature bids them be such; the habits and manners of the world confirm this precept of nature; and therefore, when they commit this offence, they excite loathing, as well as call for reprobation. For these plain and forcible reasons it is that this . . . offence is far more heinous in the wife than in the husband; and the people of all civilized countries act upon this settled distinction. Men who have been guilty of the offence are not cut off from society but women who have been guilty of it are . . . [subject to] a sentence of social excommunication for life.[68]

The double standard was particularly pronounced in the antebellum South. Any woman who engaged in extramarital sexual relations risked spousal violence, personal disgrace, divorce, and loss of contact with her children. By contrast, Southern white men enjoyed sexual privilege. Their gratification of lust was acceptable as long as indulged discreetly with poor white or black women. Occasionally, white women also crossed the racial barrier. One married woman who bore a black child explained to her white husband that she "saw no more harm in a white woman's having a black child than in a white man's having one, though the latter was more frequent."[69] That logic was not generally accepted.

Neither was adultery always the most serious crime of which the defendant was guilty. It may simply have been the crime for which a conviction was most readily attainable. A case in point is an 1870 Iowa Supreme Court case in which testimony indicated that the defendant's extramarital intercourse was against the will of the woman.[70] Why the man was not prosecuted for rape is unclear from the record. Perhaps this was an example of what we would now consider acquaintance rape, the kind of "he said, she said" case that is notoriously hard to prove. Charging the defendant with adultery made for a much easier trial because, as the Iowa court held, the woman's consent was immaterial. It was enough to show that sex occurred and that the defendant was married to someone else. Similar cases also suggest that laws against adultery and fornication were used to provide a backup position for prosecutors who believed that rapes had occurred but doubted their ability to prove them beyond a reasonable doubt.[71]

This is not to suggest that adultery cases were always themselves free of evidentiary difficulties. Courts often struggled over how much to infer from suspicious circumstances. In one 1911 case, the defendant, Trachsel, had gone to Kansas, where he committed adultery with Mrs. Blanche Snoddy. After Mrs. Snoddy returned to her husband in Iowa, the defendant also returned, and was seen going off with her toward the Chautauqua grounds, a wooded tract of land outside the city limits. A little girl who saw them alerted Mrs. Snoddy's mother-in-law, who then proceeded to the Chautauqua grounds. There she confronted the defendant and her daughter-in-law, who were sitting on a log. Mr. Snoddy subsequently accused the defendant of adultery and he was convicted at trial. The Supreme Court reversed the decision. Conceding that the evidence "tended to show an adulterous disposition" and that the parties had an opportunity to commit the act, the Court emphasized that "mere disposition and opportunity are not alone sufficient. There must be circumstances inconsistent with any other reasonable hypothesis." In this case, the Court thought one reasonable explanation of the conduct was that the parties "were conferring with reference to future adulterous relations. However improper such a conference would be it would not constitute adultery."[72]

The twentieth century witnessed an increasing liberalization of sexual norms and respect for individual privacy. Enforcement of criminal prohibitions became infrequent. In 1910, in New York City, out of 108,000 misdemeanor arrests, adultery accounted for only 34; only

6 of these individuals were convicted.[73] In 1926, in Chicago, 95 men and women were convicted of adultery. Punishments were generally light—a fine or probation—but a few were sentenced to the county jail or the house of correction.[74] Around the same time in Boston, in the first six months of 1920 there were convictions for 25 men and 20 women for adultery, with similarly light punishments.[75]

The period following World War II was a time of rapid social change. Most of the change regarding sex was in one direction— toward individual fulfillment and social tolerance and away from repression and the hypocrisy of the Victorian compromise.[76] In 1955, drafters of the Model Penal Code recommended that states abolish laws against fornication and adultery. The comments to the code noted that such laws were rarely enforced and were subject to abuses of selective prosecution and blackmail. Citing the Kinsey report, which found that about half of men and a quarter of women had engaged in extramarital sex, the drafters also concluded that the laws had little deterrent power.[77] "The extreme frequency of such behavior among otherwise law-abiding citizens suggests not only the impossibility of effective suppression, but also the toleration with which such behavior is commonly viewed." Over the next two decades, many states followed the Model Penal Code recommendation. In 1984, major cities like Baltimore and Los Angeles had only three to four arrests for adultery.[78] Adultery, as Friedman noted, was "on its last legs, penally speaking, in the age of the sexual revolution."[79]

Divorce

Adultery did, however, retain influence in family law. All the colonies recognized adultery as a ground for divorce, although most followed English traditions and did not grant absolute divorces with the right to remarry except through legislative act. What evidence is available from the late eighteenth and early nineteenth centuries indicates that adultery was the most common ground for legislative petition.[80] Beginning in the early nineteenth century, states granted courts the authority to decree divorce for certain types of marital misconduct, including adultery. Once that occurred, the most significant legal deterrent to adultery was not criminal punishment but rather a fault-based divorce system that penalized adulterers through denial of child custody and financial awards to the innocent spouse.[81] Divorce trials served to reflect and reinforce cultural beliefs about marriage, sexuality, and gender roles.

Throughout the nineteenth century, adultery was the most common ground for divorce. Between 1867 and 1906, almost 250,000 divorces were granted based on infidelity.[82] In the antebellum South, about three-quarters of men suing for divorce alleged adultery, and the great majority claimed that the adulterous partners were black. Some husbands didn't discover the adultery until after their wives had given birth to a mixed-race child. The petition of Thomas Flowers of Nash County, North Carolina, was typical. He sought a divorce from his wife, Temperance, who had gone to live with a group of free people of color, and had given birth to an illegitimate child. "This wife of his bosom, this friend of his soul," with whom he had lived in "love and confidence" for nine years, had left him for a black man. He was "stabbed to the heart." Husbands described wives who had abandoned themselves to "debauchery," "lewd and lascivious conduct," and "luridness, immorality, and vice," particularly when they gave birth to children of "various colours and complexions."[83] Men who had no difficulty with adultery committed by white masters and black slaves saw white women's relationships with black men as the height of infamy.

Typically, when Southern men had slave mistresses, the law looked the other way. Although most Southern women reconciled themselves to this double standard, some did not. About two out of five white wives who filed for divorce or separation in the antebellum period charged their husbands with infidelity. Slightly more than half of these wives alleged that their husbands' adultery involved black women. In judicial decisions, however, the double standard held force: in most states, a single extramarital sexual encounter by a wife was grounds for divorce, but the same was not true for men, particularly when they were accused of relations with women of color. When Tabitha Pope's lawyer petitioned for divorce because her husband had had sex with two slaves, an Alabama judge dismissed the case on the grounds that the evidence did not show a "habitual and continued adulterous connection." The author of *Commentaries on American Law* (1826–1830) pointed out that some judges and jurists believed that adultery by the husband "ought not be noticed" because it was not "equally injurious in its effects upon the morals, and good order, and happiness of domestic life."[84] Men who had long-standing affairs or kept mistresses generally did so with impunity, and few of their interracial affairs made it to the courts.

Most laws were gender neutral on their face, although a few states required wives who sued for divorce based on adultery to show that their husbands were living with their mistresses. However, as a practical matter, husbands were more successful when they alleged adultery. A wife had to claim additional misconduct on the part of her husband to achieve a divorce, such as a venereal disease or frequent visits to brothels. Even in cases of brothels, a husband's conduct might be overlooked. After all, as one witness acknowledged, "I ... go around considerable myself."[85]

Moreover, equal treatment for husbands and wives in grounds for divorce did not translate into equal treatment in consequences. As a Missouri Supreme Court justice summarized the situation for women found guilty of adultery in 1850, "The law deprives her of her property, of her children, of all that is dear to her, and turns her as an outcast upon the world, a miserable and degraded being."[86] Rare was the wife who rebelled against the double standard and took the view expressed by one woman in an 1833 divorce case: "My ass is my own and I will do as I please with it."[87]

Views about female chastity and the importance of women's reputations also affected how much evidence of infidelity the courts demanded. Some judges were willing to assume the worst when women failed to conduct themselves above reproach. According to the Iowa Supreme Court in 1857, because adultery "was peculiarly a crime of darkness and secrecy, it is not necessary to prove the direct fact of adultery, for if so, there is not one case in a thousand in which the proof would be attainable."[88] A typical case of circumstantial evidence involved Robert Auld's 1891 suit seeking a divorce based on his wife Isabella's adultery with Lyman Pickens. Witnesses testified that Isabella and Lyman had visited each other's rooms, reclined in a hammock together, and "showed marked intimacy." The court found that the couple had violated a "divinely ordained institution" and had undermined the "cornerstone of the social edifice." Married women "should so live that the electric light of truth, when turned upon them, will reveal nothing but honor and purity."[89]

Similar assumptions about sexual norms and gender roles underpinned many other nineteenth-century divorce cases. Aggrieved husbands often painted themselves as victims of their wives' deceit; women who presented themselves as "chaste and virtuous" were in fact pregnant with another man's child. Concerns about female chastity also led neighbors to come by evidence sufficient to warrant divorce. In a scene reminiscent of Puritan New England, a next-door neighbor of Nellie Rathburn described the suspicious circumstances that led him to the Rathburn's bedroom window to see for himself if rumors concerning her unchaste reputation were true.[90] Although he did not see her in a compromising position, the sounds of a couple's voices in the bedroom, coupled with other evidence of small-town gossip, were sufficient to justify a divorce. The townsfolk of Gilroy, California, had made up their mind about the morals of Nellie Rathburn, and the judge accepted their opinion.

Occasionally, however, courts were sensitive to the consequences of labeling a woman as an adulterer, and were reluctant to accept gossip as sufficient evidence to justify divorce. To these judges, a wife's reputation as a "lewd and unchaste woman" had little value without proof of relations with a paramour.[91] In 1866, the Illinois Supreme Court reversed and remanded a lower court decision granting a divorce based on evidence that Emma Thomas left home for several days while her husband was absent and that her moral reputation in the community was poor. A finding of adultery could not be based on "mere suspicion or even on bad reputation."[92] In 1888, the New Jersey Supreme Court reversed a lower court decision granting divorce, despite evidence that Mrs. Osborn and Mr. Stratton had traveled to Philadelphia, Niagara, and the Catskills together. Stratton also had left his own wife and children and was boarding at Osborn's home, even though it was located far from his teaching job. The lower court thought it was "unnatural, unreasonable, and highly improbable that he should go to this trouble and expense for the gratification of a friendly sentiment only." "Illicit intimacy" was the only plausible explanation for his conduct. The appellate court concluded otherwise; in its view, "adultery is not shown, nor are the elements of lust, lewdness, depravity or secrecy . . . to be found in the proofs."[93]

Indeed, some courts, equally solicitous of women's reputations, held that spreading false rumors of adultery constituted "cruel and barbarous treatment" sufficient to justify a wife's claim for divorce. As the Supreme Court of Indiana put in 1881, "a husband could hardly, by any other means, cause a sensitive wife more mental pain, torment, vexation, affliction, grief and misery, than to falsely charge her with the crime of adultery, and slanderously report the same among her neighbors."[94] The Supreme Court of North Carolina agreed, in a case where the wife showed that her husband, "upon the most frivolous and groundless pretenses, accused her of a criminal intimacy with a young physician." "And what," asked the court (rhetorically), "to a virtuous woman, can be more contumelious than a charge made by her husband of infidelity to her marriage vow?"[95]

The importance of fidelity was also apparent in child custody awards. The traditional rule, as one 1960 Maryland court expressed it in *Hild v. Hild,* is that "when a divorce is granted on the ground of adultery, the custody of the child is usually awarded to the innocent party, not as a matter of punishment or reward, but because it is assumed that the child will be reared in a cleaner and more wholesome moral atmosphere."[96] That presumption was not absolute, for when the "adulterous relationship has ceased and appears unlikely to be revived because the mother has changed her way of living, her past indiscretions may be overlooked." Merely marrying the paramour, however, was not enough. Nor were the facts in *Hild* sufficient to overcome the presumption, even though a court investigation had found that the child while living with his mother was "happy, healthy and well adjusted, and preferred to stay with his mother and brother."

The appellate court reversed a decision awarding custody to the mother, stressing her past indiscretions, as well as her attempts to prejudice the child against his father. In tones that conveyed volumes about its view of adultery, the court concluded that it would endanger the welfare of the seven-year-old boy if it permitted him "to be reared by one who has displayed a flagrant disregard of the law of the land, including the sanctity of an oath, as well as the moral code, which is well nigh universally accepted by our society. Such a person should not be entrusted to guide the physical, spiritual and moral development of the child."[97]

Similarly, in a 1949 New York case, the Court of Appeals reversed a trial court award of custody to the wife, who admitted "numerous deliberate adulteries" with a married man. As the dissent noted, the majority's decision overlooked evidence that the wife was "deeply devoted to the children," and kept her infidelity unknown to them. By contrast, the father was "inordinately preoccupied with his professional duties; that as a result he gave little of his time or of himself to the children; and that not infrequently he treated them brusquely, impatiently and even intemperately."[98] But the majority was swayed by the wife's lack of repentance and her "considered belief in the propriety of . . . extramarital sex experimentation." "It cannot be," the court concluded, that "'the best interests and welfare' of those impressionable teen-age girls will be 'best served' by awarding their custody to one who proclaims, and lives by, such extraordinary ideas of right conduct."[99]

A woman whose home was still "infested by the welcomed presence of the paramour" was by definition an unfit parent, and was not to be preferred even over a father who "drinks steadily" and is "required by the nature of his business to be absent from his family a great part of the time."[100] Even a mother who established that she was "through with her immoral conduct" and had married her paramour was typically unable to overcome the presumption of unfitness. To a 1958 Maryland court, an adulterous mother's past actions trumped the fact that the father had been "inattentive to his child . . . [and,] on at least one occasion, struck the mother." In the court's view, he still offered a more "proper environment" for raising a child.[101] Even where the father would be unable to care for his children and would instead place them with their grandparents, a 1954 Washington Supreme Court believed that such an arrangement would be preferable to granting custody to an unfaithful wife. The court was unprepared to "overlook or condone" the conduct of one who "displays such a flagrant disregard of morality, the law, a solemn oath and the sanctity of the home. It is not proper that such a person guide the spiritual, mental, moral and physical development of these children. It will endanger their welfare."[102]

As time went on, courts generally became more forgiving, particularly where the husband's own conduct was not above reproach. A 1956 Kentucky decision held that the wife's adultery would bar her from receiving alimony but not custody and child support. The record showed that the wife was "an excellent mother and never failed to give her two daughters the best of care and attention. . . . True she was indiscreet with [a paramour], but soon after her divorce she married him." Moreover, the husband had been arrested ten years earlier for an affair he had with an eighteen-year-old girl.[103]

During the mid-twentieth century, courts also struggled with the growing problem of fabricated adultery in collusive divorce cases. By the 1930s, every state that recognized divorce listed adultery as one of the grounds, and fabrication of evidence to satisfy that ground was common.[104] In New York, where adultery remained the only basis for divorce until 1966, court records revealed countless enactments of the same sordid melodrama, with the same supporting cast of paramours hired for the occasion.[105] In these cases of "soft-core adultery," the husband would check into a hotel room with a woman not his wife. She was almost always a blonde. After they partially undressed, they would be "surprised" by a knock on the door. In would come a photographer, and after pictures were taken for presentation in court, the woman would depart with her fee.[106] The practice was popularized in a 1934 article titled "I Was the Unknown Blonde in 100 New York Divorces."[107] By the 1960s, the problem of collusion was so common that a young Woody Allen incorporated it in his standup comedy routine. Allen reportedly described how he and his wife wanted a divorce but discovered that adultery was the only ground. "And that is so weird," Allen noted, "because the Ten Commandments say 'Thou shalt not commit adultery.' But New York says you have to."

The problem was not unique to New York. A study of Maryland divorce proceedings found them to involve a "largely fictitious" and needlessly expensive process.[108] In 1933, the president of the American Bar Association noted that most divorces are friendly proceedings, "the fruit of collusion."[109] The result was a form of class injustice, with divorce reserved for those who could afford to purchase witnesses.[110] The problems were a major impetus for the movement toward no-fault divorce that began in the 1960s and eventually removed the need for fabricated adultery.[111]

Criminal Conversation and Alienation of Affection

American law recognized the tort of criminal conversation, but initially restricted the claim to men. Until the passage of the Married Women's Property Acts in the mid-nineteenth century, wives had no right to sue in their own name, and the erring husband, who in other circumstances could sue for injury to his wife, was hardly a suitable plaintiff in criminal conversation cases because he was guilty of the infidelity in question. Even after the Married Women's Property Acts recognized women's right to sue, some courts were unwilling to grant wives a claim against their husband's paramour. In part, the unwillingness stemmed from a straightforward embrace of the double standard, but there was also a general skepticism about the merits of such actions. As an 1890 decision by the Supreme Court of Maine noted, a "wife's infidelity may impose upon her husband the support of another man's child, and what is still worse, it may throw suspicion upon the legitimacy of his own children. A husband's infidelity can inflict no such consequences upon his wife." Moreover, the action had been abolished in England, "and the trials we have had in this country of such actions are not very encouraging. They seem to be better calculated to inflict pain upon the innocent members of the families of the parties than to secure redress to the persons injured and we fear such would be the result if such actions were maintainable by wives."[112] However, the clear trend of the cases was to find that "what is law for the man is also law for the woman."[113] As to the argument that the consequences of a wife's infidelity were more injurious than that of a husband, one 1928 New York court was skeptical. "Are we prepared to say that humiliation, disgrace, dishonor and mental suffering afflict a husband but do not afflict a wife? The law is not so foolish."[114]

A related tort, alienation of affection, was often coupled with criminal conversation in the same action. Although not recognized in English common law, it became accepted in America in all states except Louisiana. The action consisted of depriving one spouse of the love, society, companionship, and comfort of the other. It was not necessary to show adultery, although as a practical matter it was advisable. The fact that the spouses were separated was no defense since there was always the possibility of a reconciliation. Although the defendant was typically a paramour, the action could also be brought against others, including family members who attempted to interfere with marital relations. When a complaint was for criminal conversation, proof of alienation of affection was admissible to enhance damages, and where the action was for alienation of affection, proof of adultery also affected damages. Compensation could be awarded for the "dishonor of [the husband's] bed, the destruction of his domestic comfort, and the suspicion cast upon the legitimacy of her offspring," as well as the "degradation which ensues, [and] the distress and mental anguish which necessarily follow."[115] Because punitive damages were available for both criminal conversation and alienation of affection, damage awards could be quite substantial and these "heart balm" actions were often criticized for giving rise to blackmail and extortion.[116]

However, the facts giving rise to large judgments were often sympathetic. A case in point is *Eclov v. Birdsong*, a 1948 decision upholding a hefty damage award for alienation of affection and criminal conversation. According to the appellate court, the plaintiff, Birdsong, was a "faithful and devoted husband, a hard working bread-winner, and an excellent provider." His "domestic happiness" was unquestioned until Eclov, a recent widower, seduced Birdsong's wife with false promises of marriage. Eclov's "depraved conduct" included "constantly debauching Birdsong's wife in Birdsong's own home." The result was that Birdsong's wife divorced him. In the appellate court's view, seldom had a record been presented to the court showing more "shame, degradation and duplicity in marital relations."[117]

Yet, as critics noted, the difficulty with heart balm actions was that they proceeded on the "hypothesis of a perfectly harmonious husband-wife relationship destroyed or impaired by a malicious, scheming and seductive intruder.... But the hypothesis is far from conforming to the life pattern, as indicated by the facts of the cases." Sometimes the plaintiffs were themselves guilty of adultery, a fact that did not bar their action but did mitigate damages.[118] Even where the facts fit the assumed norm, critics doubted that damage remedies would be sufficient to deter the offense. "As a rule," one law professor noted, the defendant "becomes enmeshed with [the] plaintiff's spouse without preconceived design."[119] As Chapter 3 indicates, such considerations ultimately led most courts to abolish the actions.

Moral Character

Another context in which adultery played a role was in occupations or immigration applications that required good moral character. In 1930, in *Grievance Committee of Hartford County Bar v. Broder*, an unmarried attorney with an exemplary record of legal practice was convicted of adultery for having an affair with the mother of three young children. The court held that the defendant Broder's conduct involved moral turpitude sufficient to justify disbarment. There were, in the court's view, no extenuating circumstances. Broder was a "mature and experienced man of about fifty; he knew the law and his duty to society." And the consequences of his breach were of the utmost significance: "The injury to society, to the laws, to the court, to the family relation, to the wronged husband, and to the children of tender years by this respondent's act of adultery makes of it an act of inherent baseness without alleviation or excuse. It was not the act of youth or the act of sudden temptation, or of an irresponsible moment but a . . . violent mutual infatuation . . . [that] continued for a period exceeding upwards of three years." In a case of such "public notoriety," it was "doubly imperative" for the court to uphold the profession's standards of conduct, "however high a place in the profession the attorney who violates them may hold."[120]

Broder was an unusual case. Despite the frequency of findings of adultery in divorce proceedings, a search of published decisions reveals only two other instances of bar disciplinary action against attorneys guilty of the offense. One was an 1892 decision disbarring a New York attorney who had been found guilty of various acts of financial improprieties involving clients. The attorney had also been named in a suit for alienation of affection based on adultery with his housekeeper. In justifying disbarment, the court did not single out infidelity, but referred instead to his "fraudulent and deceitful" actions, and "conduct unbecoming his profession."[121] In an 1894 Ohio case, the court declined to sanction a lawyer who had repeatedly "seduce[d] and debauch[ed] his secretary." In the court's view, an act "merely discreditable, but not infamous, and not connected with an attorney's duties" was insufficient to "expel him from office." To hold otherwise would expose members of the bar to the "whims, caprice, peculiar views and prejudices of judges." In the court's view,

> Indiscretions committed of the kind charged cannot be said to have been done in the character or capacity of an attorney, but must be ascribed to the weakness, the passions, the frailties possessed in a greater or less degree by all mankind.
>
> Grave as is the offense charged, much as the court may sympathize with the ruined girl; however great might be the hatred on the part of the court of such practices, under such circumstances; still, . . . the facts charged do not constitute unprofessional conduct involving moral turpitude.[122]

The absence of other cases on point suggests the prevalence of such attitudes. Except in the rare case of public notoriety like *Broder*, courts and bar disciplinary committees in the mid-twentieth century seemed prepared to overlook extramarital indiscretions.

A related issue arose in connection with dismissals of police officers for conduct unbecoming an officer. A series of cases in the 1970s and 1980s yielded inconsistent results. In some instances, courts sustained dismissals for adultery on grounds that the conduct contributed to a "weakening of the public confidence and trust."[123] To a 1975 Pennsylvania court, it did not matter that the state had removed adultery from the criminal code because "a great portion of our citizenry still believes it to be morally offensive."[124] And in 1982, a Virginia court rejected a police officer's constitutional claims that his adultery was private conduct protected under the Fourteenth Amendment.[125]

By contrast, other decisions set limits on the power of police departments to question or dismiss officers based on extramarital conduct. In one 1979 Philadelphia case, the court ordered the reinstatement of an officer who had been dismissed for his refusal to answer questions about living with an eighteen-year-old student while separated from his wife. Because the relationship was conducted "privately and unobtrusively," and was not shown to be relevant to the officer's job performance, the court held that the questioning violated his constitutional rights of privacy.[126] On similar reasoning, a 1983 Michigan court overturned the dismissal of a married officer who was cohabiting with a woman not his wife. In the court's view, the privacy and associational interests of the officer were sufficiently fundamental to require a showing that his job was adversely affected. The police department argued that because the officer worked in a small community, with a population of about 4,000, his conduct would be public knowledge, and that "citizens would therefore lose respect for plaintiff in particular and the police force in general." In the court's view, even if that were a relevant consideration, "constitutional rights should not depend upon popularity polls or the whims of public opinion."[127]

Similar inconsistency characterized matters involving immigration. Since the first naturalization law was passed in 1790, individuals seeking U.S. citizenship have been required to prove good moral character.[128] Whether adultery disqualified an individual was a matter of dispute among early cases. Sometimes courts held that any adultery was enough to show a lack of good moral character, regardless of the relative culpability of the petitioner. For example, in 1938, a New York trial court denied the petition for naturalization by Sophie Axelrod on the ground that her previously divorced husband had not satisfied the technical requirements for a valid marriage. Accordingly, her cohabitation with him constituted adultery. "In these circumstances," the court concluded, "it becomes necessary to deny the petition . . . however harsh such result seems to be to the petitioner."[129] A New York court reached a similar result fifteen years later in a case where the petitioner's wife had married him before her Cuban divorce decree permitted remarriage. In the court's view, there were no extenuating circumstances. Rather, the petitioner had compounded his offense by living in sin with another woman prior to his marriage. When asked why he had continued to have children with that woman if he did not really love her, the petitioner responded, "Since I am a seaman, when a seaman comes to port, we need a woman."[130]

By contrast, a federal court of appeals in New York found extenuating circumstances in its 1947 decision involving four petitioners, all of whom were technically living in adultery. In one case, the applicant's wife had been divorced from her husband but had neglected to get leave from the proper court to remarry. In two other cases, the applicants had lived with women who were separated from their husbands and had married these women as soon as death or divorce made this possible. In the fourth case, the applicant's wife, from whom he had been separated for fifteen years, had refused to give him a divorce, and he did not commence an extramarital affair until at least six years after he had left her. Discerning an "increasingly liberal trend in naturalization cases," the appellate court did not believe that the "present sentiment of the community views as morally reprehensible such faithful and long continued relationships under the circumstances here disclosed." "Morality," said the court, "is not to be measured solely by conventional formality, nor are the mores of a community static. The trend of recent naturalization decisions is to stress stability and faithfulness in the 'marital' relationship rather than the mere legality of ties."[131]

In 1952, in an effort to achieve greater uniformity, Congress passed the McCarran-Walter Immigration and Nationality Act, which included adultery as one of the grounds that would establish a lack of good moral character.[132] The legislative history sheds little light on congressional intent. However, one Senate judiciary committee report that provided the foundation for the act was critical of judicial and administrative decisions finding that extenuating circumstances for adultery would permit naturalization. The committee report went on to recommend that the "prerequisite of good moral character . . . should be . . . continued and even more strictly applied in determining the fitness of an applicant for citizenship."[133] Because the statute did not define adultery, courts were left to apply state law definitions, and they came to varying conclusions based on similar facts.[134] If, for example, the petitioner lived in a state like California, which defined adultery to require cohabitation, "intermittent" extramarital activity would not prevent naturalization. In a less permissive jurisdiction, however, a single act would be sufficient.[135] Some courts strained to find petitioners innocent of adultery where extenuating circumstances were present, notwithstanding the legislative history. A New York case shortly after passage of the act involved a petitioner who had obtained a Mexican mail divorce that was not recognized as valid in the United

States. The petitioner had remarried in New Jersey and moved to New York, where he lived in adultery. Had he remained in New Jersey, he would not have been guilty since New Jersey law retained the old common-law doctrine that extramarital intercourse did not constitute adultery unless the female participant was married. However, New York law defined adultery as "sexual intercourse of two persons either of whom is married to a third person." Under a literal interpretation of that statute, the petitioner was guilty of adultery. However, the court instead determined to follow precedent requiring criminal intent to commit adultery. And, the court asked, "How likely is it that a . . . jury would convict him" on the facts presented?[136]

By contrast, other courts considered themselves bound by the plain meaning and legislative history of the statute and found even unintentional adultery a bar to naturalization. In a 1964 decision, the petitioner and his wife had both obtained Mexican divorces that were not recognized as valid. Although they had believed themselves married, the court felt itself powerless to consider those extenuating circumstances. In its view, the judge's "personal views of whether petitioner is of good moral character" were not relevant. Accordingly, the court "reluctantly concluded that despite the obvious equities in petitioner's favor and the other evidence of good moral character," the petition for naturalization had to be denied.[137]

America's Unwritten Law

A final context in which judges and juries struggled with the legal consequences of adultery involved the "unwritten law." If a man killed his wife's lover, juries were generally reluctant to convict. Sometimes the unwritten law was written; the penal code either defined the circumstances as something short of first-degree murder or actually excused it. For example, until its repeal in 1974, a Texas statute provided that "homicide is justifiable when committed by the husband upon one taken in the act of adultery with the wife, provided the killing take place before the parties to the act have separated."[138] Courts interpreted the statute liberally. "Taken in the act" did not mean the very act of sex but circumstances that reasonably suggested to the husband that adultery had occurred or was about to occur; the phrase "before they have separated" meant while the wife and her paramour were still in each other's company.[139]

There were, however, limits to judicial tolerance. In a case in which the defendant did not kill the paramour but castrated him instead, the court held that the statute did not confer immunity. The defendant would have been justified in killing his victim but was not allowed to maim him.[140] The purpose of such statutes, courts were at pains to point out, was "not vindictive," it was "humane. It recognizes the ungovernable passion which possesses a man when immediately confronted with his wife's dishonor. It merely says the man who takes life under those circumstances is not to be punished; not because he has performed a meritorious deed; but because he has acted naturally and humanly."[141]

In states where statutes did not provide an adequate excuse, the jury could step in. A celebrated case in the late 1850s involved a New York congressman, Daniel Edgar Sickles. After learning from an anonymous letter that his young wife was carrying on an affair with a good-looking widower, Philip Barton Key, Sickles confronted his wife.[142] She tearfully confessed. Although Sickles was himself guilty of adultery, that did not apparently mitigate his rage.[143] Sickles tracked Key down and shouted, "Key you scoundrel.... You have dishonored my bed—you must die."[144] And die he did. Sickles was charged with first-degree murder but the jury found him not guilty.

The legal fiction in these cases—that the defendant was temporarily insane—often strained credulity. A notorious example is that of Major General George Cole, who learned that while he was at war, L. Harris Hiscock had prevailed upon Cole's wife to "submit to his caresses."[145] Cole appeared perfectly sane before and after he killed Hiscock. Cole consulted various friends, procured a pistol, and located his victim at a state constitutional convention. The jury's conclusion that he was insane when he pulled the trigger was, in the view of the *New York Times,* "the most extraordinary verdict ever returned by a jury made up of men supposed to be sane themselves."[146]

Even when the jury found the defendant guilty, the unwritten law sometimes kicked in to mitigate the sentence. In 1924, F. C. Gossett dropped a piece of gas pipe on the head of a man whom Gossett discovered in his wife's room when he came home unexpectedly from work. The judge imposed a fine of $5 with the explanation, "You are guilty, technically, but I would have done the same thing."[147] Lawrence M. Friedman and William E. Havemann sampled some 200 cases of the unwritten law from the mid-nineteenth to the early twentieth century, and they concluded that the law "seeped in at every pore of the system of criminal justice." "Prosecutors declined to bring charges, grand juries refused to indict . . . ; juries failed to convict or recommended mercy; judges sentenced leniently; governors pardoned; and prisons granted early parole."[148]

Somewhat surprisingly, Friedman and Havemann's study also found that although women took advantage of the unwritten law less frequently, when they did so, the defense was even more successful for them than it was for men. Female defendants were either acquitted or won light sentences in 33 out of 34 cases, compared with men's success rate of 122 out of 152.[149] A representative case involved Nancy May, who in 1924 was convicted for the murder of Alice Smith. May believed Smith was a "rival for her husband's affections." She was sentenced to ten years in prison, but the governor pardoned her before she served a single day.[150] In 1946, the murder trial of Gwendolyn Wallis ended in a hung jury. Wallis believed that Ruby Clark had stolen her husband's affections, and in a retrial of the charges, the judge dismissed the case. Although he felt that "by the written letter of the law," Wallis was guilty of murder, he believed that a second trial would end no more successfully than the first. Courtroom spectators applauded.[151] In 1956, Florence Scroggs shot her husband's lover while the adulterous couple was in a parked car outside a restaurant. The court overturned a murder verdict and required a new trial on the theory that the killing might have been justified: the evidence showed the defendant to be of "good character," the deceased to lack "virtue and chastity," and the killing designed to prevent adultery.[152]

The Scroggs case was one of the last successful examples of the unwritten law. By the mid-twentieth century, few instances occurred. Friedman and Havemann speculate that lawyers, "aware of changing times and changing mores, were less likely to trot out the unwritten law and would try something else instead—and meanwhile bargain for a lesser sentence."[153] However, as Chapter 3 indicates, some vestiges of the unwritten law lingered under a different label. But it is clear that as the twentieth century progressed, attitudes toward adultery changed significantly.

The laws concerning adultery have an undistinguished history. As a means of policing marital fidelity, legal mandates have been intrusive, inconsistent, and often ineffective. Enforcement has been marked by class, race, and gender bias; the sexual double standard has reflected and reinforced gender inequality.

By the late twentieth century, laws governing adultery were an endangered species. As Chapter 3 notes, they occasionally surfaced, often with much notoriety and handwringing over their continued viability. Legal understandings of marital fidelity evolved in tandem with social attitudes. And while the American public still overwhelmingly disapproved of adultery, it no longer saw law as the appropriate response. Deprived of a hospitable cultural habitat, legal sanctions on adultery have eroded. And, as Chapter 3 indicates, where they have survived, their enforcement leaves much to be desired.

3

The American Legal Landscape

In 2004, John Bushey, a sixty-six-year-old attorney for the town of Luray, Virginia, pled guilty to adultery and lost his job as a consequence. His infidelity was never in doubt. After his extramarital affair ended badly, the woman involved went to the police. The assistant commonwealth attorney later defended the decision to prosecute: "We're not out beating bushes and certainly we're not peeking in windows. However, in this case, it was thrown in our face."[1] Initially it looked like Bushey might challenge the law; instead, he ended up accepting a deal that required twenty hours of community service in exchange for having the charges dropped and his record cleared.

Bushey is an isolated case. But it could arise in any of the twenty-one states that still have criminal prohibitions on adultery (see Figure 3.1).[2]

Adultery also figures as a basis for demotions, as a ground for tort liability in cases alleging criminal conversation and alienation of affection, and as a factor in allocating property and custody in divorce cases. This chapter explores the lingering legal role for adultery in the United States and argues for reform. Enforcement of criminal prohibitions has been infrequent, intrusive, idiosyncratic, and ineffectual, and should be unconstitutional. In employment cases, courts should not permit dismissals or demotions based on private sexual conduct, absent some demonstrable impairment of job performance. Nor should courts tolerate speculative and vexatious actions for criminal conversation and alienation of affection. Adultery should not influence alimony and custody awards, nor should it serve to reduce the punishment for deadly violence. None of these reforms should be seen as diminishing societal respect for marriage as an institution. Rather, they simply recognize the limits of law in policing fidelity, and the excessive costs of ineffectual attempts to do so.

Criminal Prosecutions

Criminal prosecutions for adultery are rare, but they should be rarer still, given the arbitrary and idiosyncratic nature in which prohibitions are enforced, and the invasions of privacy that they entail. In the states that make adultery a crime, the majority classify it as misdemeanor, but some punish it as a felony. Penalties range from a ten-dollar fine (Maryland) to life imprisonment (Michigan).[3] Definitions also vary. Some make paramours guilty of adultery only if they are married; otherwise they are guilty of fornication. Some states require the conduct to be open and notorious. Several allow for prosecution only on complaint of the offended spouse, partly due to concerns about jeopardizing a still-salvageable marriage.[4] As the commentary to the Model Penal Code noted, these statutes are generally unenforced. Even where spouses admit their adultery in divorce cases, they are virtually never prosecuted.

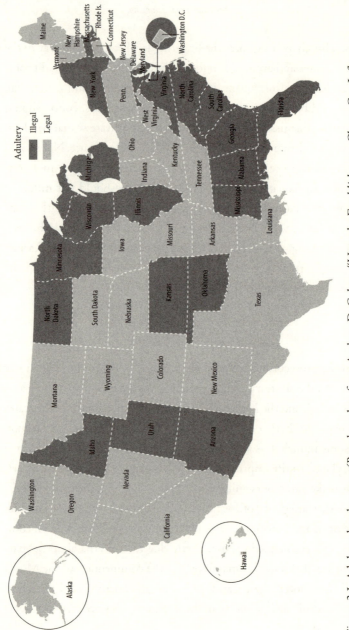

Figure 3.1. Adultery law, by state. (Based on data from Andrew D. Cohen, "How the Establishment Clause Can Influence Substantive Due Process: Adultery Bans after Lawrence," *Fordham Law Review* 79 [2011]).

The infrequent circumstances in which individuals have been charged with adultery suggest the selective and somewhat random nature of enforcement. Typically the cases involve some public behavior or a complaint by a spouse. In 2010, a forty-one-year-old New York woman became the thirteenth individual in the state's history to be arrested for adultery. She was caught having sex on a picnic table in a park near Buffalo but denied that her action was in plain sight or that any children were around. In explaining his decision to bring charges, the local district attorney emphasized that the police were "not out conducting investigations looking for people committing adultery." However, in this case there were witnesses to the act, and "no basis not . . . [to] file the charge."[5] It is unclear why the prosecutor chose adultery rather than some other offense, such as one involving public indecency. If convicted, the defendant would have been subject to ninety days in jail or a $500 fine. Although she vowed to fight the constitutionality of the charge, it does not appear that the case ever got that far.

In 1989, in South Carolina, an appellate court affirmed a conviction of a man found parking at night in a remote location with a woman other than his wife. When pressed to explain his conduct, the man declined. He told his wife, "If I tell you the truth I know you won't ever stay with me again." This admission, coupled with the other circumstantial evidence, was enough to convince the appellate court that the parties were "romantically disposed toward each other. . . . The trial judge, not having been born yesterday, was convinced that [the defendant] had committed adultery. So are we."[6]

Most contemporary adultery prosecutions have involved complaints by an aggrieved spouse. In 2005, the wife of Lucius James Penn, a twenty-nine-year-old North Dakota air force engineer, complained to police that her husband was having an affair with a sixteen-year-old.[7]

In 1991, a New York handyman's wife accused him of having had sexual intercourse on several occasions with another woman. The case attracted notice because the last case on record in New York had been in 1940.[8] In 1989, Donna Carroll's husband brought a charge of adultery during an acrimonious custody battle over the couple's young son. That charge made her the first person to be accused of the crime in Wisconsin since 1888. Although the husband also admitted having adulterous affairs, prosecutors said they could not press a complaint against him because his affairs took place while he was trucker on out-of-state hauls. If convicted, Mrs. Carroll could have been sentenced to two years in jail and a $10,000 fine. The district attorney agreed to dismiss the charge in exchange for her participation in community service and parental counseling.[9]

The most well publicized of these criminal charges involved an Arizona man's 2010 complaint that his wife of seventeen years had cheated on him at least seven or eight times. As the aggrieved husband, Dave Banks, explained to a national news network reporter, "If they used . . . [the adultery statute] all the time, maybe women or men would think twice about going and jumping in the sack and throwing away their marriage."[10] The police did not appear sympathetic. Banks claimed that it took two years for the department even to take his report, and a detective then told him that "it's about time she got on with her life and you get on with yours." Banks was unconvinced. "How do they get to pick and choose which laws they can and can't enforce? They got somebody readily admitting guilt. Seems to me that's a rubber stamp right through the court system," he told a reporter.[11] Prosecutors apparently did not agree; there is no record of a case being filed.

Occasionally, however, prosecutors claim that they are obligated to bring charges. In Wisconsin in 1989, the husband in an acrimonious divorce and custody proceeding filed a criminal complaint against his wife, who had admitted adultery in a family court hearing. In defending his decision to prosecute, the local district attorney claimed that he had no choice. "The law is on the books. There was strong evidence presented to me of a violation. For me to decide not to prosecute would be, in effect, to declare the statute null and void. And that is not my role as district attorney."[12]

In fact, prosecutors frequently decide not to prosecute for a wide variety of reasons. Even more newsworthy than the cases of prosecution are notorious cases in which adultery charges are not brought. For example, in 2008, Governor David Paterson of New York announced at a news conference that he had had several extramarital relationships but "didn't break the law." The *New York Times* followed up with a report that began, "Well, actually . . ." Adultery is a misdemeanor in New York, punishable by a fine of $500 or ninety days in jail. Rarely has it been invoked since the 1970s, and when it has, the charges are usually dropped. When asked about the prospect of a criminal prosecution of Paterson, a New York family lawyer responded, "Absent a Christian fundamentalist replacing [the local district attorney], I doubt it."[13] As Chapter 6 notes, there are many other celebrated cases involving adulterous politicians who faced no criminal liability.

This is in keeping with public attitudes. Only a third of Americans believe that adultery should be a crime.[14] Given these views, it is somewhat surprising that so many statutes remain on the books and that several have survived recent attempts at repeal.[15] No one thinks the fight to preserve these statutes has much practical significance: the issue is symbolic. As Thurman W. Arnold observed three-quarters of a century ago, "Most unenforced criminal laws survive in order to satisfy moral objections to our established modes of conduct. They are unenforced because we want to continue our conduct, and unrepealed because we want to preserve our morals."[16] The president of the Minnesota Family Council similarly explained his group's support for such laws on the grounds that "they send a message.... When you are dealing with a marriage, it's not just a private activity or a private institution.... It has enormous consequences for the rest of society."[17] In New Hampshire, opponents of adultery prohibitions disagreed. In their view, "Who we love and how we love is not something . . . the state has much business meddling in."[18] By contrast, the executive director of Cornerstone Policy Research opposed repeal of the state's criminal statute because it would "diminish . . . the harmful effects of adultery."[19] According to state senator Robert Preston, the message would be that "anything goes in New Hampshire." This would be misleading because "we do cherish some traditional values up here."[20] One of his colleagues agreed. State senator John Chandler felt that the "moral standards of the country are going downhill fast" and the legislature shouldn't encourage the trend. "If it says in the Ten Commandments 'Thou shalt not commit adultery,' it still ought to stay in the statute."[21]

But the current of public opinion is running in the opposite direction. In 1991, in Connecticut, efforts by wronged spouses to launch criminal prosecutions convinced both houses of the state legislature to decriminalize adultery, despite claims that this would turn the state into a "moral wasteland."[22] And in Colorado in 2013, a bill to repeal adultery prohibitions was successfully packaged as a way to keep the government out of people's bedrooms.[23]

Where the statutes survive, it is because state legislators worry that sponsoring repeal would "border on political suicide."[24] As Walter Wadlington, a professor of family law at the University of Virginia put it, "If people don't think anybody can be prosecuted under it anyway, why alienate a constituent by taking it off the books?"[25] Many

legislators may also share the views of Georgetown Law professor Paul
Rothstein, who told a reporter,

> I don't want to be a nut case about this, but keeping the laws on the
> books is not such an off the wall idea. Just because something is done
> doesn't mean that people want the law to reflect the baseness of human
> nature. They want the law to be aspirational and set forth our finest
> ideals. If we believe in marriage, and if the cement of that is loyalty
> and fidelity within a unit, then adultery does threaten that.[26]

But occasional, idiosyncratic enforcement does little to express those
ideals, and it compromises public respect for the rule of law. There is
no principled basis on which to distinguish adultery cases that are
prosecuted from the vast majority that are not. Nor does the rare enforcement effort constitute an effective deterrent to infidelity. Moreover, recent decisions of the U.S. Supreme Court suggest a strong basis
for claiming that adultery prosecutions are unconstitutional.

Constitutional Challenges

In 1977, in a case involving minors' access to contraceptives, the Supreme Court disclaimed any intention to answer "the difficult question
whether and to what extent the Constitution prohibits state statutes
regulating [private, consensual sexual] behavior among adults."[27] A year
later, the Court again declined to address that question in the context of
adultery. *Hollenbaugh v. Carnegie Free Library* involved a librarian and a married janitor who were dismissed for "living together in open adultery"
with their illegitimate child.[28] In affirming their dismissal, a federal
trial court rejected the couple's claims that the library had infringed on
their fundamental right to privacy, and that there was no "rational connection between their conduct and their fitness to perform their jobs."

The Court noted that the library had received complaints about the couple's living arrangement. "As employees of a library in a relatively small community, plaintiffs were frequently called on to deal directly with the community," so the library's concern for their reputation was not, in the trial judge's view, "arbitrary, unreasonable or capricious."[29]

The U.S. Supreme Court denied review. Justice Thurgood Marshall dissented, and wrote separately to protest an "unwarranted governmental intrusion into the privacy of public employees." From his perspective, the trial court's decision allowed a public employer "to dictate the sexual conduct and family living arrangements of its employees, without a meaningful showing that these private choices have any relation to job performance." As he noted, the state had decriminalized adultery, and the library board members did not demand that the couple end their relationship. They insisted, rather, that the couple normalize it through marriage or stop living together. Thus, the library board "apparently did not object to furtive adultery, but only to petitioners' refusal to hide their relationship. In essence, [the board] sought to force a standard of hypocrisy on their employees and fired those who declined to abide by it." Such discrimination seemed to Marshall "particularly invidious." The petitioners' "rights to pursue an open rather than a clandestine personal relationship and to rear their child together in this environment closely resemble the other aspects of personal privacy to which [the Court has] . . . extended constitutional protection." To Marshall, the library board's action could not even satisfy rational basis review because it never showed that community disapproval of the couple's living arrangements affected use of the library or compromised the librarian's ability to discharge her duties. Nor was there any indication that the custodian's job called for contacts with the community or that his performance was affected in any way by his extramarital relationship.[30]

Hollenbaugh is the closest the Supreme Court has come to passing on adultery issues. In dicta in two cases involving access to contraception, concurring or dissenting justices suggested that adultery prohibitions were constitutionally permissible.[31] In lower court decisions, constitutional challenges have been unsuccessful. In 1983, the Massachusetts state supreme court upheld the state's adultery statute. The case involved a defendant arrested for having sexual intercourse with a woman not his wife in a van parked in a secluded wooded area. The court held that there was no "fundamental personal privacy right implicit in the concept of ordered liberty" protecting extramarital sex. Rather, the state has a legitimate interest in prohibiting conduct which may threaten that institution [of marriage]. ... We take judicial notice that the act of adultery frequently has a destructive impact on the marital relationship and is a factor in many divorces."[32] If lack of prosecution of the crime "indicates a general public disfavor with the statute," then the court believed that the appropriate response rested with the legislature, which had the power to repeal that statute.

Another unsuccessful constitutional challenge arose in 1982, when a federal trial court in Illinois held that the associational and privacy interests of a "swingers" club were not infringed by police harassment. Police officers had instructions to record the license plate numbers of club patrons and, where possible, to ticket them for minor traffic and vehicle violations. Because the patrons had not been dissuaded from attending meetings, the court held that their First Amendment interests had not been impaired. Interestingly, the court held that the club was not in violation of the state's adultery law, which prohibited sexual activities that were "open and notorious." Although the adulterous activities of the swingers' club were well known, they took place behind closed doors, which was enough to shield them from criminal prosecution.[33]

However, a more recent Supreme Court pronouncement on privacy raises questions about whether adultery prohibitions could withstand constitutional challenge. In 2003, in *Lawrence v. Texas*, the Supreme Court overruled its prior decision in *Bowers v. Hardwick* and struck down a criminal sodomy statute. According to the majority, decisions concerning intimate relationships are a form of liberty deserving constitutional protection. The Court also disagreed with *Bowers's* conclusion that sodomy prohibitions were deeply rooted in the nation's history; rather, the *Lawrence* court stressed that such statutes were rarely enforced and had been abolished in many states. That trend reflected "an emerging awareness that liberty gives substantial protection to adult persons in deciding how to conduct their private lives in matters pertaining to sex." In the Court's view, the Texas statute "further[ed] no legitimate state interest which can justify its intrusion into the personal and private life of the individual."[34]

Lawrence was not a conventional due process decision. As Harvard professor Cass Sunstein notes, such a decision would have taken one of two approaches.[35] First, the Court might have declared that engaging in private, consensual sexual activity constitutes a fundamental right and the state cannot interfere with that right absent a compelling justification. Alternatively, the Court might have said that the state lacks a rational basis for prohibiting private, consensual sexual activity. The Court did neither. Nowhere in its analysis did the Court use the terms "fundamental interest" or "rational basis." Nor did it explain the implications of its holding beyond sodomy laws.

In his dissent, Justice Antonin Scalia criticized the majority's decision as signaling the "end of all morals legislation, such as prohibitions on fornication, bigamy, adultery and incest."[36] Of all those statutes, Sunstein believes that adultery prohibitions present the hardest case.[37] On the one hand, adultery involves an intimate, consensual, sexual relationship analogous to the ones in *Lawrence* and other cases involving procreation and sexuality that have received constitutional protection.[38] And, as in *Lawrence,* the infrequency of prosecution reflects a broad consensus that the practice at issue should not be punished. On the other hand, the state has a legitimate interest in prohibiting adultery that is not present in cases involving sodomy, namely, protection of the institution of marriage and the interests of the innocent spouse. The Court has traditionally held marriage in the highest esteem; indeed, the right to privacy originated in cases concerned with marital privacy.[39] The seminal case in constitutional privacy law, *Griswold v. Connecticut,* struck down a state's ban on contraceptives on the ground that it intruded on the "sacred precincts of the marital bedroom."[40] And in *Loving v. Virginia,* which invalidated bans on interracial marriage, the Court called marriage "fundamental to our very existence and survival."[41] However, the frequency with which adultery occurs, and the infrequency with which adultery statutes are enforced, suggests that criminal prohibitions are an ineffective means of shoring up marital relationships.

Only one federal case since *Lawrence* has involved an adultery prosecution. In the North Dakota case noted earlier, the defendant air force engineer objected that the prosecution violated equal protection guarantees. The trial court agreed. It held that the state had the right to protect the institution of marriage and criminalize adultery but that the statute unlawfully discriminated by exempting those who disclosed adultery during a divorce or separation proceeding and by requiring a complaint by a spouse.[42]

Another post-*Lawrence* decision arose in a somewhat odd factual context. In a 2009 District of Columbia case, a former hair salon employee sued her employer for sexual harassment and alleged as damages the loss of desire for intimacy with her husband. However, she was not legally married at the time. Although she thought she had divorced her prior husband, the divorce was not finalized until after the harassment occurred. This was relevant because any intimate relations in which she engaged with her second husband would technically constitute adultery, a criminal act under Virginia law. And, as the defendant noted, the "impairment of the ability to do something you do not have the legal right to do is not an actionable damage." The federal trial court, however, rejected this defense on the ground that the Virginia Supreme Court had struck down the state's fornication statute, and language in that decision suggested that the adultery prohibition was also invalid. In effect, the Virginia court had suggested that it considered "statutes criminalizing private consensual sexual intercourse irrelevant for the purposes of civil litigation."[43]

Taken together, intermittent enforcement of adultery prohibitions does little to enforce marital fidelity or reinforce confidence in the rule of law. Given the lack of public support for criminal prohibitions, legislatures should repeal them. Where legislatures decline to act, courts should strike down adultery prohibitions as an infringement of constitutionally protected rights of privacy. There is no rational basis for believing that infrequently and arbitrarily enforced prohibitions on adultery are an effective way of advancing the state's interest in protecting innocent spouses and the institution of marriage. There are better ways to signal respect for that institution and better uses of law enforcement resources than policing private, consensual sexual activity.

Employment

So, too, in employment cases, courts should resist seeing adultery as a ground for sanction unless it is demonstrably related to job performance. Lower courts have long grappled with constitutional objections to the termination or demotion of public employees who had engaged in extramarital affairs. Typically, the courts found that such conduct involved no constitutionally protected rights, and that there was a rational basis for sanctioning the employee. The Supreme Court's decision in *Lawrence* does not appear to have altered such reasoning.

For example, in 1980, a Texas court held that a junior college violated no rights of privacy in demoting a registrar based on his extramarital affair with a librarian.[44] The conduct violated the college's policy on professional conduct, which stated that "faculty members are expected to accept responsibilities in practicing, developing and promoting high standards of moral, ethical, and professional conduct. The image of any faculty member at all times should be such that any student striving to emulate [the] same could be assured of being a good stable citizen." The court held that the policy was a rational means of serving legitimate interest in "maintaining community respect for the College" and "providing students high standards of behavior to emulate."[45]

Pre-*Lawrence* cases involving police officers usually came to a similar result. In some instances, the state's interest in dismissal seemed clearly compelling, but not because of adultery by itself. In a 1986 Arizona case, a federal appellate court had no difficulty finding that two married police officers who had sex with a prostitute while on duty "created conflicts of interest, compromised their performance as officers, raised the possibility of blackmail, threatened the morale of the department and jeopardized the department's reputation in the community. The department's prohibition on 'conduct unbecoming an officer' while admittedly vague, was clearly intended to protect the legitimate interests of the department."[46] However what was objectionable about that conduct was prostitution, not adultery. The actions of the police officers would have been equally problematic if they had been unmarried.

In a harder case, a North Carolina court sustained the demotion of a police officer for engaging in "immoral and indecent" conduct and bringing the "department into disrepute" by having an extramarital affair with another officer. Rejecting the officer's claim that the prohibitions were unconstitutionally overbroad, the court accepted the department's conclusion that the conduct at issue "casts a poor light on the Department as a whole," that morale and discipline within the department could suffer as a result of community disapproval, and that the "effectiveness of the particular officer could be greatly limited."[47]

Community disapproval was also the justification for a Virginia state trooper's dismissal. The trooper, a married man with two daughters, was accused in an anonymous complaint of having an affair with a married neighbor. During the course of the affair, the neighbor gave birth to a child whom she claimed was fathered by the trooper. The Department of State Police claimed that these circumstances were widely known in the small town where the trooper lived and that his actions tended to bring "the reputation of the Department into disrepute."[48] The court dismissed without discussion the trooper's claim that his conduct involved a constitutionally protected right to freedom of association and privacy. It also rejected his equal protection claim that other officers who had engaged in adultery had not been similarly punished. The court reasoned that, under Virginia law, participation in an immoral or unlawful act precludes recovery for injuries sustained as a result.[49]

Similarly, in 2000, a Michigan police officer unsuccessfully challenged his dismissal for having an affair with the wife of another officer. When the officer refused to end his relationship, he was dismissed for "unprofessional conduct" that "discredits the officers and/or the department" and for "moral turpitude" that impairs an officer's "ability to perform as [a] law enforcement officer or causes the department to be brought into disrepute." In rejecting the officer's claim that his conduct involved constitutionally protected rights of intimate association, the court noted that adultery constituted a felony under Michigan law and was the "very antithesis of marriage and family," principles that had formed the basis of constitutional privacy protections. Refusing to second-guess the "fairness" of the department's decision, the court concluded that it was not "arbitrary, irrational or unreasonable," which was all the constitution required. The fact that other officers may have engaged in adultery but escaped discipline did not suggest otherwise, because their conduct did not involve an affair with another officer's wife, which threatened the cohesiveness of the department.[50]

With similar reasoning, courts in 2002 and 2003 came to similar conclusions.[51] As one judge put it, the officer had failed to suggest how his decision to enter into an intimate sexual relationship with a married woman was a fundamental right deeply rooted in the nation's history and tradition or implicit in the concept of ordered liberty. Though "perhaps unfair," his dismissal did not infringe his right of association as guaranteed by the First and Fourteenth Amendments.[52]

The Supreme Court's decision in *Lawrence* does not appear to have altered courts' reluctance to second-guess dismissals for adultery. In 2005, a county clerk challenged her termination for maintaining a "romantic relationship" with an attorney married to a woman who worked in another county court down the hall. The court rejected the clerk's claim that her dismissal infringed her constitutional rights of freedom of association. The county had concluded that the clerk's relationship was "unacceptably disruptive to the workplace," and this, in the court's view, constituted a rational basis for her termination.[53]

In 2010, a federal appellate court held that a county's interest in "discouraging intimate association between supervisors and subordinates is so critical to the effective functioning of its Fire Department that it outweighed the [couple's] interest in [their] relationship."[54] Similarly, in a 2008 Utah case, a federal court of appeals upheld the reprimand of a married police officer for having sex while she was at an out-of-town training seminar. The case arose after an inquiry triggered by her estranged husband. The city alleged that her personal life interfered with her duties as an officer, although there was no evidence of what exactly the interference involved since she was presumably off duty when the affair took place. However, the court distinguished *Lawrence* on the ground that the decision had not found a fundamental right covering all intimate sexual activity. In the Utah court's view, the police department could reasonably admonish an officer when it believes that will "further internal discipline or the public's respect for its police officers and the department they represent."[55]

Finally, in 2013, two individuals unsuccessfully challenged their termination from a residential FBI training program. The couple had committed curfew violations in connection with an adulterous affair. Their relationship, according to the court, lacked "the hallmarks of marital, familial or otherwise long term relationships," and thus was not "the type of relationship the Supreme Court considered when invoking a right to privacy."[56]

Such an analytic approach misses the point. The issue in employment cases should not be simply whether adulterous relationships are different from marital relationships, but whether the extramarital conduct impairs job performance. Vague invocations of community disrepute should not be sufficient. As long as off-duty conduct does not pose a demonstrable threat to the functioning of the workplace, employees' private sexual activities should remain private.

Immigration and Naturalization

A related context in which adultery should not matter is that of immigration and naturalization. As Chapter 2 indicated, in 1952, Congress made adultery a bar to citizenship. However, the statute did not define adultery. Until legislative reform in 1981, courts struggled with whether to defer to state law or to establish a uniform national standard.[57] Courts opting for a federal standard barred citizenship only where the petitioner's extramarital affair tended to destroy an existing marriage and thus posed a threat to public morality. Accordingly, in one 1971 New York case, the court found no impediment to citizenship where the petitioner had never lived with his first wife and married her only to give his children legitimacy. Before his divorce was final, he began an extramarital affair with a woman he later married. The court held that it would be "ironic and unjust" to penalize the petitioner for doing the "honorable thing" and marrying his first wife. Because that marriage was in name only, his extramarital affair did not hurt his first wife or demonstrate bad moral character.[58] Similarly, in a 1966 Michigan case, the court permitted citizenship for a petitioner whose adultery involved only "isolated acts of intercourse" occurring well after his wife had abandoned the marital relationship. The petitioner's conduct, "while not to be condoned, should not be viewed as so morally reprehensible as to . . . [suggest that the petitioner] is a man of bad character."[59]

In 1981, Congress clarified matters by amending the Immigration and Nationality Act. As modified, the act declared that applicants should be found to lack good moral character if they "had an extramarital affair which tended to destroy an existing marriage."[60] So, for example, in a 2009 Maryland case, the court held that the petitioner's adulterous relationships with two other women did not destroy his marriage. The couple had already stopped living together, and his former wife testified that the affairs "had nothing to [do] with why the two of us divorced."[61] Under those circumstances, the petitioner's adultery would not bar his citizenship. As that case indicates, the new standard for extramarital affairs is a clear improvement over its predecessor, but there remains a question as to why private, consensual sexual conduct should be a consideration at all. As Chapter 1 indicated, the most recent polls show that a majority of Americans do not believe that adulterers should be disqualified from leadership positions, so such conduct is not universally viewed as an indication of bad moral character.

Criminal Conversation and Alienation of Affection

In a celebrated case that inspired a major motion picture, Dorothy Hutelmyer won a million-dollar verdict from Margie Cox, her husband's former secretary. The evidence suggested that Hutelmyer and her husband had a "fairy tale marriage" that was "loving, warm and devoted," and included an "active sexual relationship." Then Cox divorced her husband and became "openly flirtatious" with Mr. Hutelmyer, She also changed her "matronly" appearance and began wearing "short skirts, low-cut blouses, and tight clothing to the office." Cox and Hutelmyer began spending increasing amounts of time alone, and Cox claimed that Hutelmyer told her that he had separated from his wife, a claim that the judge and jury seem not to have believed.[62] Cox also "publicly displayed the intimate nature of her relationship" in front of coworkers, "and 'welcomed' Hutelmyer into her home" at all hours of the day and night, despite her knowledge of the harm that their relationship would cause his wife and three young children.[63] That, in the court's view, was ample evidence to justify the

$500,000 in compensatory damages and $500,000 in punitive damages that the jury awarded.

Hutelmyer is not unique. Six states still permit lawsuits for criminal conversation, an oddly named offense that, as Chapter 2 indicated, involves neither crimes nor conversation; it is a civil action that allows aggrieved spouses to sue for damages from the paramour. Six states recognize the related action for alienation of affection.[64] Judgments in such suits, though infrequent, can be substantial; million-dollar awards are not uncommon.[65] The amounts of awards seem exceptionally idiosyncratic. A wrestling coach recovered $910,000 in compensatory damages and $500,000 in punitive damages from a man who had sex with his wife in a hotel room.[66] By contrast, a husband who learned during a marital counseling session of his wife's affair with one of his employees received less than a quarter as much. He recovered $100,001 in actual damages and $250,000 in punitive damages, based on his testimony that the affair caused him severe emotional distress, eroded his self-respect, and "broke [his] heart very badly."[67] The highest verdict on record came in 2010, an award of $9 million to Cynthia Shackelford against the woman she sued for breaking up her thirty-three-year marriage. Shackelford told reporters that she hoped the verdict would send a simple message to "would be homewreckers": "Lay off."[68]

Most states, however, have given that message to aggrieved spouses instead by abolishing actions for criminal conversation and alienation of affection, either by statute or judicial decision. Mississippi put an end to criminal conversation in a lawsuit based on Patricia Alford's affair with her boss. He was "forty years old and wealthy"; she was "twenty-four years old and unhappy." Divorce followed, as did a trial verdict against the boss. The state supreme court reversed. As it noted, criminal conversation made any extramarital involvement, regardless of circumstances, open to vexatious lawsuits.[69] In 2014, the West Virginia Supreme Court came to a similar conclusion in a case involving Maria Miller. After twenty years of marriage, she began a romantic affair in the less-than-romantic setting of retirement planning; she fell in love with a life insurance employee who was helping her with her 401(k) account. Mark Miller, her enraged husband, sued the employee for over half a million dollars, including damages for emotional distress stemming from fear of contracting a "loathsome disease." Miller also sued the employer, New York Life, for failure to train and supervise its promiscuous employee. The court rejected both claims, and in effect suggested that he get on with his life.[70]

Courts give a number of reasons for abolishing criminal conversation and alienation of affection, all of which make sense.[71] As the Mississippi Supreme Court pointed out, criminal conversation requires no actual injury; the doctrine was "born of the notion that the cuckold spouse . . . has some property interest in the chastity of the other. Such [a] presumption . . . ha[s] no vitality in today's society."[72] Another concern is that the action may be vexatious or extortionate, and may even be "counterproductive if it is used for vindictive purposes by a spouse whose marriage has failed for reasons attributable to the fault of that spouse."[73] Two other objections are that "the nature of the [sexual] activities underlying criminal conversation . . . are not such that the risk of damages would likely be a deterrent" and that, "since the injuries suffered are intangible, damage awards are not governed by any true standards, making it more likely that they could result from passion or prejudice."[74] The cases lend themselves to highly speculative damage awards. Aggrieved spouses can recover for injury to their "social position," "disgrace in the community," "humiliation, mortification . . . and shame," "mental anguish," and "loss of support."[75] Commentators have suggested that courts could curb excessively punitive damages awards by requiring that the amounts bear some close relationship to the actual injuries sustained.[76] However, that is an impossible task when the actual injuries are as inherently speculative as shame, anguish, and disgrace.

A final concern is the lack of defenses in criminal conversation actions. Damages are possible even if the parties had separated, and even if the defendant did not know the wife was married or the marriage was not significantly affected.[77] *Feldman v. Feldman*, a 1984 New Hampshire decision, was a textbook case in the argument for the abolition of actions for criminal conversation. The plaintiff, Joan Feldman, had married Ben Feldman, who traveled extensively for his job. The couple had three children and a home in Massachusetts. Some nine years later, Ben Feldman misrepresented himself as a divorcé and married Darlene Feldman, with whom he had a child and a home in New Hampshire. Four years later, Joan discovered Ben's marriage to Darlene. She filed suit for divorce and sued Darlene for criminal conversation and alienation of affection. A special master found for Darlene on the claim of alienation of affection on the ground that Ben had deceived her and she had no intent to alienate his affections for Joan. However, on the criminal conversation claim, the master awarded damages of $35,000. Darlene appealed, and the court found in her favor by eliminating actions for criminal conversation entirely. In the court's view, "viable contented marriages are not broken up by an outsider," and the action " 'diminishes human dignity' by treating spousal affection as a property right." There was no "viable legal rationale for the continued existence of a tort action which essentially seeks to punish an activity without reference to either the activity's motivation or its results."[78]

Not all courts and legislators agree. Some see their role as protecting the marital relationship and "its sanctity against someone who through persuasion, enticement, or inducement" had destroyed a marriage.[79] As one judge put it, "Because we happen to be living in a period of loose morals and frequent extramarital involvements is no reason for a court to put its stamp of approval on this conduct."[80]

But, precisely because we do live in an age of widespread sexual permissiveness, courts should be reluctant to offer the vehicle for vindictive and speculative damage awards. Legislatures should abolish such actions, and, where that has proven politically impossible, courts should take the initiative.[81] Criminal conversation and alienation of affection were initially created by courts, and they should be abolished by courts as outmoded and ineffectual attempts to police marital fidelity. Aggrieved spouses should get a life, not a lawsuit.

Divorce

Adultery plays a continuing but declining role in divorce cases, and that decline should be encouraged. In some jurisdictions, adultery is a bar to alimony or a justification for alimony for the innocent spouse; in others it is a factor in alimony and custody decisions.[82] Even adultery occurring after the spouses have separated can result in denial of alimony.[83] Application of this doctrine occasionally has involved courts in indelicate inquiries into which sexual acts constituted adultery. In one 1986 Louisiana case, the wife admitted undressing and engaging in certain "enumerated sexual activities" that did not involve sexual intercourse. Rejecting the dictionary definition of adultery, the court held that the wife's acts were sufficient to qualify. "It would be fatuous of this court to believe that human passion, kindled in so frank a manner as [the wife] confessed, would not be ultimately consummated."[84] On similar reasoning, a 1997 South Carolina court determined that it did not have to decide exactly which sexual acts constituted adultery. It was enough for the husband to establish that his wife had shared a room with another man on several occasions, and had the "opportunity and inclination" to be "sexually intimate," even though a medical condition made intercourse unlikely.[85]

Courts have, however, divided over whether a same-sex relationship constitutes adultery within the meaning of divorce statutes. In a 2003 New Hampshire case, the court relied on the "plain and ordinary" meaning, as defined by the dictionary, to conclude that adultery involved sexual intercourse, which required persons of the opposite sex.[86] By contrast, other courts have found "no substantial distinction" between homosexual and heterosexual extramarital sexual activity because both involve "marital misconduct."[87] As the dissenting judges in the New Hampshire case noted, it would be "hard to comprehend how the legislature could have intended to exonerate a sexually unfaithful or even promiscuous spouse who engaged in all manner of sexual intimacy . . . except sexual intercourse."[88]

On the whole, courts in divorce cases are less judgmental than in earlier eras. In some jurisdictions, marital misconduct is only one among twelve to fifteen factors affecting property distribution, and courts do not always find it significant in determining financial awards.[89] Other courts have held that adultery should not be used as a "severe penalty" in allocating property.[90]

In custody cases, the Missouri Court of Appeals summarized recent trends: "Adultery is usually insufficient, without more, to stigmatize a mother as an unfit custodian." Such conduct is relevant only if it has an "effect upon the child."[91] Although courts occasionally have talked about adultery as evidence of a mother's moral values, the focus generally has been on whether a child had been exposed to, or harmed by, the mother's illicit conduct.[92] It is no accident that the Missouri court used the term "mother." Although the doctrine governing parental fitness is gender neutral, it is applied disproportionately to mothers in contexts of marital infidelity. In cases in 2009 and 2012, a Mississippi court emphasized that adultery should not be used as a sanction against the guilty parent in awarding custody, but evidence that the mother had sacrificed time with her child to be with her lover was a critical factor in assessing parental fitness.[93] In another Mississippi case several years earlier, the court overturned a custody award to the husband that was based largely on the wife's "poor judgment" in engaging in an extramarital affair. The affair occurred after the wife had left the home, and the record established that she had "good parenting skills."[94] Similarly, in a 2009 South Carolina case, the court held that "flagrant promiscuity" will affect a child's welfare, but that a wife who had two extramarital affairs and brought a lover to her daughter's dance recital did not rise to that level.[95]

Such case law is headed in the right direction. Marital infidelity bears no necessary relationship to parental fitness, and it is far less relevant in financial determinations than are factors such as spousal need. The likelihood of a gender-based double standard in custody cases is a further reason to avoid the use of adultery in assessing parental conduct.

Provocation

Modern cases do not recognize an unwritten law that would excuse the killing of adulterous spouses or their lovers as a form of temporary insanity. However, learning of a spouse's adultery can sometimes constitute provocation sufficient to reduce charges of murder to voluntary manslaughter.[96] The traditional rule is that a defendant must actually confront the couple in a compromising position; just hearing about adultery through "words alone" is insufficient.[97] However, a growing number of jurisdictions, following the Model Penal Code approach, allow juries to consider the totality of circumstances in determining whether verbal provocation is adequate to support a verdict of manslaughter.[98] For example, in two cases from the early 1980s, courts permitted juries to consider a verdict of voluntary manslaughter in cases involving only words. In a Massachusetts case, the wife pointed to her crotch and told her husband "You will never touch this again because I have got something bigger and better for it."[99] In a Georgia case, the husband, who was paralyzed from the waist down, confronted his wife with a letter from her boyfriend. She then taunted him about his disability and said that he "couldn't have sex relationships with her the way other men do."[100] In both cases, the court reversed the murder convictions and left it for a jury on retrial to consider whether a reasonable person would justifiably lose control in such circumstances.

The trend, however, has been to disallow manslaughter verdicts based on purely verbal provocation, and this trend should be encouraged.[101] An early example can be seen in a Massachusetts case involving a defendant who had separated from his wife for several weeks. When he went to see her and their baby, his wife, using an obscenity, told him, "I don't need you around here, I have got another man." When she then told him to get out, he shot her. The court declined to find that the wife's admission of adultery constituted sufficient provocation to support a manslaughter verdict. In the court's view, "past adultery lacks the peculiarly immediate and intense offense to a spouse's sensitivities which has led courts to recognize present adultery as adequate provocation."[102] Similarly, in a 1992 Ohio case, the defendant strangled his fiancée after she told him that she had been sleeping with other men and no longer cared for him. The court found that insufficient provocation to justify a voluntary manslaughter instruction.[103] Similarly, in two consolidated 1989 cases, the Illinois Supreme Court declined to find sufficient provocation where a defendant's wife admitted adultery and either disparaged the defendant's sexual abilities or flaunted the fact that she had slept with her lover in the marital bed. Because in each case the husband suspected his wife's infidelity prior to the admission, the court found that the provocation was insufficient to cause sudden passion that would reduce the crime to voluntary manslaughter.[104] On similar reasoning, a 1999 Massachusetts court refused to reduce charges where a wife reportedly "blurted out that she was with a black guy and his dick was bigger than [the defendant's]." Because the admission of infidelity came as no surprise, it was not the sort of "sudden discovery" that would justify a charge of manslaughter rather than murder.[105] Nor was a man's learning that a child is not his own, a wife's threat to "find someone else to have sex with," or an argument over the wife's infidelity sufficient to show adequate provocation.[106] As a 2000 South Carolina court put it, "spousal adultery is not a license to kill."[107]

Given the large number of spouses who learn of a partner's adultery, these decisions make obvious sense. There is, moreover, evidence suggesting that for most people, even the sight of their spouses committing adultery would not prompt them to lose control.[108] Accordingly, some judges and juries are reluctant to absolve defendants of murder, even where they witness infidelity. In a 1995 New York case, Carl Beck entered the bedroom of his estranged wife while she was having sex with Joseph Valvo. Beck shot Valvo, and after his wife fled to the kitchen to call 911, he shot her as well. At trial, the defendant claimed that Valvo had lunged at him and caused him to fear for his life, and that the gun went off accidently in a struggle. Beck also claimed that he had killed his wife under the influence of extreme emotional disturbance. The jury rejected that claim and the appellate court affirmed. In the court's view, the evidence supported the conclusion that the "actions of the defendant were deliberate, rational, 'and the result of his malevolence' rather than an uncontrolled response to his wife's faithfulness."[109] Similarly, a Georgia court dismissed as "utterly barbarous" a claim that voluntary manslaughter was justified in a case where a husband caught his wife and her lover in a compromising setting; he had been following her for some time, and the act reflected premeditated murder rather than sudden passion.[110] More courts should follow this approach and decline to normalize deadly violence as a reaction to infidelity.[111]

Where courts fail to do so, the legislature can step in. One Maryland lawmaker was moved to act after she saw two men "get away with murder."[112] In one of the cases, a defendant received a sentence of eighteen months in jail for killing his wife hours after finding her in bed with another man. In explaining his sentence, the judge stated, "I seriously wonder how many men married five, four years would have the strength to walk away without inflicting some corporal punishment."[113] In the other case, the defendant received a ten-year sentence for killing his wife after suspecting that she may have been unfaithful. Maryland law permitted a fifteen-year sentence for stealing a television set, but only ten for manslaughter provoked by adultery. In response to lobbying by women's organizations, the legislature removed adultery from the list of provocations that can reduce a murder charge to manslaughter.[114]

Taken together, recent prosecutorial, judicial, and legislative decisions have eroded the legal significance of adultery. Criminal statutes are rarely enforced, and actions for criminal conversation and alienation of affection have been abolished in the vast majority of jurisdictions.

When citizenship is denied or employment terminated for adultery, the rationale is generally unconvincing. In divorce and custody matters, adultery plays a declining role. And in homicide cases, infidelity is less likely to justify reducing the charge from murder to manslaughter. Such changes should not be taken as a sign of greater tolerance for infidelity. As the opinion polls cited in Chapter I make clear, society's condemnation of adultery has increased rather than decreased over the last two decades. What has changed, however, is the public's increased respect for privacy and its decreased confidence in law as a means of policing marital fidelity. The preceding discussion makes clear why courts should get out of the business of monitoring extramarital conduct altogether. Adultery in this age seems to be nobody's business but that of the players in these family dramas.

4

Sex in the Military

Lieutenant Kelly Flinn gained national attention not only because she was the first woman to pilot a B-52 bomber, but also because she lost that job as a result of charges stemming from adultery. She had had a brief affair with a married enlisted man who was not in her chain of command, and then fell in love with a married civilian, Marc Zigo, whose wife was a junior enlistee. When the two began their affair, Zigo assured Flinn that his marriage was breaking up.[1] It was not. Zigo's wife complained to her supervisor, who advised Flinn to stop interfering with the marriage and warned her that she was risking her career.[2] Flinn ignored the advice. An investigation began as a "nasty bit of payback." Flinn had encouraged a friend who had been sexually assaulted by another lieutenant to file a complaint. The lieutenant was sentenced to nine months in prison for various sexual offenses, and got even by telling investigators about Flinn and Zigo. When questioned about the relationship, Flinn claimed that it was "platonic." She didn't know that Zigo had already given the military police detailed accounts of their affair, including her sexual preferences and their methods of birth control.[3] Flinn's commander ordered her to have no further personal contact with Zigo. Despite this order, Flinn hoped to salvage her relationship with Zigo, and allowed him to remain living at her off-base house, where he had moved after his wife kicked him out of their home.

The air force initiated a court-martial, based not only on Flinn's adultery but also on her false statement and failure to obey the order of a superior. She faced a nine-and-a-half-year prison term as well as dishonorable discharge. Flinn did not submit quietly. She hired a team of civilian attorneys and a public relations firm, which launched a national media campaign. It portrayed her as the victim of an archaic law, intrusive investigation, and double standard of enforcement. Many members of the public were appalled that the tactics of a "pajama police" could end a distinguished career, particularly when male officers facing similar charges escaped with less stringent sanctions.[4] New York congresswoman Carolyn Maloney wondered, "If an equally accomplished male pilot had made the same mistakes, how many high-ranking Air Force members would have looked the other way?"[5] Flinn later speculated,

> Maybe the military brass wanted to even the score, to show that women were every bit as capable of sexual peccadilloes as men are—a kind of perverse equal opportunity project. Or maybe, as many women's advocates have suggested, this was a way of saying, without having to say it, that women have no place in the military; let them in and all hell breaks loose.[6]

Whatever the motivation, the air force saw little to be gained from proceeding with the court-martial, in light of the public reaction. In popular-opinion surveys, Americans were closely divided: 43 percent thought Flinn was treated fairly while 47 percent thought that the treatment was unfair. Moreover, 47 percent said that the treatment was worse for Flinn than it would have been for a man, only 17 percent thought the converse, and 27 percent thought the treatment was the same.[7] Almost half of Americans (49 percent) thought that the military should not have special rules prohibiting adultery.[8] Over half (53 percent) thought that the military rules about adultery should be changed.[9]

In the wake of strong public criticism, the military offered, and Flinn accepted, a general discharge, which is given to someone when their service has been "honest and faithful," but when "significant negative aspects of the member's conduct or performance of duty outweigh positive aspects of the member's military record."[10]

Kelly Flinn was not alone. In the five years preceding her discharge, the military court-martialed nearly 900 individuals on charges that included adultery. Many more cases were handled administratively.[11] At the same time that civilian adultery prosecutions have declined, military prosecutions have escalated. This chapter argues that the disparity cannot be justified by military necessity, and that the armed forces have paid an excessive price for their prohibitions on adultery. Extramarital affairs should only be subject to sanctions when they pose a demonstrable threat to good order.

Historical Background

Adultery has always been part of military life, although prior to the 1980s, it was rarely prosecuted.[12] The prohibition has its origins in the British military ethos, which was influenced by Christian views on sexuality. The amendments of 1677 to England's Articles of War made adultery punishable by court-martial or expulsion from the armed forces.[13] During the Revolutionary War, the colonies adopted the English Articles of War.[14] Subsequent U.S. military codes preserved the prohibition on adultery, although it was not explicitly enumerated in the Uniform Code of Military Justice (UCMJ) enacted in 1950.[15] In 1984, as part of a broader reform effort, adultery was added to the Manual for Courts-Martial (MCM) as a substantive offense that could trigger a maximum penalty of dishonorable discharge and confinement for a year.[16]

Although no statistics are available, adultery in the military has long been reported to be widespread.[17] Separation from spouses presents obvious opportunities and temptations. Married servicemen have often patronized prostitutes, and many have had overseas "TDY wives," temporary-duty-assignment mistresses.[18] Air force pilots traditionally greeted each other with the phrase "Wings up, [wedding] rings off."[19] "Do what you want, just don't get caught" was the prevailing wisdom.[20] The most notorious example is that of Dwight D. Eisenhower. While Supreme Allied Commander in Europe during World War II, Eisenhower had a prolonged affair with his driver, Kay Summersby, a member of the Women's Auxiliary Corps. Although most historians believe that the affair was never fully consummated because of Eisenhower's impotence, Summersby's memoir leaves no doubt that the couple was sexually intimate.[21] In 1952, rumors began to circulate that Eisenhower had written to General George Marshall indicating his plans to divorce his wife and marry Summersby. Marshall reportedly responded that if Eisenhower "even came close to doing such a thing, he'd not only bust him out of the Army, he see to it that never for the rest of his life would he be able to draw a peaceful breath."[22] Eisenhower was never disciplined for his actions, and details of the affair did not surface until after his death, with the publication of Summersby's memoir and some of their correspondence.[23]

During the 1980s and 1990s, prosecutions for adultery escalated, partly in response to the inclusion of an explicit prohibition in the MCM, as well as to the rapid influx of women in the armed forces. Gender integration created more opportunities for unlawful "fraternization," relationships between officers and enlisted personnel, which often involved adultery. A 2013 overview by the Associated Press revealed that about a third of military commanders fired over the past eight years lost their positions because of sexually related offenses, including harassment and adultery.[24] According to one female air force captain, "many of us have often said that if we had a dollar for every married man that hit on us ... when we were in the service we'd be living in mansions and driving Rolls."[25]

Legal Standards

The military's standard for prosecuting adultery requires three elements:

(1) That the accused wrongfully had sexual intercourse with a certain person;

(2) That, at the time, the accused or the other person was married to someone else;

(3) That, under the circumstances, the conduct of the accused was to the prejudice of good order and discipline in the armed forces, or was of a nature to bring discredit upon the armed forces.[26]

The MCM provides a detailed explanation of the circumstances under which sanctions for adultery are appropriate.

To constitute an offense under the UCMJ, the adulterous conduct must either be directly prejudicial to good order and discipline or service discrediting. Adulterous conduct that is directly prejudicial includes conduct that has an obvious and measurably divisive effect on unit or organization discipline, morale, or cohesion, or is clearly detrimental to the authority or stature of or respect toward a servicemen. Adultery may also be service discrediting, even though the conduct is only indirectly or remotely prejudicial to good order and discipline. Discredit means to injure the reputation of the armed forces and includes adulterous conduct that has a tendency, because of its open or notorious nature, to bring the service into disrepute, make it subject to public ridicule, or lower it in public esteem.... Commanders should consider all relevant circumstances, including but not limited to the following factors....

(a) The accused's marital status, military rank, grade, or position;

(b) The co-actor's marital status, military rank, grade, and position, or relationship to the armed forces;

(c) The military status of the accused's spouse or the spouse of co-actor, or their relationship to the armed forces;

(d) The impact, if any, of the adulterous relationship on the ability of the accused, the co-actor, or the spouse of either to perform their duties in support of the armed forces;

(e) The misuse, if any, of government time and resources to facilitate the commission of the conduct;

(f) Whether the conduct persisted despite counseling or orders to desist; the flagrancy of the conduct, such as whether any notoriety ensued; and whether the adulterous act was accompanied by other violations of the UCMJ;

(g) The negative impact of the conduct on the units or organizations of the accused, the co-actor, or the spouse of either of them, such as detrimental effect on unit or organization morale, teamwork, and efficiency;

(h) Whether the accused or the co-actor was legally separated; and

(i) Whether the adulterous misconduct involves an ongoing or recent relationship or is remote in time.[27]

Officers can also be held liable for adultery that constitutes conduct "unbecoming an officer and a gentleman." The Manual for Courts-Martial describes such conduct as including "action or behavior in an unofficial or private capacity which, in dishonoring or disgracing the officer personally, seriously compromises the person's standing as an officer." Acts of "indecorum" or crimes of "moral turpitude" qualify.[28]

Commanding officers often have discretion concerning whether to punish the offense by court-martial or by nonjudicial punishment.[29] In 1998, in the wake of the Flinn case, the Defense Department conducted a year-long review of sexual misconduct cases. One upshot was a rule revision that called on commanders to deal with adultery at the lowest appropriate level, namely punishment or counseling within a company, as opposed to a court-martial. At the same time, the rules call for more uniform but tougher treatment of fraternization between officers and enlisted personnel.[30]

Justifications

In justifying its prohibition on adultery, the military relies on three main arguments. The first is that it is necessary to preserve good order and morale. The Supreme Court has recognized that "no military organization can function without strict discipline and regulation that would be unacceptable in a civilian setting."[31] As one air force captain reasoned, if servicemen under an officer's command learn of the officer's adultery, they may cease to respect the officer because "there is widespread moral disdain for adulterous behavior." This could lead to a breakdown in the chain of command, because it's "tough to follow a moral maggot, especially in combat."[32] The problems are compounded when the parties involved are in the same chain of command. As one officer noted, "Where people are in very close proximity, if you've got Joe Smith shacking up with So-and-So's wife, or vice versa, that has a very damaging effect on the morale of that unit."[33] A second concern is that if the public learns of adulterous conduct, it will erode popular respect and support. A third concern is that the frequent separations necessitated by military service may cause spouses to worry about their partner's fidelity.[34] Prohibitions on adultery are seen as a way to shore up marriages strained by separation.

These are the justifications that the court invoked in the only recent case that challenged the constitutionality of the military's adultery prohibitions. There, a twenty-three-year-old married officer was convicted of adultery based on a rendezvous with a civilian at the base quarters that the serviceman shared with his family. The serviceman challenged his conviction under *Lawrence v. Texas,* discussed in Chapter 3. *Lawrence,* he argued, extended a constitutional right of privacy to "discreet consensual adultery ... where there is no other legitimate government interest furthered by prosecuting the offense." In addressing that claim, the appellate court acknowledged the limits on the military's power to enforce adultery prohibitions. In order to constitute an offense under the Uniform Code of Military Justice, the conduct must either be "directly prejudicial to good order and discipline or service discrediting." In the court's view, the conduct at issue met those criteria and therefore forfeited constitutional protection. The serviceman was not separated from his wife, his conduct persisted after discovery by his wife, and it occurred in quarters where other soldiers could find out about it. Such conduct, the court reasoned, could lead "the general public [to] think less of a military service whose noncommissioned officers are free to engage in multiple acts of adultery on board a military installation." In addition, the court cited the military's "particular interest in promoting the preservation of marriages within its ranks." "Because military families are often required to endure extended separations from a spouse," the military had a "unique responsibility to ensure that the morale of their deployed personnel (and that of the spouses left behind) is not adversely affected by concerns over the integrity of their marriages."[35]

But, as the discussion below indicates, enforcement of adultery prohibitions ill serves those interests and comes at excessive cost. The current inconsistent application of those prohibitions does not effectively foster either internal morale or public respect.

Enforcement Practices

No systematic information is available concerning enforcement of the military's ban on adultery. Unless it is accompanied by more serious charges, adultery is rarely subject to court-martial.[36] Because most violations are dealt with at lower levels than court-martial, few cases result in reported decisions. What information is available points to a number of problems. For example, many experts believe that women are treated more harshly than men.[37] In addition to the case of Kelly Flinn, critics point to a 2008 court-martial of Lieutenant Commander Syneeda Penland. She was convicted of conduct unbecoming an officer, failure to obey an order, and making a false statement. All of these charges stemmed from a sexual relationship between Penland, who was single, and a married junior officer in a separate chain of command, who was not punished. As a result of the conviction, the navy dismissed Penland a few months short of retirement, causing her to lose her severance pay, health benefits, and military pension. Penland unsuccessfully argued that the charges were brought in retaliation for her efforts to expose financial improprieties.[38] The prosecution presented no evidence that the affair was notorious, misused government time or resources, or had a detrimental effect on either party's unit or individual performance.[39] The prosecution stated that the case was not about adultery, but about Penland using her rank to try to persuade her lover's wife, an enlisted service member, to divorce him.[40] Given the limited information available about the facts, it is unclear how the government proved that the affair was prejudicial to good order or constituted conduct unbecoming an officer. The case does, however, suggest that the factors in the MCM designed to limit adultery prosecutions may have little effect in practice. And the personal costs are substantial. In addition to the loss of pay and benefits, Penland has a felony conviction on her record. As she told reporters, "They've ruined my life; not just my career but my life."[41]

Adultery investigations also have been needlessly humiliating. In some instances, the military has pursued adultery charges to embarrass a service member when more serious charges "turned to crap."[42] In 2014, Brigadier General Jeffrey Sinclair was reprimanded and fined $20,000 for his affair with an officer under his command. His sentence came after the army dropped claims that he had assaulted the officer.[43] Another celebrated example involved the prosecution of James Yee, a Muslim Guantanamo Bay chaplain who was charged with adultery and possession of pornography after espionage charges proved groundless. If convicted, Yee faced a sentence of thirteen years in prison.[44] In the wake of claims that the prosecution was a vindictive effort to cover up a botched investigation, the military dropped the charges and issued a reprimand.[45] But the harm to Yee's marriage had already been done. His wife told the *New York Times* that the shame of the adultery proceedings was more devastating than the espionage investigation.[46]

Even when the underlying adultery charge is legitimate, the process can be unnecessarily intrusive. Once activated, "military investigations tend to be very very through," as was clear in the Flinn case.[47] Of what relevance was information about her foreplay preferences, favorite positions, and birth control techniques? The potential for invasive oversight is compounded by the telephone hotlines that military officials have established for complaints about sexual abuse. The intention was to "provide a channel of communication for service men and women who felt they could no longer trust their chain of command." "Now," critics charge, "the hot lines seem to have evolved into a funnel for malicious gossip and anonymous back-stabbing."[48]

Inconsistency is another problem. The military has long been charged with providing "different spanks for different ranks"; the "higher the person who commits the offense, the less happens to him."[49] A textbook case of leniency involved Major General David Hale, the army's deputy inspector general in charge of overseeing personnel misconduct, including sexual abuse. Hale allegedly blackmailed the wife of his deputy into having sex with him by falsely claiming that her husband was involved in an adulterous affair of his own. Hale reportedly offered to protect the deputy from court-martial if his wife slept with him. The wife claimed that Hale had promised to marry her, but that their affair collapsed when she learned that he had lied about her husband's affair. She subsequently filed a complaint. While the investigation was pending, Hale asked to be allowed to leave the military. The request was granted and he was honorably discharged, an action widely criticized as emblematic of the "kid gloves" treatment reserved for high-ranking officers.[50] The criticism escalated when a report by the inspector general subsequently disclosed that Hale had engaged in sexual relationships with wives of four officers under his command during overseas assignments. In response, the army tightened its retirement procedures for senior officers.[51] It also subsequently required Hale to be tried by court-martial.[52] He pled guilty to eight counts of misconduct including lying to his superiors about his affairs. The penalty appeared relatively light given the seriousness of the charges. He paid $22,000 in penalties and was demoted to a one-star brigadier general, which reduced by only $9,000 his annual pension of $75,744.[53]

Criticism of the seeming double standard for high-ranking officers and other soldiers has led to the opposite problem: overly punitive treatment of officers for conduct posing little threat to good order or public respect. In 2005, the army removed four-star general Kevin Byrnes from command amid allegations that he had had an extramarital affair with a civilian. The removal occurred just three months before the general was set to retire after thirty-six years of service. Experts believed that the military was "trying to make it clear that four-stars don't get special treatment." Recent scandals created a "need to send that message."[54] According to one experienced military defense lawyer, further sanctions were unnecessary because the army was already "taking his career and flushing it down the toilet. There's not much more that you can do to a high-ranking officer like that. His legacy is ruined."[55]

In a similar case, army major general John Longhouser announced he was retiring early and at one rank beneath his current standing because of revelations that five years earlier he had had an affair. Although he was separated from his wife at the time and had subsequently reconciled with her, he was forced to leave his command. According to Secretary of Defense William Cohen, "There is no witch hunt out there. . . . I am not the secretary of morality. But the military has very high standards. . . . And when those standards are breached, then there are consequences that flow from it."[56]

Cohen subsequently walked the statement back when it was revealed that a respected four-star general of the air force, Joseph W. Ralston, had had an affair thirteen years ago with a civilian woman while he was separated from his wife. This time, Secretary Cohen vowed to "draw a line" against a "frenzy" of sexual allegations that threatened to derail General Ralston as the leading candidate to become chairman of the Joint Chiefs of Staff, the president's top adviser on military matters. "We need to come back to a rule of reason instead of a rule of thumb," Secretary Cohen said. At the same time, the secretary warned against those who would "have the military define decency down."[57] Ralston nonetheless withdrew his candidacy. His decision may have been influenced by the hard line that he himself had taken two years earlier when he relieved Lieutenant General Thomas Griffith of his command because of an affair. Ralston's explanation was that he had "lost confidence in Griffith's ability to command due to inappropriate personal conduct."[58]

In commenting on Ralston's withdrawal, Senator John McCain stated that "the long and distinguished career of a fine Air Force general in its entirety surely says more about his qualifications for continued service than does an allegation of a single mistake in his personal life."[59] A marine private saw it differently, given Flinn's treatment: "Our contract says flat out you can't mess around . . . and if it applies to her [Flinn], it should apply to him."[60] The American public, however, saw a distinction. Half of those surveyed thought that Flinn should be forced to resign, while less than a third (31 percent) thought that Ralston should be forced to resign.[61] In a separate Gallup poll, 57 percent of respondents also said that the military should make exceptions to its policies for cases of adultery that occurred "many years ago." When respondents were given the choice between making such exceptions and eliminating the ban on adultery in the military, almost half (49 percent) thought there should be no prohibition at all, and 29 percent thought that exceptions should be made.[62] When asked if they thought that adultery and sexual misconduct were widespread in the military, three-quarters of Americans answered affirmatively.[63] More than half (58 percent), however, thought that the military over-enforced its rules on adultery.[64]

The costs of over-enforcement came home in 2012 when General David Petraeus, the director of the Central Intelligence Agency and one of America's most decorated four-star generals, resigned after an investigation revealed his extramarital affair. The affair was discovered in the course of an FBI inquiry into whether a computer used by Petraeus had been compromised. The woman involved was Paula Broadwell, the coauthor of a biography of Petraeus. Press accounts tended to be more judgmental of Broadwell than of Petraeus; she was commonly portrayed as a "shameless, self-promoting prom queen" who had enticed a much older man into career suicide.[65] Petraeus's own statement accepted full responsibility. He stated, "After being married for over 37 years, I showed extremely poor judgment by engaging in an extramarital affair. Such behavior is unacceptable, both as a husband and as the leader of an organization such as ours."[66] Some commentators agreed and thought it "looks bad for the military." If other soldiers committed that crime, they could be dishonorably discharged, so Petraeus was "getting off easy."[67] Other commentators agreed about Petraeus's poor judgment, but thought the problem was not sex but stupidity: Petraeus had posted sexually explicit messages in a Gmail folder. "Got that," wrote Roger Simon in *Politico.* "The head of the Central Intelligence Agency thinks Gmail accounts are secure and untraceable. What, he couldn't have checked with a tech-savvy 12-year-old first?"[68]

Many commentators, however, questioned the need for Petraeus's resignation and criticized the "antiquated" code that seemed to make it necessary.[69] If the concern was that an affair could lead to blackmail, what was the point of resignation once the conduct became public? One *Washington Post* commentator drew an analogy to an apocryphal French diplomat who was confronted by a Soviet agent during the Cold War and shown pictures of himself having sex with a woman not his wife. The Frenchman peered at the pictures and then pointed to one and another. "I'll take this one and yes, that one too."[70] Although American culture may be less permissive, Petraeus could hardly be blackmailed after the affair went viral. Other commentators questioned whether there wasn't some better use of national security resources than combing through military emails looking for inappropriate communications, as happened not only to Petraeus, but also to another commander, John Allen. "Is this the country we want to live in?" asked one critic.[71] When the American public was asked if Petraeus should resign, 47 percent thought that he was right to do so. However, 62 percent thought that adultery should not be a military crime, a figure even higher than the majority of Americans who said the same following the Flinn affair.[72]

Directions for Reform

As poll results indicate, prohibitions on adultery are not necessary to ensure public respect. Nor is giving individual commanders so much discretion to set punishments an effective way of fostering consistent treatment and internal morale. The Cox Commission, a group brought together by the National Institute of Military Justice in 2001 to evaluate changes to the Uniform Code of Military Justice, pointed out that most adultery is not prosecuted, and that when it is, there is a widespread perception that enforcement is "arbitrary, even vindictive."[73] Moreover, as cases like those of Flinn, Petraeus, Longhouser, Byrnes, and Ralston demonstrate, the military is paying a high price in lost talent for enforcement of rules that are out of step with prevailing public views.

The obvious solution is for the military to remove adultery as a basis for discipline. Existing sanctions for fraternization and conduct unbecoming an officer could accomplish similar goals in situations in which adulterous affairs pose a demonstrable threat to morale and good order.[74] The military could still prosecute conduct that poses a conflict of interest and prejudice to the unit, such as a sexual relationship between an officer and a solider or the spouse of a solider under his or her command.[75] The punishment would not stem from the fact that the soldier was married, but from the potential for sexual coercion and damage to unit cohesion. Adultery that distracts individuals from their military duties should be dealt with like any other personal problem.[76]

Such a regime would result in different outcomes in cases that have been subject to military oversight. For example, in one mid-1990s case, a military court upheld criminal penalties against a married officer separated from his wife who had sex in the barracks with a civilian. In the court's view, such conduct tended "to reduce the other soldiers' confidence in his integrity, leadership, and respect for law and authority . . . [and] to cause the other soldiers to be less likely to conform their conduct to the rigors of military discipline."[77] Such purely speculative damages should not trigger prosecution. If adultery was removed as an offense, presumably other soldiers would not view it as contrary to respect for law and authority. So, too, removal of the ban on adultery would require a different result in a case involving Lieutenant Colonel Ronald Kroop, who was court-martialed for two adulterous affairs. The first was an off-base liaison with a sergeant not in his chain of command. The second affair was with a design engineer under Kroop's command. Sexual relations occurred in hotel rooms while the two were on temporary duty assignments. The woman in the second affair gave mixed signals about whether she wanted to end the relationship. The result was a confrontation between the woman, her husband, and Kroop in his office during on-duty hours.[78] Under the reforms proposed here, only the second affair would be prosecuted; it runs contrary to rules on fraternization. It would also be appropriate to force resignation and demotion in the case of a major general who had affairs with the wives of two subordinate officers, given the potential for abuse of power and disruption of unit cohesion.[79]

A 2014 proceeding demonstrates the risks of exploitation. It involved charges against Brigadier General Jeffrey Sinclair, a former deputy commander of American forces in southern Afghanistan. His affair with a subordinate officer began consensually but ended in what the woman claimed was forced oral sex and a threat to kill her if she disclosed the relationship. The case ended in a plea to charges including adultery and maltreatment, and a sentence demoting him two ranks and fining him $20,000.[80] But again, the threat posed to military order did not stem from the fact that Sinclair was married; the conduct would have been equally objectionable if it had not involved adultery.

The point of these examples is to underscore the rationale for less oversight and more consistency in the military's response to sexual misconduct. As recent reports make clear, the armed forces face a major challenge in dealing effectively with sex, but the problem involves assault, not adultery. Over the last quarter century, more than half a million uniformed men and women have experienced rape or attempted rape.[81] Reports of sexual assault and rape were up 50 percent in 2013, and another 8 percent in 2014.[82] Only one in four cases of sexual assault in 2014 was reported.[83] Of the 5,061 cases in 2013, fewer than one in ten, only 484, went to trial, and only 376 resulted in convictions.[84] An armed service member who sexually assaulted a fellow service member had a 92 percent chance of avoiding a court-martial.[85] As an army nurse told the cochair of a new bipartisan caucus on military sexual assault, "I'm more afraid of my own soldiers than of the enemy."[86] Resources that are now expended on adultery investigations should be redirected to more serious cases of sexual assault. For most extramarital affairs, what the military needs is an effective version of a policy no longer appropriate in its original context of sexual orientation: "Don't ask, don't tell."

5

Alternative Lifestyles

Although taboos on adultery are almost universal, monogamy is not.[1] According to some historical research, it has been the cultural ideal in a minority of known societies. In the majority, men have been able to have more than one wife.[2] Given these norms, it is striking that nonmonogamous marital arrangements receive such little public or academic attention in our own society. In one survey of popular marriage and family textbooks, alternative lifestyles received virtually no mention.[3] After a brief flurry of interest in the topic in the late 1960s and early 1970s, discussion in the United States waned. "Whatever Happened to Swingers, Group Marriages, and Communes?," reads the title of one contemporary overview.[4]

The answer is that they are still around but in less visible forms. They are aided by a burgeoning self-help literature on alternative lifestyles and an ever-expanding number of websites for couples seeking extramarital sexual encounters.[5] There are no reliable figures on the number of people in consensual multiple-partner relationships, but estimates for the United States generally range from 0.5 million to 9.8 million.[6]

These relationships take a variety of forms, which typically involve adultery, although they are virtually never prosecuted under adultery statutes. One alternative lifestyle is swinging, in which married or committed couples exchange partners for sexual purposes.[7] The practice, once labeled "wife swapping," is generally described as casual, recreational sex. It is distinguished from polyamory, a term coined in the 1990s to describe the practice of having more than one loving sexual relationship at the same time, with the consent of all partners involved.[8] A subgroup of polyamory involves open marriage, in which partners allow each other to have sexual relationships with others.[9] Such marriages may involve groups that pool resources and share sexual partners. Another form of polyamory is polygamy, in which husbands have multiple wives (polygyny) or, less commonly, wives have multiple husbands (polyandry).

This chapter argues that alternative lifestyles should receive greater social and legal tolerance. To better understand their dynamics, it is useful to begin with a historical perspective.

Historical Background

In 1820, the Scottish immigrant Frances Wright lectured on free love throughout the United States. Her doctrine stressed the right to change partners at will.[10] It was not well received. Critics charged that she had "unsexed herself" by launching a "crusade against Religion, marriage, chastity, order and decency, and the very foundations of civil society."[11] Another advocate of alternative lifestyles was John Humphrey Noyes, a former protestant minister expelled for his heretical doctrines. In 1844, he founded a commune in Putney,

Vermont, that practiced complex marriage. All the men were married to all the women, and children were raised by the group. If any couple seemed to be developing exclusive attachments, the parties were forbidden to visit one another or banished to another part of the community.[12] Individuals had to request permission to become parents; requests were granted to those who demonstrated spiritual perfection and an optimal physical condition.[13] In 1847, Noyes was arrested for adultery, and warrants were issued for several of his followers. Noyes was released and group members left for Oneida, New York, where they established the best-known of the nineteenth-century utopian communities. It grew to 300 members before threats of legal action and leadership issues caused Noyes to flee to Canada. He then proposed that community members abandon complex marriage and obey laws on fornication and adultery, which they did. Commitment to communal goals died out, and the group became a joint stock company that was highly successful in silverware production.[14]

Some historians estimate that as many as 500 utopian communities existed in the United States in the nineteenth century.[15] Those that practiced alternative lifestyles denied that free love entailed promiscuity. Rather, it meant that parties should stay in a relationship only as long as mutual love remained. This stance often provoked responses by law enforcement officials. They frequently made arrests with the aim of forcing free-love residents to leave the area to avoid prosecution for adultery or related moral offenses.[16]

Those associated with the free-love movement generally agreed with a tract by Stephen Pearl Andrews, which began, "I reject and repudiate the interference of the State in my morals."[17] Beyond that point, however, there was no consensus on the value of marriage or the legalization of divorce. Some believed that marriage could be good as long as it did not outlast the love that inspired it.[18] Others wanted an alternative to exclusive marital relationships.

The concept of alternative lifestyles reached a wider audience in the late nineteenth century, when the celebrated lecturer and newspaper editor Victoria Woodhull advocated sexual freedom. She argued that sex should occur only when a man and a woman loved each other and that they had an inalienable right to love for as long or short a period as they chose. Marriage restricted this ideal by allowing sex without love between husbands and wives, and by preventing loving sex between those not married to each other.[19] To highlight the hypocrisy of opponents of free love, she publicized the affair that a prominent Brooklyn minister and moralist, Henry Ward Beecher, was having with a married parishioner, Elizabeth Tilton. Tilton's husband sued Beecher for criminal conversation and alienation of affection in a sensational trial that scandalized America. Beecher won the case, and Woodhull was widely condemned and briefly imprisoned on federal charges of sending obscene material through the mail. Although she was eventually acquitted, she immigrated to England and withdrew from public attention.[20]

This was not the end of free love as a movement. Ezra Heywood founded the Free Love League in 1873. He then published a free-love tract, *Cupid's Yokes*, which claimed that the human heart was capable of loving any number of times and persons: "The more it loves the more it can love."[21] *Cupid's Yokes* described marriage as a form of prostitution. This earned the moral indignation of the famous anti-vice crusader Anthony Comstock, who had Heywood jailed for obscenity.[22] Another advocate of free love was feminist anarchist Emma Goldman. In 1930, she wrote, "I demand the independence of woman, her right to support herself; to live for herself; to love whomever she pleases, or as many as she pleases. I demand freedom for both sexes, freedom of action, freedom in love and freedom in motherhood."[23]

Polygamy became controversial in the nineteenth century as a practice associated with the Mormon Church. The church was established in 1830 by Joseph Smith, who claimed a right to practice polygamy inspired by the Old Testament. Smith and his successor, Brigham Young, both had dozens of wives, and, in 1852, polygamy was officially announced as a part of the religion.[24] This resulted in a firestorm of protest. As a consequence, the polygamy doctrine was renounced by the church in 1890 under federal pressure that made renunciation a condition for Utah's statehood.[25] However, until the 1950s, practitioners of breakaway polygamous sects were routinely jailed. That ceased after a major 1953 raid evoked a negative public reaction to photographs of children being torn from their parents to be placed in foster care.[26] After that debacle, law enforcement typically intervened only on reports of child abuse, underage marriage, or welfare fraud.

The "sexual revolution" of the 1960s attracted increased interest in alternative lifestyles. By the turn of the twenty-first century, there were an estimated 3,000 to 4,000 communes operating in the United States, some of which practiced nonmonogamous living arrangements.[27] One of the most celebrated communes was the Sandstone Retreat, based in the hills above Los Angeles. Founded by John and Barbara Williamson in 1967, Sandstone combined humanistic psychology with sexual freedom. All the doors of the rooms were removed and clothing was optional. During its five years of operation, about 8,000 people passed through, almost all from the upper-middle class. To some, it was a place where they could play out their sexual fantasies. For others, it was a turning point in their lives, and it influenced authors such as Alex Comfort, the author of *The Joy of Sex*. According to Barbara Williamson, the only difference between a Sandstone party and one that you would go to at a friend's home was the fact that most of the people did not have their clothes on and sexuality was permitted. "But everything else would be the same."[28]

Kerista, another well-known commune, started out in the Haight Ashbury district of San Francisco in the aftermath of the 1967 Summer of Love. During that summer, some 100,000 individuals gathered in the Haight, many of whom practiced a version of free love. In the Kerista commune, some thirty members participated in three different group marriages that lasted twenty years.[29] Kerista was well known for creating a rotational sleeping schedule to prevent pair bonding, and for punishing infractions of group rules by withholding sex or threatening banishment.[30]

The publication of Gilbert Bartell's 1971 book, *Group Sex: An Eyewitness Report on the American Way of Swinging*, stimulated interest in swinging. Bartell's research, confirmed in later studies, found that swingers were overwhelmingly white, middle class, married, politically conservative, and secretive about their activities.[31] By the turn of the twenty-first century, some estimates put the number of swingers, or "lifestyle practitioners," at close to three million.[32] A smaller number of stable polyamorous families were also in existence, sometimes estimated at about half a million.[33]

Although the "mainstream" polyamory community has had a decidedly heterosexual focus, gays and lesbians have played a role in the spread of polyamorous concepts. Celeste West, author of *Lesbian Polyfidelity*, was among the first lesbians to take a stand for polyamory in the early 1990s.[34] Bisexual women are common in polyamorous communities but gays and lesbians are not; they tend to have their own communities.[35] Because the phenomenon of same-sex marriage is too recent for research to have developed on alternative lifestyles among married gay and lesbian individuals, the discussion that follows focuses on heterosexual couples and the rationale for their greater social and legal acceptance.[36]

Swinging and Open Marriage

Although swinging is widely perceived as a deviant and objectionable lifestyle, supporters point to a number of benefits.[37] Swinging allows individuals to experience sexual variety and to live out their fantasies without secrecy or deceit. The vast majority of swingers report being happy with that lifestyle and most credit it with improving their marriages.[38] In one online survey of over 1,000 couples, almost two-thirds (62 percent) said their marriages were happier after swinging.[39] Another study found that the divorce rate among swingers was lower than the norm.[40] As one swinger reported, "It did a lot for our own sex life. We had much better sex after we started switching than before. I don't know why, but we did." Another woman similarly noted that swinging allowed sex that was "pure and uninhibited" with "no guilt." She stopped, however, when the fantasy wore off and people began to talk.[41]

Swinging tends to attract white, middle-class, and well-educated participants. People of color often feel uncomfortable at largely white parties. One worried about being seen as the "token black," or "novelty," and didn't want to feel that "people are attracted to me ... because they're trying to figure out something. Like I'm some anthropological experiment." Black people who are having nonmonogamous relationships may be less likely to label them as polyamorous. One African American woman who engaged in poly relationships thought that "a lot of African American men are poly and just not open about it." She also felt that there was a double standard. Women who were poly were seen as "hoes."[42]

When asked about the disadvantages of swinging, practitioners mainly voiced concerns about sexually transmitted disease and AIDS. In one study, almost two-thirds had changed their behaviors because of the AIDS epidemic, typically becoming more selective in their partners and practicing safe sex. Other concerns included jealousy, anxiety about performance, fear of public exposure, and the time and effort required.[43] Some swingers discontinued the lifestyle because of legal or community sanctions. As one female lawyer noted,

> If I told anyone at work how I lived or what is my philosophy, I'd be fired first and disbarred second. The courts might even take my child from me. What I am doing in my private life could be interpreted as a crime against public morality. There are laws against that sort of thing.... Maybe no one would care. But it is just not worth taking the risk to find out. It is difficult enough to get a job under ordinary circumstances these days.[44]

Her husband worried about writers who might infiltrate swingers' parties. "And before you knew it, you might turn up on the front page of a newspaper. And that was not something that we wanted to happen to us."[45]

Open marriages carry somewhat different advantages and disadvantages. These marriages take various forms. Some involve group marriages, typically consisting of more than one man and more than one woman who live together in a single family unit. Others involve multiple adults who share living arrangements but do not consider themselves married to all other group members. Because polyamorous individuals do not attempt to take out multiple marriage licenses, they are not generally violating bigamy laws.[46] They are, however, violating many states' laws against fornication and adultery, although studies of alternative lifestyles report no enforcement of such statutes.[47] In some open marriages, dubbed "the new monogamy," each partner assumes that the other will remain the main attachment, but that outside relationships may occur as long as they are transparent and don't threaten the primary connection.[48] Often, polyamorous couples pass as monogamous, a practice that protects them from stigma and discrimination.[49] One of the rare cases of law enforcement intervention involved commune members charged with lewd and lascivious behavior stemming from nude sunbathing. The jury acquitted.[50] Still, the possibility of criminal sanctions adds a layer of fear, guilt, and shame that discourages people from coming out.[51]

Cases in which polyamorous parents have lost custody add another deterrent. In one prominent case, a triad who appeared on an MTV series, *Sex in the 90s*, lost custody to the child's grandmother.[52] The court ruled against custody for the mother without even allowing her to testify. In explaining that ruling, the judge stated, "I am not about to put that child back into a situation where all three of these people are in the same bed." Although the mother's attorney protested that the three did not all sleep together, the court viewed their lifestyle as conclusive evidence of unfitness. "Parents have to set the correct example for the kids," the judge reasoned. "And part of the statute says that you have to be concerned with the moral upbringing of the child."[53] In response to such cases, the nonprofit Polyamory Society posted a warning on its website: "If your PolyFamily has children, please do not put your children and family at risk by coming out to the public or by being interviewed [by] the press!"[54]

Many individuals do not start out consciously choosing polyamory, but "find that polyamory has chosen them."[55] As one wife put it, "I never believed that a piece of paper could stop you from being attracted to somebody." Her husband added, "We never decided to have anything called 'an open marriage.' We just decided to allow what happens to happen. . . . Our marriage is just whatever it is." What happened was that the husband had brief sexual encounters and the wife had long-term affairs based on emotional attachment. Occasionally they found another couple with whom they could switch partners. "Some people would be horrified by the idea," the husband reported. "But these were our friends. It was no big deal."[56] In another case, after a husband had an affair with a neighbor, his wife and the neighbor's husband decided they also felt an attraction; things developed to the point where they combined households, including their children, for over a decade. The husband who initially had the affair then struggled with a desire to engage in a second, secret affair.[57] In a third case, a couple had been married for twenty-three years when the husband fell in love with another woman. He wanted to include her in the relationship rather than divorcing his wife. Both women were initially skeptical, but ultimately developed a close friendship and enjoyed sharing the husband in bed.[58]

In a less happy example, a couple had been married for twelve years and although they had agreed from the beginning that their marriage would be open, neither had gone beyond playful flirtation. Suddenly the wife found herself in love with another man. She didn't want to upset her husband so she kept the affair a secret. When she finally confessed that she was in love, her husband felt angry and betrayed, and wanted to retreat to monogamy.[59]

Nonmonogamous couples often go through an explicit process of negotiating boundaries, in which the spouses define particular behaviors, emotions, and kinds of partners as either acceptable or off limits. For example, out-of-town sex is OK, sex in our bed is not; emotional or long-term involvement is unacceptable; and sex with friends or co-workers is impermissible. Boundaries are often set, transgressed, and renegotiated over time as individuals and circumstances change.[60]

The polyamorous community is important in bringing together practitioners because it provides a pool of potential partners and support in a world where nonconformists are often stigmatized. Some people seek out or stumble on a polyamorous subculture (usually on-line). Others are recruited by lovers or potential lovers who hope to involve them in multiple relationships. Individuals often establish multiple partner relationships and only later come to identify as poly-amorous when they discover the term. Polyamorous groups provide emotional assistance in the form of empathy, advice, and a new frame of reference to help normalize the lifestyle. They offer an environment where individuals can discuss relationships and expect under-standing rather than condemnation. One woman recalled receiving sympathy and advice from a support meeting after a relationship be-tween two men she loved degenerated into bitterness and jealousy. "I needed to hear something else from people besides, 'well, what did you expect to happen, you little slut?'"[61]

Couples in open marriages generally report equal or higher levels of satisfaction than do couples in monogamous relationships.[62] The most commonly cited benefits include shared resources; greater ful-fillment of physical, emotional, and social needs; and the excitement of new experiences.[63] Couples report that their sex lives improve as they discover new skills, techniques, and possibilities.[64] To minimize jealousy and insecurity, many use a rotation schedule to determine sleeping arrangements.[65]

Although research on polyamory's impact on children is fragmen-tary, some studies find that polyamorous parenting increases resources and adds flexibility to parent-child relationships. Because the family involves more than two adults, it is often able to afford to keep one parent at home. Children also get more attention from a larger number of adults. Of course, children may experience difficulties when a parent's partner leaves. As one child asked, "I know why you guys are breaking up but why does he have to break up with me too?"[66] However, the same problem arises when monogamous couples divorce, and the consequences may be greater for conventional marriages because the entire family unit is destroyed. Moreover, one study has found that polyamorous relationships last as long as monogamous ones.[67] The majority of children say they have no problem with their parents having multiple partners, or that the disadvantages outweigh the advantages.[68] Few experience stigma, partly because the lifestyle is invisible to outsiders. Many families operate with a don't ask, don't tell policy, so "it just doesn't come up that much."[69] One study found that children in open marriages were above average in terms of academic performance, self-esteem, and social skills.[70]

Yet polyamory also has its problems. Research suggests that 80 percent or more of couples in open marriages experience jealousy.[71] The resulting conflict can seriously damage relationships. Open marriage is a primary cause of divorce in a substantial minority of the couples who have this arrangement.[72] Some research suggests that divorce is more likely for couples in open marriages than for couples in monogamous relationships.[73] One five-year study found that many couples shifted from open to sexually monogamous relationships because participants "felt that non-monogamy was too time consuming, took too much energy or was too complicated. They also thought that it got in the way of developing love, trust, and more intimate relationships with a partner."[74]

Polygamy

Some polyamorous relationships are polygamous: the man (it is almost always a man) is married to more than one spouse, either formally, as in certain religions, or informally. Estimates of the number of Americans who practice polygamy vary widely, ranging between 20,000 and 500,000.[75] Many are Mormon Fundamentalists. They are in about a dozen extended groups of members of the Fundamentalist Church of Jesus Christ of Latter-Day Saints. The mainstream Mormon church, the Church of Jesus Christ of Latter-Day Saints, has excommunicated polygamists and insisted that none of their splinter groups should be called "Mormon."[76] Members of these groups sometimes face sanctions for welfare fraud, or for child abuse and statutory rape when wives are underage, but otherwise they generally live undisturbed.[77] It is difficult to prosecute them under bigamy laws because they typically record only the first marriage and witnesses to later marriages are unwilling to cooperate.[78] According to a Utah attorney general, "We all know what's going on. But trying to do anything about it legally would be opening one Pandora's box after another."[79] The same patterns of nonenforcement are typical for other polygamist groups as well.[80]

In recent years, polygamy has been in the news, partly because of high-visibility litigation and televised coverage. In 2008, Texas authorities raided a fundamentalist Mormon compound and arrested its leader, Warren Jeffs. Jeffs was convicted of sexual assault of two teenage girls after forcing the girls into marriage and fathering a child with one of them.[81] Around the same time, polygamist Kody Brown costarred, with his four wives and seventeen children, on a reality show, *Sister Wives*. The show was promoted as an effort to demonstrate how the Brown family attempted to "navigate life as a 'normal' family in a society that shuns their lifestyle."[82] *Sister Wives* was joined by HBO's series, *Big Love*, which ran for five seasons before airing its final episode in 2011. It followed the life of a fundamentalist Mormon husband who balanced three wives and eight children while maintaining a small business and ultimately running for political office.

Increased public attention to polygamy also resulted from suggestions that it might be entitled to constitutional protection. Some have cited court decisions striking down prohibitions on sodomy and protecting same-sex marriage as forerunners to broader safeguards for unconventional sexual relationships.[83] In a widely publicized interview, former Republican senator and presidential candidate Rick Santorum warned that this was possible: "If the Supreme Court says that you have the right to consensual sex within your home, then you have the right to polygamy, you have the right to incest, you have the right to adultery."[84] In his dissent in the Supreme Court's decision invalidating sodomy laws, Justice Scalia made a similar prediction. Opponents of same-sex marriages also doubted that there was any "logical reason" to prevent courts' extension of the same right to polygamous couples.[85]

Many disputed that logic. As they noted, prohibitions against polygamy have long withstood constitutional challenge. In 1878, in *Reynolds v. United States*, the U.S. Supreme Court upheld an anti-bigamy statute against claims that it infringed Mormons' religious freedom.[86] A subsequent decision sustained the convictions of six fundamentalist Mormon men for transporting their plural wives across state lines in violation of the Mann Act. That act criminalized the use of interstate commerce to move women from one state to another for purposes of prostitution or "other immoral purposes." In affirming the convictions, the Court described polygamy as a "return to barbarism," "contrary to the spirit of Christianity," and a "notorious example of promiscuity."[87] In 2004 and 2006, the Utah Supreme Court affirmed bigamy convictions, claiming that the practice was associated with harms to wives and children.[88] However, in 2013, in *Brown v. Buhman*, a federal district court struck down a portion of the Utah law against bigamy that criminalized cohabitation by married persons with people other than their spouses. The court viewed the law as void for vagueness and a violation of the constitutional right to free exercise of religion. The court noted that the act had rarely been enforced, and then only in the context of religiously motivated cohabitation. This enforcement pattern had created "substantial uncertainty" as to whether individuals would be prosecuted under the statute.[89] The court did, however, uphold the law's ban on any attempt by a married person to enter into a second marriage that would be recognized by the state. The case is under appeal.

In none of these cases did the courts undertake any comprehensive review of the evidence for and against prohibiting polygamy. *Reynolds* simply summarized the conventional view that "polygamy has always been odious among the northern and western nations of Europe," and concluded that it would undermine the "sacred obligation" of marriage.[90] In one of the Utah decisions, the court relied on a student-written law review article for the proposition that "crimes not unusually attendant to the practice of polygamy include incest, sexual assault, statutory rape and failure to pay child support." The court added that "the closed nature of polygamous communities makes obtaining evidence of and prosecuting these crimes challenging."[91]

A review of the evidence supporting anti-polygamy legislation by the British Columbia Supreme Court suggested grounds for concern. Unlike commentators who found children benefiting from open marriage, this court concluded that children in polygamous families suffered more emotional, behavioral, and physical problems than other children, as well as lower educational achievement.[92] These problems are thought to reflect higher levels of conflict and tension in polygamous families, as well as the inability of fathers to give sufficient attention to all of their children. Other researchers find similar harms to children, including higher risks of infant mortality, abuse, and neglect.[93] Early marriages for girls have negative health implications and significantly limit their education and socioeconomic opportunities. Recent prosecutions have detailed horrendous cases of child rape of wives as young as thirteen. In one instance, a sixteen-year-old girl accused her father of whipping her and dumping her, semiconscious, in a remote area when she rebelled against marrying her uncle as his fifteenth wife. She walked seven miles to a gas station and called 911. Her father was convicted of child abuse and the uncle was convicted of incest and unlawful sexual conduct.[94] Plural wives are also vulnerable to domestic abuse, from other wives as well as husbands.[95] Although some research finds that the incidence of abuse is no greater in polygamous than monogamous families, the secrecy and social isolation that polygamy invites make it more difficult for victims to seek assistance.[96] Polygamy also leads to a surplus of young unmarried men, sometimes labeled "lost boys," who cannot find wives and therefore feel forced to leave their fundamentalist Mormon communities with few skills or social support structures.[97] Welfare and tax fraud are also thought to be common in fundamentalist Mormon families.[98]

Yet, all too often, popular debate falls into the trap of comparing the worst forms of polygamy to ideal forms of monogamy, and ignoring the benefits that multiple wives provide. Some Mormon women consider polygamy a solution to such difficulties as single motherhood, poverty, loneliness, and work / family conflicts. Many of these women have a strong sense of sisterhood with their fellow wives and rely on them for help with childcare.[99] The British Columbia court heard testimony from some women who noted the advantages of polygamy for wives pursuing a career because "they are not 100 percent responsible for the care and feeding of their husbands."[100] One lawyer who lived with her husband and his eight other wives wrote in the *New York Times* that polygamy "enables women, who live in a society full of obstacles, to fully meet their career, mothering and marriage obligations." When she left for her commute to the courthouse at 7 a.m., her daughter was "happily asleep in the bed of my husband's wife."[101] Some wives urge their husband to marry another wife and even participate in the selection.[102] When confronted with a husband who "gets out of line" or neglects his responsibilities, wives can unite against him to force change.[103]

So, too, for some African Americans, polygamy is a way to achieve a stable family in communities suffering from a shortage of marriageable men. Imprisonment, substance abuse, and chronic unemployment have reduced the number of eligible male partners. The result is "man sharing," a form of de facto polygamy similar to various practices in urban Africa.[104] Parties don't always hold themselves out as married, so they don't meet the formal definition of polygamy, but their lifestyle looks much the same.[105] Some African Americans support legalization of polygamous practices on the theory that it would foster greater social and legal responsibility in black men for their children, as well as provide black women with supportive networks that would increase their social and economic resources.[106]

Policy Implications

At issue in the debate over alternative lifestyles are fundamental questions about the nature of love, the role of marriage, and the appropriateness of legal regulation. "Why should sexual love be regarded as more exclusive than any other kind of love?" ask some feminists. "No one suggests that a woman who has two children loves each of them less than a woman with only one, yet we assume that she cannot love two lovers."[107] At least not legally.

Critics of legal prohibitions fall into two camps. One group believes polygamy should not be criminalized. The other group believes it should be affirmatively recognized as legitimate. Although they acknowledge abuses such as underage marriage, reformers argue that criminalization forces polygamy underground, into isolated, rural areas removed from legal and community oversight.[108] Not all who support decriminalization support polygamy. Law professor Jonathan Turley "personally detest[s]" the practice. But, he argues, "if we yield to our impulse and single out one hated minority, the First Amendment becomes little more than hype and we become little more than hypocrites. For my part, I would rather have a neighbor with different spouses than a country with different standards for its citizens." "The rights of polygamists," Turley believes, "should not be based on popularity, but principle." And, in his view, it makes no sense that "a person can live with multiple partners and even sire children from different partners so long as they do not marry. However, when that same person accepts a legal commitment for those partners 'as a spouse,' we jail them."[109]

Some critics of the existing regime go further and claim that polygamy is an acceptable lifestyle for an increasingly multicultural society and should be recognized as such. Polygamy, after all, is practiced not only by Mormon Fundamentalists, but also by Muslims. According to feminist law professor Drucilla Cornell, the government's recognition of only monogamous relationships is an "illegitimate incorporation of moral or religious values into the basic institutions of a constitutional government." In her view, the government should protect "all lovers who choose to register in civil marriage or some other form of domestic partnership."[110] Other researchers argue that multiple adults should be allowed to have custody of children in order to "distribute the extensive emotional, practical and financial needs associated with raising a child. By officially recognizing multiple parents, policies can help to attach more adults more securely to children.

In a society with a crumbling social safety nets, the more ways in which people can care for each other the better."[111] On the rare occasions when the polyamorist community is asked, it supports governmental recognition. In a survey of readers of *Loving More,* a magazine for polyamorists, over two-thirds favored state approval of group marriage. Even the opponents wanted decriminalization. Their desire was to "get the government out of the bedroom and people's intimate lives."[112]

There are, however, practical problems that supporters of polygamy have failed to address. For how many partners is it reasonable to expect health insurance coverage by employers, or welfare benefits from the government? Opponents of legalization point to the French experience as a cautionary tale. Following World War II, France attempted to increase its labor supply by permitting the immigration of polygamous families from Africa. The result was to create problems of spousal neglect, coerced marriage, and excessive access to government benefits. In 1993, after protests from African women's advocacy groups, France ended the policy.[113]

Most Americans share such concerns. In a 2013 Gallup poll, only 14 percent of Americans accepted polygamy. Of all the issues polled, it received the second highest disapproval rating, second only to adultery.[114] In a 2008 poll, two-thirds of the public thought that the government had the right to pass laws to prohibit polygamy. Seventy-nine percent considered marriage between an adult man and a girl seventeen years of age or younger to be sex abuse. In an earlier survey, Americans were split equally on whether a man living with more than one wife should be arrested.[115]

The polyamorous community is ill equipped to overcome such opposition. With few exceptions, its members have not been active politically. As one man put it, "We are neither the crusade type nor the martyr type; we just want to lead the style of life that we have found, without interference."[116] "Make Love, Not Law" was the title of one article on the lack of activism among polyamorists.[117] A recent World Polyamory Association annual conference included no coverage of marriage as a potential legal option. Polyamorist self-help books are filled with advice on jealousy, conflict resolution, and other relationship concerns but almost none on legal issues.[118] A survey of *Loving More* magazine found only one article on law in forty issues.[119] The individualist utopian values shared by most polyamorists are not conducive to collective mobilization. And the differences in political and religious ideology between fundamentalist Mormons and other members of the polyamorous community make coalitions unlikely.

In this political climate, perhaps the most plausible solution is for courts to follow the approach of *Brown v. Buhman* and invalidate criminal bans on polygamous cohabitation while retaining the prohibition on multiple marriage licenses. This partial legalization would remove the pressures that have forced polygamy into isolated, rural communities, while limiting eligibility for the benefits that accompany marriage. Such an approach could be coupled with other efforts to address risk factors associated with underage marriage and domestic abuse— isolated, rural environments; the absence of a strong female network; overcrowded conditions; and an ideology of male supremacy.[120] Education and support structures aimed at polygamous wives, as well as heightened enforcement of child sex abuse statutes, may be the most productive way of reducing the harms associated with polygamy. At the same time, values of individual privacy and religious liberty counsel tolerance for adults who have freely chosen an alternative lifestyle.

6

Sex and Politics

Anyone writing about adultery and American politics is awash in material. Among presidents alone, seventeen have had known sexual affairs, almost all involving adultery.[1] At issue in this chapter is how marital infidelity shapes political careers. What does it say about fitness for public office? When and why does private conduct become a matter of societal concern? How much does the public want or need to know about the intimate lives of politicians? Because those lives are fodder for journalists and historians, they also provide a window on the dynamics of adultery in real life. And when exposed, these affairs shed light on the public attitudes that shape legal and cultural norms.

We, the people, cannot resist a sexual scandal. Nor can we sometimes help but relish the satisfaction of seeing the privileged brought down to size for violating norms that may inconveniently constrain our own behavior. This chapter argues that we should resist that impulse. Adultery is not a good predictor of politicians' performance in office, and the publicity accompanying sexual scandal jeopardizes the careers of many talented public servants. Whether fidelity in marriage should matter in assessing fitness for political positions depends on context. The discussion that follows identifies factors that are relevant, such as whether the conduct involves womanizing, hypocrisy, abuse of office, or other legal improprieties. But, as a general matter, society suffers if it restricts its leadership choices to politicians whose sex lives are above reproach. This is not to deny that politicians' infidelity raises legitimate concerns about moral values and public credibility. But stripping individuals of public office is not always the answer, and American voters have often, and appropriately, decided as much.

Love Affairs

Franklin D. Roosevelt

Consider Franklin D. Roosevelt, consistently regarded as among the country's best presidents and unquestionably unfaithful to his wife, Eleanor. Thirteen years into their marriage, she was sorting through his mail while he was recovering from pneumonia. She discovered love letters by Lucy Mercer, her former social secretary. Eleanor confronted Franklin and said that she would divorce him if he did not end the affair. His mother was opposed to divorce and threatened to cut him off financially, which would have dramatically affected the family's lifestyle.[2] Even more to the point, a key adviser, Louis Howe, warned Roosevelt that he would have no political future if he ended the marriage.[3] The only ground for divorce in New York was adultery, and the details of his affair, if revealed in court proceedings and press accounts, would result in political ruin. He might even lose his position as assistant secretary of the navy, because his superior was extremely conservative on sexual matters.[4] In effect, a divorce would amount to career suicide; as one biographer put it, Roosevelt was "no businessman, and no great shakes at the law." In response to the dilemma, Roosevelt fell back on deception. Just as he had once deceived Eleanor about the affair, he now deceived Mercer by telling her that Eleanor would not grant him a divorce.[5] He also broke his promise to Eleanor. Mercer married, and after her husband died, she began visiting Roosevelt again and was with him when he died, a fact concealed from Eleanor.[6]

By all accounts, the affair transformed both Eleanor and the marriage. She later wrote, "The bottom dropped out of my own particular world, and I faced myself, my surroundings, my world, honestly for the first time. I really grew up that year." And, as she confided to friends, "I have the memory of an elephant. I can forgive, but I cannot forget."[7] The Mercer affair ended the Roosevelts' sexual relationship, and turned it into a working partnership. Instead of a lover, she became in effect a "cabinet minister without portfolio." It is doubtful that this transformation upset Eleanor much. On the eve of her daughter's wedding, Eleanor told her that sex was an "ordeal to be borne."[8] What the affair did accomplish, according to historian Doris Kearns Goodwin, was to show Eleanor "a possibility of standing apart from Franklin. No longer did she need to define herself solely in terms of his wants and his needs. . . . With the discovery of the affair, however, she was free to define a new and different partnership with her husband, free to seek new avenues of fulfillment." She discovered that she had "real talents for leadership and public life, . . . and her role expanded after Franklin's paralysis, when he turned to her to keep the Roosevelt name in the public eye."[9]

After the affair, the couple began to seek affection elsewhere. Franklin began a close relationship with his secretary, Marguerite

"Missy" LeHand. She lived with him at New York's Governor's Mansion and in the White House, and was often found in Roosevelt's bedroom at night in a nightgown and sitting on his lap in the Oval Office. Accounts differ over whether she was Roosevelt's mistress.[10] His son Elliott believed that the relationship was sexual and maintained that "everyone in the closely knit inner circle of father's friends accepted it as matter of course." His brother Jimmy disagreed: "I suppose you could say they came to love one another but it was not a physical love. . . . Besides, if it had been a physical love, I believe mother would have known . . . and had she thought it was, she would never have accepted the situation as fully as she did."[11] When an interviewer asked his daughter, Anna, point blank whether her father was having an affair with Missy, she answered, "Who could tell?"[12]

What is clear is that Franklin was the love of Missy's life, and that he cared for her deeply. Their relationship formed a "triangle of mutual advantage. Franklin gave Missy her reason for being. Missy provided the adoring female companionship that Franklin required. And his dependence on Missy freed Eleanor to pursue the life she wanted."[13] "Missy alleviated Mother's guilt," Elliot observed. "Knowing Missy was always there allowed Mother to come and go as she pleased without worrying about Father or feeling she was neglecting her wifely duties."[14] Nowhere does Eleanor seem anything but solicitous of Missy and grateful for her attentions to Roosevelt. As Eleanor confided to a friend, "He couldn't have lived without me, but neither could he have lived without Missy."[15] Missy provided the unconditional affection that Eleanor could not. As she recognized, Roosevelt "might have been happier with a wife who was completely uncritical. That I was never able to be, and he had to find it in some other people. Nevertheless, I think I sometimes acted as a spur, even though the spurring was not always wanted or welcome. I was one of those who served his pur-

poses."[16] In commenting on the affair after the couple's death, Eleanor's distant cousin Alice Roosevelt Longworth said, "Well, Franklin
was entitled to a little fun. After all, he was married to Eleanor."[17]

Missy was rewarded in the end. After she was incapacitated by a
cerebral hemorrhage, Roosevelt left her half his estate, valued at nearly
$2 million, to pay for her medical bills.[18]

Some speculate that Eleanor may have had her own affair during
this period with Associated Press reporter Lorena Hickok. The two
wrote between 2,000 and 3,000 letters, some of which hinted at sexual
involvement.[19] Friends, however, doubted that it was a lesbian relationship. Whether or not the attachment was physical, Hickok's love for
Eleanor provided what Goodwin terms "a mix of tenderness, loyalty,
confidence, and courage that sustained her in her struggle to redefine
her sense of self and her position in the world."[20] By all accounts, both
Eleanor and Franklin benefited immeasurably from their relationships,
in ways that enriched their political as well as their personal lives.

Mark Sanford

A politician not nearly as influential or revered as Roosevelt, South
Carolina governor Mark Sanford, also had an affair of the heart. In
June 2009, Sanford vanished for six days. His wife, staff, and security detail all had no idea where he was. A spokesperson issued a statement that he was hiking the Appalachian Trail.[21] On his return, he
was met at the airport by a reporter who had received a tip that the
governor might be seeing a mistress in Argentina. Several hours later,
Sanford held a press conference where he tearfully admitted that he
had been "unfaithful to [his] wife," but said that he would die knowing
that he had met his "soulmate."[22] And, in what was widely viewed as
an excess of candor, he confessed to spending the past five days "crying

in Argentina."[23] Adding to his humiliation, the local newspaper published copies of steamy e-mails he had written to the woman.

His wife was not at his side during the press conference. She later issued a statement indicating that although she still loved her husband, she had asked him to leave the family two weeks earlier for a trial separation. "We reached a point where I felt it was important to look my sons in the eyes and maintain my dignity, self-respect, and my basic sense of right and wrong."[24]

The *New York Times* called for Sanford to resign and most voters (54 percent) agreed.[25] As the *Times* noted, he had failed to transfer emergency powers to the lieutenant governor, lied to the state and his staff, and tapped taxpayer funds to drum up a trade mission that allowed him to see his lover.[26] But Sanford vowed to stay on, and the Judiciary Committee of the South Carolina House of Representatives rejected a resolution to impeach him.[27] Sanford's wife then filed for divorce on grounds of adultery, and published a book detailing her husband's deception.[28] Sanford subsequently became engaged to the woman from Argentina.

His political career was far from over. After finishing his term as governor, Sanford successfully ran for his original congressional seat.[29] Some conservatives withheld support. As one commentator put it,

> Let me say upfront: I would rather we lived in a society where adultery had a higher social cost. That's not to say people shouldn't be forgiving or that there should be no such thing as second chances. But ideally, I'd like it if things were less loosey-goosey. Cheat on your wife, and maybe you don't get to run for public office anymore.... Or, if that's too much to ask, maybe the interval between scandal and rehabilitation could last a little longer than the maturation time of a fruit fly.[30]

Most voters disagreed; substantive issues trumped sex.[31] Nate Silver crunched the numbers and, after extrapolating from the congressional district's Republican electoral record, estimated that the scandal had cost Sanford 13 percentage points. That was not enough to tip the election. Voters in South Carolina may not like infidelity, Silver concluded, "but they appear to like Democrats even less."[32]

Womanizers

John F. Kennedy

A different order of scandal involves chronic philanderers. But for the presidents who have fallen into this category, adultery did not necessarily impair their ability to lead the country.

Womanizing ran in the Kennedy family. Joseph Kennedy, John F. Kennedy's father, facilitated his romances by investing heavily in Hollywood. He had a string of starlets, some of whom he brought home with him.[33] But John Kennedy's escapades were on a different order of magnitude. They led him to take risks that even his father thought foolhardy. Aides called him "mattress Jack."[34] The women were so interchangeable that he had trouble keeping them straight and he didn't always bother to learn their names.[35] Not much changed after his marriage to Jacqueline Bouvier, whose father was also a notorious womanizer. She hadn't expected fidelity, but she was unprepared for the flagrancy of his philandering. He sometimes brought lovers to receptions where she was present or left her stranded at official functions, including one of his inaugural balls, while he ducked out for a quick tryst.[36] After he was elected president, Jackie often seated a lover next to him at state dinners. That way, at least he would have no access to fresh talent.[37] In one of his most notorious displays, he had his lover, Marilyn Monroe, sing a sensuous version of "Happy Birthday, Mr. President" in a see-through gown at his forty-fifth birthday celebration in Madison Square Garden. Jackie did not attend.[38]

Kennedy's tastes were eclectic, and his partners included movie stars, high-class call girls, stewardesses, socialites, campaign workers, and government employees. He had no reservations about taking advantage of White House staff, either as targets of his affection or facilitators of his affairs. He had relationships with at least two White House secretaries who traveled frequently with him, although they were not assigned any routine secretarial duties; they were on call for late-evening "work."[39] Kennedy's aides had few qualms about arranging the president's liaisons; they "took less time than tennis and partners were often easier to find."[40] White House staff were also asked to comb apartments for evidence of infidelity, but they were not always as thorough as they needed to be. On one occasion, they overlooked a pair of panties stuffed in a pillowcase, which Jackie discovered.[41]

This was not, however, the worst moment in their relationship. That came in 1956, when Jackie gave birth to a still-born child. Kennedy was cruising in the Mediterranean with several attractive young women and declined to fly home immediately to be with his grief-stricken wife. The situation worsened when Jackie discovered that their fifteen-year-old baby sitter was pregnant, and was naming Kennedy as the father. Joseph Kennedy reportedly salvaged the situation by offering to make a financial settlement on Jackie, provided that she did not leave her husband.[42] By all accounts, Kennedy was as perfunctory as a lover as he was as a husband. Actress Angie Dickinson reportedly described her affair with Kennedy as "the best twenty seconds of my life."[43]

Lyndon Baines Johnson

Lyndon B. Johnson was also a womanizer and proud of it.[44] He enjoyed boasting about his sexual conquests and claimed to have had "more women by accident than Kennedy had on purpose."[45] There were rumors of illegitimate children; one filed a paternity suit against Johnson's widow in 1987. It was widely known that Johnson had sex with numerous secretaries, who were picked for attractiveness. Aides referred to them as "the harem." Many of his liaisons were not particularly discreet. He had sex in the Oval Office and on Air Force One.[46] Not all of his advances were welcome. One attractive aide recalled being awakened in her room at the LBJ ranch by Johnson's voice saying, "Move over. This is your president."[47]

Part of what fueled such behavior was a sense of invulnerability. Johnson was unusually candid about his expectations. He reportedly told a group of reporters, "You may see me coming in and out of a few women's bedrooms while I am in the White House, but just remember, that is none of your business."[48]

Reporters largely agreed. As a consequence, Johnson's infidelities remained a well-kept secret, and did not demonstrably affect his domestic triumphs or foreign policy disasters. Johnson's legacies are his Great Society programs, his civil rights leadership, and his Vietnam debacle. His extramarital affairs are barely a footnote.

Gary Hart

A watershed in press coverage of adultery occurred with presidential candidate Gary Hart. His sheer recklessness shattered the boundaries of discretion that had previously marked media coverage. For the first time, reporters asked a candidate about infidelity. And the answer doomed the candidacy of a man who had been the front-runner in the 1988 presidential race.[49]

Gary Hart was raised in the Nazarene faith, a strict religion that forbade dancing, drinking, and even watching movies. Commentators often attributed his relentless womanizing to desires that had been repressed growing up.[50] He lost little time in compensating. Charges of philandering surfaced early in his political career. So did charges of hypocrisy. He launched his campaign for the presidency with the claim that "all of us must try to hold ourselves to the very highest standards of integrity and ethics, and soundness of judgment."[51] He displayed none of these qualities. When aides raised concerns about his womanizing, he resisted discussion: "You can't take my privacy away from me. Back off. I need space."[52] A campaign aide recalled that Hart had responded to press inquiries by saying that "adultery was a matter between himself and God and he doesn't have to answer to anyone else."[53] With unparalleled recklessness, Hart not only denied charges of infidelity, but also invited the media to prove him wrong: "Follow me around. I'm serious. If anybody wants to put a tail on me, go ahead. They'll be bored."[54]

They weren't. Acting on an anonymous tip even before Hart issued his challenge, *Miami Herald* reporters staked out Hart's Washington, D.C., townhouse.[55] When confronted while he was with a young blonde woman not his wife, Hart denied being involved in any sexual "relationship" with her.[56] As a *New York Times* editorial wryly inquired, "Would 'political' or 'business' relationship better describe it?"[57] When *Herald* reporters asked if Hart had taken the woman on a yachting trip in Florida, Hart implausibly responded, "I don't remember."[58]

The woman was Donna Rice, a twenty-nine-year-old model, described in the press as an "action girl."[59] Hart had met her aboard a yacht aptly named *Monkey Business*. The *Herald* published its account of the stakeout, and the story went viral. Hart initially tried to sidestep the scandal. He attacked the paper for its "misleading and false" account of the weekend, which he attributed to "spotty surveillance." "Did I make a mistake by putting myself in circumstances that could be misconstrued? Of course I did," Hart conceded. "Did I do anything immoral? Absolutely not."[60] When asked point blank if he had ever committed adultery, Hart responded, "I don't think that's a fair question. . . . I'm not going to get into a theological definition of what constitutes adultery."[61]

The scandal didn't blow over. Reports of other affairs surfaced. Five days after the *Herald*'s report, and less than a month after he had announced his candidacy, Hart was forced to suspend his campaign. His press statement was defiant: "I refuse to submit my family and my friends and innocent people and myself to further rumors and gossip. It's simply an intolerable situation. . . . The presidential nominating system is just a mockery that reduces the press of this nation to hunters and presidential candidates to being hunted. . . . And if it continues to destroy people's integrity and honor, then that system will eventually destroy itself."[62]

In the final analysis, what doomed Hart's candidacy had less to do with sex than with judgment. As *Washington Post* columnist William Raspberry put it, Hart's problem was a "deadly lack of ordinary wisdom [and] common sense."[63] For a position like the presidency, which involves moral leadership, appearances matter. The reckless self-indulgence that caused Gary Hart's monkey business is not what the public wants in a leader of the free world.

Yet, at the same time, the price Hart paid after his presidential campaign seems excessive. He became the "iconic adulterer," a perpetual political pariah who never gained another meaningful opportunity for public service. As he told *New York Times* reporter Matt Bai in 2009, "I made a mistake." It was "a single incident fifteen years ago. I think I've paid my dues. . . . I'm not even asking for forgiveness, but fairness. . . . This whole business of '87 is flypaper to me. It's so frustrating. It's like being in a time warp. I want to get unstuck."[64] Because he never did, the public lost out on a potentially gifted public servant.

William J. Clinton

Bill Clinton holds the record for the most meticulously documented extramarital affairs. He set the tone for his relationship with his future wife, Hillary Rodham, when she followed him to Arkansas to act as his campaign manager in the 1974 congressional election and he slept with another of his campaign workers.[65] However, they married in 1975 and she stood beside him while he served six terms as governor despite constant "bimbo eruptions."[66] Clinton strayed so often and so flagrantly from his marriage that his aide Betsey Wright talked him out of a run for president in 1988. She compiled a list of women with whom he had had sexual relationships and suggested that he would suffer the same fate as Gary Hart, whose campaign had imploded just months earlier.[67]

Four years later, Clinton launched his campaign for the 1992 presidential nomination and publicly confessed that he had caused "problems" in his marriage. This did not, however, inoculate him from scandal once Gennifer Flowers had sold her story of a twelve-year affair with him to a tabloid and began appearing on talk shows.[68] Four state troopers confirmed that they regularly took Clinton to Flowers's apartment and that they overheard him using his influence to find her a state job.[69] The scandal was later compounded by other claims of Arkansas state troopers that they had facilitated Clinton's extra-marital involvements and bought gifts of lingerie for his partners. They also alleged that they had been offered employment in exchange for their silence.[70]

What salvaged Clinton's political career was his national television appearance on *60 Minutes*, in which he denied the affair and Hillary was stoically supportive. According to Bill, Flowers was a "friendly acquaintance" and her disclosures were motivated by payments from the tabloid. Bill acknowledged causing "pain in my marriage" but was not prepared to say more. No married couple, he asserted, should have to discuss the details with anyone outside the marriage. Hillary agreed, and emphasized the dangers for the country if a "zone of privacy was lost."[71] She also stated, "I'm not sitting here because I'm some little woman standing by my man, like Tammy Wynette. I'm sitting here because I love him and I respect him and honor what he's been through and what we've been through together. And you know, if that's not enough for people, then heck, don't vote for him."[72]

Despite the scandal, Clinton won the nomination and the presidential election. During his first term, he continued to be dogged by allegations of infidelity and sexual exploitation. The one that proved his undoing involved only an attempt at adultery with an Arkansas state employee, Paula Jones. She charged Clinton with severe emotional distress and deprivation of civil rights after a state trooper implied that she had had sex with Clinton while he was governor. According to Jones, during a 1991 quality management conference, a state trooper summoned her from her post behind a registration table to come to Clinton's Little Rock hotel room. She claimed she thought they were going to discuss a better state job for which she had applied. Instead, Clinton unzipped his fly, dropped his pants, and invited her to kiss his penis. She refused, and he suggested that they keep this "between ourselves."[73] After Jones filed the suit, Clinton's lawyer denied at a press conference that the incident had ever taken place and said that the president had "no recollection of ever meeting Jones, though he couldn't rule it out."[74] Ostensibly to establish that Clinton had a habit of soliciting sex with other government employees, but also to embarrass the president, Jones's lawyers named a substantial number of other women as potential trial witnesses. One of them was Monica Lewinsky.

Lewinsky was a twenty-two-year-old White House intern who was pitching in with West Wing tasks during a 1995 government shutdown prompted by congressional budget fights. While passing by Clinton, she flashed her thong underwear at him.[75] Days later, when he invited her into his office, she blurted out, "You know, I have a really big crush on you."[76] The two kissed and later retired to an aide's office, where Clinton received oral sex. The next night, she managed to be alone with him by delivering him some pizza, and they "fooled around" in his bathroom.[77] The affair continued, and despite their precautions, Lewinsky's presence was noted. The deputy chief of staff for operations received information that Lewinsky had a habit of hanging around the Oval Office.[78] Lewinsky was then told that her unit was being reorganized, and that she was being transferred to the Pentagon. She hated her new job, and Clinton promised that if he won reelection, "I will bring you back here, just like that."[79]

Although he did not keep that promise, the affair continued on and off, and Lewinsky complained when he didn't call or exert sufficient effort to find her a new job. When asked later why she had persisted in a dead-end relationship, she responded, "I fell in love."[80] In retrospect, she said,

I feel that he should have shown more restraint and left it as a flirtation and as an unacted-upon fantasy. I'm not blaming him for what happened, but it was just too much. It was too much of an emotional burden for someone my age. If I had really understood everything I would have seen him more as President than a man. And I would have realized the ramifications of ever telling anybody about it.[81]

One of the people she told was a colleague at the Pentagon, Linda Tripp. On advice of a New York literary agent, Tripp taped their phone conversations. She ultimately tipped off Jones's lawyers. They turned the tapes over to Independent Counsel Kenneth Starr, who was investigating the Clintons' involvement in Whitewater, a series of Arkansas land deals.[82] Starr then broadened his inquiry to include possible perjury and obstruction of justice in connection with the *Jones* case.

Two years into his relationship with Lewinsky, Clinton finally broke it off, telling Lewinsky, "It was wrong for me, wrong for my family, and wrong for her."[83] The man whom *TIME* magazine designated "the nation's Libido in Chief" had finally had enough. In the aftermath of the affair, Clinton reminded her that she had told him when this affair started that when it was over she would not give him "any trouble." With unintended prescience, Lewinsky responded, "Trouble? You think I have been trouble? You don't know trouble."[84]

The trouble came in several forms. Lewinsky filed an affidavit in the *Jones* case denying that she had ever had a sexual relationship with Clinton. Clinton, on national television, claimed, "I did not have sexual relations with that woman, Miss Lewinsky."[85] His decision to lie was partly driven by poll numbers. Adviser Dick Morris had run some surveys and had told Clinton that voters weren't ready for a confession.[86] His lawyer also represented to the judge in the *Jones* case that "there is absolutely no sex of any kind in any manner, shape or form." When asked about that statement in a subsequent grand jury proceeding, Clinton tried to take advantage of verb tenses, stating with a straight face, "It depends on what the meaning of the word *is*, is. If . . . 'is' means is and never has been, . . . that is one thing. If it means there is none, that was a completely true statement." Although he acknowledged having had "inappropriate intimate physical contact" with Lewinsky, he refused to supply details. He was equally evasive about whether he and Lewinsky had ever been alone. "It depends on how you define alone," he explained.[87] On eighty-four occasions during his grand jury testimony, he claimed to have no recollection concerning the question asked. Clinton's professed inability to recall facts such as whether he and Lewinsky were alone during oral sex seemed like an exercise in "optional amnesia."[88] As *New York Times* columnist Maureen Dowd noted, "He is like the cursed girl in the fairy tale: every time he opens his mouth, a toad jumps out."[89]

Denials of a sexual relationship were short lived. Starr pressured Lewinsky into cooperating with his investigation by threatening her with a perjury prosecution for the false affidavit in the *Jones* case. While under oath, Lewinsky was forced to testify about who touched whom when and where and whether orgasm resulted.[90] Starr also had physical evidence of the affair, including a semen-stained dress that Lewinsky had worn during sex with Clinton. On the day before he was called by Starr to testify before a grand jury, Clinton disclosed his relationship with Lewinsky to his wife. Then, following his grand jury testimony, in a nationally televised address, he acknowledged his infidelity to the nation. Sounding more combative than contrite, he admitted engaging in a relationship that was "not appropriate. In fact it was wrong. It constituted a critical lapse in judgment and a personal failure on my part for which I am solely and completely responsible." He added, "I know that my public comments and my silence about this matter gave a false impression. I misled people, including even my wife. I deeply regret that. I must put it right, and I am prepared to do whatever it takes to do so." However, "the fact that these questions were being asked in a politically inspired lawsuit, which since has been dismissed, was a consideration too." The president then lashed out at the independent counsel, and claimed that the investigation of Whitewater land deals had spiraled into an investigation of intensely private matters; it had "gone on too long, cost too much and hurt too many innocent people. Now, this matter is between me, the two people I love most—my wife and our daughter—and our God.... It's nobody's business but ours. Even presidents have private lives. It is time to stop the pursuit of personal destruction and the prying into private lives and get on with our national life."[91]

Although the speech functioned more as an attack than an apology, subsequent polls found that 62 percent of Americans gave Clinton a favorable job performance rating, and 63 percent thought that his relationship with Lewinsky was a private matter. By a margin of 65 to 31 percent, Americans also thought Clinton's testimony and subsequent speech should have ended the matter.[92]

Clinton's standing with his aides and family was considerably worse. Members of the Clinton administration were furious that the president had squandered his chances to become one of the nation's great leaders. The country was enjoying unprecedented economic prosperity and had achieved significant foreign policy successes. Now these achievements had been eclipsed, "all for a reckless fling with a chubby-cheeked female who was the age of Clinton's own daughter."[93] By her own account, Hillary was "furious ... dumbfounded, heartbroken and outraged that I'd believed him at all.... I didn't know whether our marriage could—or should—survive such a stinging betrayal. . . . This was the most devastating, shocking and hurtful experience of my life." Although his standing in the polls remained high, his standing with Hillary had "hit rock bottom." When the Clintons left for vacation, Hillary recalled, "Buddy, the dog, came along to keep Bill company. He was the only member of our family who was still willing to." At the same time, Hillary echoed much of the country in her belief that her husband's "failing was not a betrayal of his country." "I believed that he ought to be held accountable for his behavior—by me and by Chelsea—not by a misuse of the impeachment process."[94]

Republicans in Congress thought otherwise. They voted to impeach him for lying under oath concerning his affair with Lewinsky and for obstructing justice by enlisting his close friend Vernon Jordan in finding her a job in exchange for her silence. The matter then moved to the Senate for trial, where Clinton denied the charges. In essence, he claimed that receiving oral sex from Lewinsky did not constitute "sexual relations" as that term was defined for purposes of the *Jones* proceeding. There, the parties agreed that such relations occurred when a person "knowingly engages in or causes . . . contact with genitalia, anus, groin, breast, inner thigh, or buttocks of any person with an intent to arouse or gratify the sexual desire of any person."[95] By that definition, Clinton claimed, Lewinsky had engaged in sex with him but he had not engaged in sex with her. He also denied that Jordan's efforts to assist her job search were in exchange for silence.[96] Clinton's lawyers further asserted that none of the conduct alleged amounted to "high crimes or misdemeanors," the constitutional standard for removal from office. The Senate agreed, and, on a largely partisan vote, acquitted him on the charges.[97]

That was the result most Americans wanted. They appeared ready to separate private and public conduct. In a 1998 ABC poll, two-thirds of respondents said that the Lewinsky affair had nothing to do with Clinton's job as president. Throughout the scandal, Pew surveys found that two-thirds of the pubic repeatedly said that they didn't like Clinton as a person, but over 60 percent consistently liked his policies.[98] Moreover, the personal dislike was relatively short lived. A 2014 poll showed that Clinton was, by a wide margin, the most admired president of the last quarter century.[99]

The Clinton-Lewinsky affair also highlights Americans' ambivalence about media coverage of politicians' private lives. As a *Boston Globe* editor noted, "People are intrigued by it and they don't like that they're intrigued by it. There's a revulsion at their own level of interest."[100] The report of Starr pandered to that interest. The Starr team seemed "weirdly prurient" in their approach to the investigation.[101] The report was simultaneously salacious and sanctimonious. Although Starr insisted that the issue was not sex, but lying, the term "sex," or some variation of it, appeared 581 times in the 445-page report.[102] The press reported the sexual findings in loving detail. "For the better part of a year, watchdogs and pundits...nipped at the presidential underwear, exposed it, analyzed it, and in the process stained themselves."[103] Fifty-nine percent of the public disapproved of how the news media was handling the scandal.[104] Most Americans reported that the affair was receiving too much attention.[105] When asked how the country could avoid future scandals, 34 percent of the public said, "elect presidents with high moral character"; 60 percent said, "make sure a president's life stays private."[106] *New York Times* columnist Anthony Lewis spoke for most Americans in claiming, "We do not want...prosecutors looking into the sex lives of presidents. We should not have tawdry tales of their investigations filling our newspapers and television screens."[107]

But a substantial gulf exists between what the public says it wants— or wishes it wants—and what it actually consumes. Sex sells, and in a world of intense competition among media organizations, it is hard for journalists to resist titillating details. Television networks devoted more airtime to Clinton's scandal in 1998 than to all other news stories put together.[108] In the first ten days after allegations of Clinton's affair surfaced, the three largest television networks devoted two-thirds of their news coverage to the scandal. CNN posted a 40 percent increase in viewers. Several news programs recorded their highest-ever audiences during the scandal.[109] Some sixty-seven million Americans watched Clinton's address admitting the affair, and seventy-four million tuned into Barbara Walters's post-impeachment interview with Monica Lewinsky. Only the Super Bowl drew a larger audience.[110] "The personal is political" was popularized as a feminist slogan, but it also has evolved into a "journalistic axiom."[111] How many members of the public wouldn't prefer to read about a semen-stained dress than about economic policy? The boundaries between news and entertainment have blurred, and politicians' private lives are a casualty. When legal remedies are added to that mix, effective governance can also suffer.

Hypocrisy

For many politicians involved in sexual scandals, the problem is not adultery per se, but the gap between their public image and their private conduct. That gap does not always end political careers, but it makes leaders more vulnerable to challenge. And the more notable the hypocrisy, the greater the vulnerability.

Helen Chenoweth

Idaho Republican Helen Chenoweth is the only American woman leader to have been publicly implicated in adultery. One of the most conservative members of the House of Representatives, Chenoweth had been highly critical of Clinton's personal behavior. She used his relationship with Lewinsky as the basis for a 1998 television commercial in which she spoke out against the president and asked her opponent, "Where do you stand . . . ?"[112] The commercial angered the wife of a former lover of Chenoweth. The wife felt that Chenoweth was being hypocritical, and she disclosed Chenoweth's six-year affair to the *Idaho Statesman.* Chenoweth acknowledged the affair with a married business colleague, but sought to distinguish her behavior from that of the president. Her affair occurred after her divorce, when she was not a public official. Since her election, she had "lived [her] personal life uprightly."[113] Anyone who followed her around after her election "would be utterly bored" with her social life.[114] Moreover, she had "asked for God's forgiveness and . . . received it."[115]

However, disclosure of the affair complicated Chenoweth's reelection campaign, which emphasized family values. Chenoweth had won her seat four years earlier partly by capitalizing on the extramarital affair of her opponent. But the candidate opposing Chenoweth in 1998 was disinclined to do the same. His sense was that "the people out here care a lot more about real issues that affect their families' lives than they do about anyone's personal life, whether it's Helen Chenoweth's or Bill Clinton's."[116] He was right, and Chenoweth won reelection.

John Edwards

In 2008, John Edwards, former U.S. senator from North Carolina and Democratic Party presidential candidate, admitted to having an extramarital affair with Rielle Hunter. It began in 2006, when Hunter joined Edwards's presidential campaign to produce a series of webisodes that portrayed life behind the scenes on the campaign trail. The project threw Hunter and Edwards in close proximity, and she cemented the relationship by supplying exactly what he wanted to hear: that he had "the power to change the world," and that he could be as great a leader as Gandhi or Martin Luther King Jr.[117] The affair soon became obvious to staff, and Edwards's wife, Elizabeth, discovered it through a cellphone left in her husband's luggage. Edwards told her it was a "one-night stand." Hunter's contract was terminated, the webisodes were pulled off the campaign website, and she disappeared. But not for long.

By all accounts, the Edwards had an unhappy marriage, but neither of them wanted a divorce. Elizabeth's ambitions were tied to her husband's presidential campaign. John believed that his wife was more popular than he was and that a divorce would torpedo his political career.[118] The risks of separation became even greater in March 2007, when Elizabeth learned that the cancer she had been fighting was incurable. She insisted that John remain in the race. He did, and rumors circulated that Hunter had appeared at hotels where the candidate was staying. Elizabeth began closely monitoring his movements and the tabloids were sniffing at his door. But, according to campaign aide Andrew Young, Edwards

> never seemed to grasp the magnitude of the trouble he faced. Instead he would tell me that if the truth ever came out it would be, at worst, a one day news story because "everyone knows" that politicians screw around on their wives. What this position denied was the fact that his wife had cancer and he had sold himself to the American public as a devoted husband and family man who talked about his faith in order to appeal to Christian voters.[119]

In October 2007, the *National Enquirer* published an exposé of Edwards's affair with an unnamed campaign worker, and followed it up in December with a piece titled, "Update: John Edwards Love Child Scandal." The article featured a photo of Hunter six months pregnant, and identified Edwards as the father, although Young, as a favor to Edwards, had claimed paternity.[120] Edwards dismissed the story as "lies" and "tabloid trash."[121] Major television networks and newspapers did not report the accusations, but the story took on new legs when *Enquirer* reporters confronted Edwards after he met with Hunter and the baby in a Beverley Hills hotel room. In an ignominious effort to escape, Edwards locked himself into a restroom and had to be escorted out by security guards.[122]

Claiming that he was "dogged by tabloids," Edwards tried to put the matter to rest by appearing on ABC's *Nightline*.[123] There, he acknowledged the affair and conceded that becoming a national figure had "fed a self focus, an egotism, a narcissism that leads you to believe that you can do whatever you want. You're invincible. And there will be no consequences. And nothing, nothing could be further from the truth."[124] A profile of Edwards in *New York Magazine* made a similar point: "Edwards's story is equally, lastingly resonant; an archetypical political tragedy in which the very same qualities that fuel any presidential bid—ego, hubris, vanity, neediness, a kind of delusion—became all-consuming and self-destructive."[125] Yet Edwards's confession, however self-revelatory, was also strikingly tone deaf. As *New York Times* columnist Maureen Dowd noted, the "creepiest part of his creepy confession was when he stressed . . . that he cheated on Elizabeth in 2006 when her cancer was in remission. His infidelity was oncologically correct."[126]

In 2010, Edwards finally admitted he was the father of Hunter's child and separated from his wife. She died shortly thereafter. A survey that year by Public Policy Polling revealed that he was the "most unpopular person we've polled anywhere at any time."[127] Edwards's troubles were compounded in 2011 when he was indicted on six felony charges. They concerned payments made to Hunter and Young that allegedly violated campaign finance laws. After a mistrial on one charge and an acquittal on five others, the Justice Department chose not to retry the case.[128] Edwards then struggled to rebuild his career as a trial lawyer.[129] As one friend put it, "He doesn't want his legacy to be he had a toot with this gal from nowhere and that's the sum of his life."[130]

As was true of Hart, Edwards's conduct over the course of his political campaign raised serious questions regarding his integrity, judgment, and ability to lead. His carelessly cultivated public image was simply too far from the truth to make him a viable candidate.

David Vitter

The combination of infidelity and hypocrisy is not always toxic. In 2007, the phone number of David Vitter, Republican congressman from Louisiana, was included in a published list of phone records of a company run by "DC Madam" Deborah Jane Palfrey. After *TIME* and *Hustler* magazines called the senator's office for comment, he provided a press statement that read,

> This was a very serious sin in my past for which I am, of course, completely responsible. Several years ago, I asked for and received forgiveness from God and my wife in confession and marriage counseling. Out of respect for my family, I will keep my discussion of the matter there—with God and them. But I certainly offer my deep and sincere apologies to all I have disappointed and let down in any way.[131]

Following on the heels of that statement was the disclosure by a different madam that Vitter had been a client of her high-priced New Orleans brothel in the 1990s.[132]

Vitter's embarrassment was compounded by the fact that he had positioned himself as a champion of "family values." He was pummeled by the press and his opponent (although not by voters) because of his hypocrisy. He had opposed gay marriage and funding for Planned Parenthood, supported abstinence-only sex education, and condemned Bill Clinton as "morally unfit to govern."[133] His opponent for reelection sought to capitalize on the disparity between Vitter's public statements and his private conduct. "David, you never had family values. You've sinned, you've lied, you've broken the law, you've embarrassed the state—yet you've not hinted once that you think you should step down."[134] But Vitter's job approval ratings remained high; two-thirds of voters either strongly or somewhat approved his job performance.[135] He was reelected in 2010, and, in 2014, he announced plans to run for governor. Vitter was aided by his wife's support, despite an earlier statement predicting that if her husband strayed, she would act less like Hillary Clinton than like Lorena Bobbitt, the wronged wife who castrated her sleeping husband: "If he does something like that, I'm walking away with one thing and it's not alimony, trust me."[136] But like Vitter's constituents, she instead found a way to forgive if not forget.

Eliot Spitzer

A year after Vitter's scandal surfaced, New York governor Eliot Spitzer faced similar prostitution charges with dramatically different results. On March 12, 2008, he resigned in the wake of disclosures that he had patronized an elite escort service. Threatened with impeachment if he did not resign, Spitzer stated, "I cannot allow for my private failings to disrupt the people's work. Over the course of my public life, I have insisted—I believe correctly—that people take responsibility for their conduct. I can and will ask no less of myself. For this reason, I am resigning from the office of governor."[137] For viewers of his press conference, seeing his demonstrably mortified wife standing beside him was "like watching someone swallow a hand grenade in real time."[138]

Spitzer's misconduct came to light as a result of several bank reports of suspicious activity. That activity related to wire transactions that Spitzer had made to a shell company connected to a Web-based prostitution service.[139] Internal Revenue Service agents began investigating the transactions, and a federal wiretap caught Spitzer, known as "Client 9," discussing arrangements to meet and pay a prostitute.[140] Details of the transaction surfaced, including Spitzer's reputation as a "difficult" client who sometimes asked prostitutes "to do things you might not think were safe."[141]

What gave the scandal further traction was Spitzer's hypocrisy. He had prosecuted several prostitution rings in his career, and one of his first acts as governor was to increase the penalty for patronizing a prostitute.[142] Now Spitzer himself numbered among the men that this law was designed to punish. Some women's groups and anti-trafficking organizations that had worked with him on the prostitution statute felt betrayed.[143] Spitzer also had a reputation as an arrogant and self-righteous official, and many New Yorkers were not particularly grieved by the fall of a man whom the *Wall Street Journal* had dubbed the "Lord High Executioner."[144]

Spitzer was not, however, without defenders. University of Chicago professor Martha Nussbaum argued that "Eliot Spitzer's offense was an offense against his family. It was not an offense against the public.

If he broke any laws, these are laws that never should have existed and that have been repudiated by sensible nations. The hue and cry that has ruined one of the nation's most committed political careers shows our country to itself in a very ugly light."[145] But Spitzer had knowingly violated the law he had sworn to uphold and had worked to strengthen; ignoring that would hardly show the nation in a better light.

Most New Yorkers seemed to agree. Spitzer lost his bid in 2013 to become New York City comptroller. His wife, however, received her reward: a sympathetic portrayal in the television series *The Good Wife*, which premiered in 2009, and was inspired by the scandal.[146] The affair took an obvious toll on their marriage and, in 2013, the couple announced they were separating.[147]

Implications: The Personal and the Political

Scandals, notes Laura Kipnis, will always be with us, "sniffing at the back door, nosing around for cracks in the façade." Because the "human personality is helpless against itself," we will always see leaders "orchestrating their own downfalls, crashing headlong into their own inner furies."[148] And the public will always find "something secretly gratifying about nabbing so many national leaders with their pants—and their contradictions—around their ankles."[149] What is, however, distinctive about the modern era is that social, economic, and technological forces have publicized conduct that might once have remained private. Most obviously, the public's increased comfort in discussing sex has created a market for scandal that the press has been all too willing to supply. The rise of the women's movement has decreased tolerance for behavior that was once overlooked. Competition among media has pushed in similar directions. The proliferation of news sources and the round-the-clock news cycle have increased the demand for coverage. Technology has provided more ways to obtain information and to make it instantly accessible.

In this climate, what accounts for the belief of so many politicians that they can get away with adultery? Psychologists have identified several cognitive dynamics that contribute to risk-taking behavior. One is people's tendency to see themselves as unique and superior to others, particularly concerning moral conduct.[150] This uniqueness bias is exacerbated by conditions of power. Political leaders live in what consultant Eric Dezenhall labeled a "mental aquarium," an environment of admiration that leads to an inflated sense of self-confidence and self-importance.[151] A second cognitive bias is the tendency of individuals to view their own transgressions as less objectionable than identical actions by others.[152] Power again increases the likelihood of such bias.[153] Although social disapproval normally helps check self-interest, feelings of power reduce sensitivity to that constraint.[154] Recent research also suggests that individuals who need to exert a great deal of control in their working lives have less ego strength to regulate their private lives.[155]

Given these dynamics, why are so few women politicians involved in sexual scandals? One reason is that they appear more risk averse, partly due to lingering double standards of morality that make promiscuity more costly for women than men (particularly if they are married and have children).[156] Anthropologist Lionel Tiger has argued further that women have fewer sexual opportunities because power is not as alluring in women as in men.[157] Others have suggested that women in positions of leadership have less time for, less interest in, or less sense of entitlement to extramarital sex. These women also tend to be older than their male colleagues, and older women have fewer opportunities for affairs than do men of their age. Whatever the reason, it is clear that female politicians are less likely to be implicated in sexual scandal, and that their increased involvement in leadership positions may reduce its frequency.[158]

How much scandal should matter is, however, open to debate. Where should the boundaries lie between public and private? If a politician hires a hooker or has an affair, does that call into question his leadership capacities? Most Americans believe that it does and want those facts disclosed. In a 2009 poll, 61 percent of respondents thought voters should know about a politician's infidelity.[159] In a 2007 poll, 43 percent of Americans said they wouldn't vote for a candidate who had an extramarital affair.[160] In practice, however, as the preceding examples of Clinton, Chenoweth, and Vitter illustrate, most people appear more morally flexible. As one *New York Times* headline put it, "Politicians Are Slowed by Scandal, but Many Still Win the Race."[161] Still, there is a strong feeling that character can't be compartmentalized and that the qualities that politicians display in their personal lives spill over into their professional lives. In an age in which divorce is readily available and acceptable, a politician's choice to remain married, while repeatedly violating marital commitments, raises questions of moral values. In suggesting that Mark Sanford was unfit for office, former cabinet member and conservative commentator William Bennett maintained that "someone who lies in private is going to lie in public and you can't trust someone who does that."[162]

A further reason for caring about private conduct involves public credibility. Leaders charged with making or enforcing standards of conduct should follow them as well. In order to maintain respect and serve as appropriate role models, politicians should behave responsibly in their personal as well as their professional lives. Hypocrisy is also a factor. Part of what made the conduct of Edwards, Vitter, Spitzer, and Chenoweth problematic was the distance between their public pronouncements and their private conduct. And while the law should not police private sexual lives, it should hold politicians accountable for any illegal behavior or abuse of office. The use of campaign funds or taxpayer dollars to subsidize infidelity compounds its impact, as Sanford discovered. Powerful House committee chair Wayne Hays lost credibility when the public learned that he had hired a mistress as an administrative assistant, although, by her own account, "I can't type, I can't file. I can't even answer the phone."[163] David Paterson's reputation as New York governor was compromised by reports that he had used campaign funds to pay for hotel rooms for his affairs, which were billed as "constituent services."[164]

Yet to suggest that adultery is always disqualifying is problematic on several grounds. A threshold difficulty involves the assumption that character reflects consistent personality traits, and that individuals who exhibit dishonesty or disrespect for ethical standards in one context will do so in another. Yet a vast array of social science research suggests that this assumption is, to a large extent, a "figment of our aspirations."[165] Context is critical in shaping moral behavior, and there is often little correlation between seemingly similar character traits such as lying and cheating.[166] Even slight changes in situational factors can substantially affect tendencies toward deceit.[167] Whatever else one may say about infidelity in marriage, history does not indicate that it is an accurate predictor of ethics or effectiveness in office. Compare, for example, Richard Nixon, who was faithful, and Franklin Delano Roosevelt, who was not. John F. Kennedy lied frequently about his sexual affairs but was honest with the public about the botched invasion of the Bay of Pigs.

A second problem with drawing inferences from sexual conduct is that it encourages a kind of Gresham's law of journalism. All it takes is one reporter with a peephole perspective. As soon as a scandal breaks in any major media outlet, it becomes difficult for other members of the press to remain above the fray. The prevailing philosophy of "Let the public decide" often encourages the media to pander to our worst instincts, and to divert its attention from more substantive issues. As a famous article on privacy by Samuel Warren and Louis Brandeis noted, gossip about scandal "both belittles and perverts. . . . It usurps the place of interest in brains capable of other things."[168] Details about politicians' sex lives can demean not only politicians but also ourselves.

The costs of such coverage are not borne by politicians alone. Society also suffers when its choices for leadership narrow to those willing to put their entire sexual histories on public display. Under the watchful eye of reporters scrambling for a scoop, large numbers of Americans have something frayed around the ethical edges. Our nation has a limited supply of gifted leaders, and many who might serve are either unwilling or unable to withstand the widening gauntlets of journalists.

The point is not that adultery is irrelevant in assessing qualifications for leadership. It is rather that context matters. Much depends on the nature and consequences of the conduct and what other issues are at stake. Did the affair involve other illegal conduct such as prostitution or financial improprieties? Did it involve abuse of office or unduly reckless behavior? Is the position one such as the presidency, which necessarily entails moral leadership? What will happen in terms of other policy concerns if the politician is impeached, defeated, or forced to resign? How a public servant treats women in private must be balanced against how he treats women's issues in his political capacity. Bill Clinton had an abysmal record on marital fidelity but an excellent one on gender equality. What makes for personal goodness is not always the same as what makes for the common good. As journalist Matt Bai notes, American history is rife with examples of people who were "crappy husbands . . . but great stewards of the state, just as we had thoroughly decent men who couldn't summon the executive skills to run a bake sale."[169] In politics, it may often make sense to hate the sin but vote for the sinner.

7

International Perspectives

In 2005, at former French president François Mitterrand's state funeral, his long-time mistress Anne Pingeot appeared alongside his wife and their two sons.[1] Meanwhile, in Islamic countries, women could be stoned for adultery, and at least 75 percent of Muslims in Egypt and Pakistan favored that penalty.[2] As those examples suggest, attitudes toward infidelity vary widely and provide a window into global norms concerning sex, gender, religion, and law. This chapter offers a brief overview of differing regional views regarding adultery. The point is not to attempt a comprehensive summary, but rather to provide a comparative perspective that can inform America's own evolving legal standards.

Among developed societies, the percent of married people who admit to having been unfaithful over the previous year typically ranges from 2 percent to 25 percent.[3] One survey of thirty-six countries found that poor countries had higher rates of infidelity.[4] Togo topped the list: 37 percent of male partners admitted to cheating during the previous year. In Haiti, it was 25 percent of men; Nigeria, 15 percent; Peru, 13.5 percent; the United States, 4 percent; Switzerland, 3 percent; and Australia, 2.5 percent. In only a few countries did more than 2 percent of women say they were unfaithful in the last year. Sex differences were greatest in poor countries. In the Dominican Republic and Burkina Faso, less than 1 percent of women were unfaithful, compared to 20 percent of men. In accounting for the gender differences, some researchers speculate that married men are cheating with single women or prostitutes and are more likely than women to exaggerate their affairs. Women may underreport them, given the sexual double standard that prevails in many countries.

Two other surveys also offer some interesting international comparisons. One is an Internet poll on sexual behavior, conducted by Durex, a condom manufacturer.[5] The survey methodology was not calculated to give accurate measures of countrywide infidelity rates because respondents had to have an Internet connection and be willing to respond to a poll by a condom manufacturer. Still, the comparative statistics are illuminating. Thailand and Malaysia topped the list.[6] In another survey of twenty-four industrialized countries, a higher percentage of adults in the United States viewed adultery as always wrong (80 percent), compared to those in most other industrialized countries such as Sweden (68 percent), England (67 percent), Italy (67 percent), Australia (59 percent), Japan (58 percent), Canada (55 percent), and Russia (36 percent). Only two countries had higher rates than the United States: the Philippines (88 percent) and Northern Ireland (81 percent).[7]

The discussion that follows offers a snapshot of regional attitudes and practices. Although reliable data is limited, the information available highlights a broad range of cultural norms, which is reflected in differing legal regimes. In many countries, these norms and laws reveal a sexual double standard. The picture that emerges also makes clear that decriminalization of adultery is increasingly the trend outside Islamic countries, which has obvious implications for the evolution of American legal norms. And within those Islamic countries, the brutality of criminal enforcement makes adultery a human rights issue.

Europe

In 2004, controversy centered on a proposal by Turkish politicians once again to criminalize adultery in order to "preserve the family."[8] After intense criticism from the European Union and various advocacy groups, the governing party of Turkey abandoned its efforts, at least partly in hopes of eventual admission into the European Union.[9] Although the Turkish controversy has subsided, the debate reflects a larger ideological split that persists in a number of European nations, where secularist norms collide with religious and moral values.

Although most of Europe once prohibited adultery, statutes criminalizing infidelity have disappeared. In 2006, Romania was one of the last to abandon such laws.[10] International norms helped to propel this decriminalization movement.[11] The International Covenant on Civil and Political Rights includes a right to privacy, which some commentators argue prohibits the criminalization of sexual relations between consenting adults.[12] The United Nations Working Group on the Issue of Discrimination against Women in Law and in Practice has taken this position. It has also concluded that laws prohibiting adultery violate the UN's Convention on the Elimination of All Forms of Discrimination against Women (CEDAW).[13] Specifically, Article 16 states that "parties shall take all appropriate measures to eliminate discrimination against women in all matters relating to marriage and family relations."[14] In addition, the CEDAW Committee, the Human Rights Committee, and the UN Working Group have called for an end to laws criminalizing adultery, which they characterize as discriminating against women.[15] According to the UN Working Group, "Maintaining adultery as a criminal offence—even when, on the face of it, it applies to both women and men—means in practice that women will continue to face extreme vulnerabilities, and violation of their human rights to dignity, privacy and equality, given continuing discrimination and inequalities faced by women."[16] In nations where adultery prohibitions are truly neutral both on their face and in practice, such laws are usually no longer enforced and overdue for repeal.[17]

Even though Europe has abolished criminal prohibitions on adultery, public disapproval of the practice remains high. In one survey across twenty-four nations, only 4 percent reported that it is not wrong at all for married people to have sex with someone besides their spouse. Sixty-six percent described extramarital sex as always wrong, and the remaining 30 percent said it was sometimes wrong.[18] In a 2013 study by the Pew Research Center, more than half of those surveyed in almost every nation agreed that having an affair was "morally unacceptable."[19] France was a notable exception; only 47 percent of French respondents agreed.[20] Many European nations, however, topped the list of those being most amenable to such relationships, and showed significantly lower percentages of disapproval than the United States. Apart from France, the nations with the lowest percentages saying adultery was morally unacceptable were Germany (60 percent), Italy (64 percent), and Spain (64 percent). Notably, Britain and Greece were higher on the list, at 76 percent and 79 percent, respectively, while the United States came in at 84 percent. Turkey topped the list with 94 percent finding adultery morally unacceptable.[21]

France's tolerance of extramarital affairs is long standing. The country's political leaders set the tone. "French Politicians Stray Early and Often" was the lead of one representative article. It noted that a French president around the turn of the twentieth century died in the bed of his mistress, and that Charles de Gaulle was the only post–World War II French leader to avoid an extramarital relationship.[22] One of France's most notorious philanderers in recent memory is the former head of the International Monetary Fund, Dominique Strauss-Kahn. He was forced to resign after an American hotel maid accused him of sexual assault, and he was implicated in a prostitution ring.[23] Following his resignation, one of Strauss-Kahn's former mistresses wrote a tell-all book purporting to detail their relationship. Strauss-Kahn opposed the publication and eventually won the right to place a card detailing his objections inside of each copy.[24] Although acknowledging that his sex life (including wife swapping) was "out of step with French society," he nonetheless insisted that there was nothing wrong with "free behavior between consenting adults" and that authorities investigating his involvement with prostitutes were trying to "criminalize lust."[25] Despite the scandals, Strauss-Kahn rebounded to head a prominent global investment firm.[26]

Contrary to popular perception, however, the French report no higher rates of adultery than do Americans. Fidelity is the top quality French women seek in a partner. According to Pamela Druckerman's comparative study, what distinguishes adultery in France is not its frequency but the lack of guilt that typically accompanies it. The French typically view infidelity as a "transgression, but one that's forgivable and even understandable." Part of the reason may be that they are less religious than many other cultures. Only 11 percent say that religion is "very important" to them, compared to 59 percent of Americans. As Druckerman concludes, the French "don't commit rampant adultery.

But when the French have affairs they do a better job of enjoying them than Americans do."[27]

Adultery is also common among other European leaders. One of the most celebrated affairs in recent history involved England's Prince Charles and Camilla Parker Bowles. The relationship transformed Bowles into a public pariah following the tragic death of Princess Diana, even though she, too, had been unfaithful.[28] The scandal was compounded by tabloids' publication of transcripts of secretly recorded telephone conversations, complete with references to Charles's desire to live inside Camilla's trousers.[29] Years later, when the pair finally announced their engagement, the Church of England refused to host the wedding of the two adulterers.[30]

In January 2010, neighboring Ireland was rocked with its own salacious scandal when news broke that the wife of Irish first minister Peter Robinson had been having an affair with a nineteen-year-old boy who was forty years her junior. Compounding the scandal was evidence that the minister's wife had used political kickbacks to help her young lover fund his first business venture.[31]

In a more serious scandal, former Italian prime minister Silvio Berlusconi faced criminal charges for (among other things) soliciting sex with a seventeen-year-old girl known by the stage name "Ruby the Heartstealer."[32] While Berlusconi admitted to giving Ruby thousands in euros, he claimed that the sums were "gifts," and that he never engaged in improper relations with the young belly dancer. Prior to the "Rubygate" scandal, Berlusconi had been married twice. His second wife, a former nude dancer with whom he had begun an affair during his first marriage, divorced him after he attended the eighteenth birthday party of an aspiring lingerie model and allegations surfaced that he had been soliciting sex with minors.[33] Berlusconi announced plans to marry his twenty-seven-year-old fiancée at the end of contentious divorce proceedings with his second wife.[34] As for Rubygate, an initial conviction in the lower courts was overturned on appeal in 2014. In spite of this and other scandals, Berlusconi remained head of the right-wing Forza Party in Italy.[35]

Adultery has also figured in employment disputes. The European Union recognizes both the right of individuals to respect of their private lives and the right of religious groups to remain free from undue state interference.[36] Conflicts occasionally arise where religious organizations dismiss employees because of sexual indiscretions. The European Court of Human Rights has taken a case-by-case approach to such issues. For example, in *Schüth v Germany*, the court determined that the Catholic Church had acted improperly when it dismissed an organist and choirmaster on grounds of adultery. The court noted that the choirmaster lacked alternative employment opportunities, and that the connection between the employee's infidelity and the overall mission of the Catholic Church was minimal.[37] By contrast, in *Obst v. Germany*, the court sided with the Mormon Church in its decision to dismiss a public relations director because of adultery. In this case, the credibility of the director was impaired, and he was able to obtain employment outside the church.[38]

Adultery also plays a role in family contexts. In two Spanish cases, the court rejected claims for damages by husbands who alleged economic and emotional harm suffered as a result of their wives' adultery and deception as to the paternity of several children. In rejecting the claims, the court reasoned in one case that the wife had not intentionally hidden the third party's paternity, and in the other, it concluded that the only legal consequence of infidelity should be divorce. Otherwise "any disturbance of matrimonial life would give rise to liability for damages."[39]

Countries vary as to whether adultery constitutes grounds for divorce. Many allow it, but Germany and France have eliminated it.[40] A new French law created a general fault-based provision for divorce, which no longer separately listed adultery but rather subsumed it within the more general category of fault. This means that adultery is no longer a "peremptory grounds" for divorce in France; it no longer automatically entitles the innocent spouse to a divorce on favorable terms. Also, modern French divorce law allows parties to obtain a no-fault divorce on the basis of "prolonged disruption of the life in common," defined as a separation for six or more years. This controversial provision became colloquially known in France as "divorce by repudiation," and in England, an analogous provision in the English Divorce Reform Act of 1969 was more colorfully termed "Casanova's Charter." Debate regarding this provision has centered on whether the spouse who has brought about the "disruption" should be allowed to freely divorce the other spouse, who had committed no wrongdoing. To address this concern, both the French and British laws give judges discretion to deny this no-fault option if they deem it inappropriate under the circumstances.[41]

Adultery has also figured in the law of provocation in Europe. As in some parts of the United States, many European countries allow adultery to be considered as a mitigating factor in homicide cases. England weathered controversial debates on the topic in 2009 and 2012. Under the relevant statute, defendants could not be convicted of murder if they "suffered from a loss of self-control that had a 'qualifying trigger,' and a reasonable person 'in the circumstances' of the defendant might have acted in a similar way."[42] In 2009, the British Equalities minister proposed reforming the law to prevent murder charges from being reduced to manslaughter in cases of adultery. The proposal met with vehement opposition in the House of Lords. According to one lord, a retired judge, "We will make ourselves look extraordinarily foolish if we say a jury cannot take account of what most people recognize as being the most dominant cause of violence by one individual against another." The Ministry of Justice expressed disappointment with the opposition, stating that "the history of the partial-defence of provocation has led to a commonly-held belief that this is a defence which can be abused by men who kill their wives out of sexual jealousy and revenge over infidelity. This erodes the confidence of the public in the fairness of the criminal justice system."[43] In 2012, the Court of Appeal for England and Wales controversially determined that adultery could still be considered within a broader "loss of control" framework, creating what has been dubbed the "infidelity plus" defense.[44]

Russia

When it comes to adultery, Russia is an outlier among nations. In 2010, *Russia Today* published the results of a poll that surveyed 4,200 Russians about marital infidelity. It found that 28 percent of men and 17 percent of women reported committing adultery at least once. Many Russians believed that "having an affair is not catastrophic for a marriage"; 42 percent stated that they would work to salvage their marriage after discovering their partner's infidelity.[45]

These findings are consistent with those published a dozen years earlier in a cross-national comparison of attitudes toward adultery. Of the twenty-four countries studied, Russia stood out as the most tolerant of infidelity. Only 36 percent of Russians described extramarital sex as "always wrong," compared to an average of 66 percent for all twenty-four countries. And 17 percent of Russians described adultery as "not wrong at all," compared to an average of 4 percent for all the countries surveyed and an average of 2 percent for most Western countries.[46]

The law in Russia reflects these attitudes. No references to adultery occur in the nation's criminal or family code. Adultery is not even grounds for divorce.[47] The relative permissiveness of contemporary Russian society may in part reflect a backlash against the severe treatment of infidelity under communism. Adultery then was "a career-wrecking scandal." Today, "wandering spouses" are an "accepted and even expected" part of life in Moscow. A "boys' night out" often includes prostitutes. In some elite circles, having a mistress is expected; and many Russian women "shrug off the fooling around. It's seen as unavoidable and natural."[48] As one sociologist put it, women view "faithfulness in marriage . . . as something that is nice but unrealistic."[49] Russians do not consider it adultery if a married man has sex with a stranger on vacation.[50]

Given these attitudes, the sex lives of politicians rarely cause much scandal, except when the facts are lurid. In the late 1990s, just as the Clinton-Lewinsky affair broke in the United States, the Russian public got its own taste of "sex, lies, and videotapes." A state-owned television station aired excerpts from a secretly recorded video that showed a man resembling Russia's prosecutor general (that is, attorney general), Yuri Skuratov, having sex with two women prostitutes. Then-president Boris Yeltsin immediately condemned Skuratov for "moral unscrupulousness and scheming," but rumors swirled that Yeltsin himself was involved in the screening of the video.[51] Skuratov had antagonized Yeltsin when he began to investigate corruption that implicated Yeltsin's family.[52]

In 2012, President Vladimir Putin fired his defense minister, Anatoly Serdyukov, over allegations of corruption and adultery. When police launched an early-morning raid on the apartment of a woman who was Serdyukov's neighbor and former employee, Serdyukov opened the door in his bathrobe.[53] The raid, which was part of a corruption investigation, figured on Russian television, and reports indicated that Serdyukov's mistress lived in a "13-room apartment worth about ten million dollars filled with expensive jewelry and art masterpieces."[54] Claiming that his aim was to ensure an impartial investigation, Putin then fired Serdyukov. The mistress was placed under house arrest, and both were subsequently indicted. She is facing trial; Serdyukov received amnesty.[55] Underlying the scandal—and Serdyukov's sacking—was a tangle of political and family loyalties. As a *New Yorker* profile explained,

> Serdyukov's wife is the daughter of a former Prime Minister who used to be a colleague of Vladimir Putin . . . and is believed to be a member of Putin's current inner circle. Serdyukov's father-in-law was arguably a key driving force in his career. . . . Serdyukov owes to his marriage "his dashing transformation from an owner of a furniture business to a cabinet minister." . . . Serdyukov's dismissal looked like a most unusual move for Putin, who has a reputation of a leader who "never gives up his own," corrupt or not. A possible explanation that the Russian rumor mill is suggesting: in the adultery scenario, Putin's loyalty would have been to the father-in-law.[56]

Given Putin's own marital history, if he sided with the father-in-law in firing Serdyukov, odds are that it was due more to political calculations than to moral affront. In 2014, he finalized a divorce from his wife of thirty years. Putin described the divorce as "a joint decision: we hardly see each other, each of us has our own life," and his wife called the divorce "civilized."[57] Nevertheless, rumors have circulated since 2008 that Putin was involved in an affair with a younger woman, a former gymnastics champion turned lawmaker. The Russian tabloid that published the rumor was promptly forced to close. Foreign media have continued printing the rumors, however, and suggested that Putin has children with his mistress. While Putin denies such rumors, the electorate seems largely indifferent.[58] As one commentator explained, "In a country still sorting itself out after 70 years of communism and six years of anything-goes capitalism, the private predilections of elected leaders don't seem to have much bearing."[59]

Asia

China presents a particularly interesting case in the evolution of attitudes toward adultery. Traditionally, men were allowed to keep concubines and visit prostitutes. When Mao Zedong took power in 1949, however, he declared that relationships with concubines constituted bigamy and were therefore illegal. Adultery was not a criminal offense, and Mao was himself famously promiscuous, but the practice was discouraged.[60] Finding a place to cheat was difficult, and neighborhood committees could report anyone having "lifestyle problems" to Communist Party officials.[61] Leaders of work groups could demote or fire someone guilty of infidelity, or make them undergo a humiliating "self-criticism."

Reforms following Mao's death led to more privacy and more liberal sexual attitudes. A 2012 study revealed rates of infidelity of 13.6 percent among Chinese men and 4.2 percent among Chinese women.[62] Chinese men hovered around the median 13.2 percent infidelity rate of the thirty-six other countries included in the report, but Chinese women were far more likely to cheat than women elsewhere—well above the median of 0.8 percent. James Farrer, a professor of sociology who studies the sex cultures of China, suspects that its emphasis on gender equality prompts Chinese women to "feel as though they have a right to do the things that Chinese men have a right to." He explains that "when you talk to women about infidelity in China, they will often say, 'Well, men do it. Why can't we?' "[63] Farrer also sees the widespread participation of Chinese women in the workforce as a contributing factor, as it increases the opportunities for married women to meet men.

The frequency of adultery has spawned a flourishing industry of private investigators, known colloquially as "mistress killers." Their primary function, to gather evidence for divorce proceedings, was highlighted in a celebrated case involving the Sherlock Holmes Agency in Sichuan Province. Members of the agency, together with a local television camera crew, aggrieved wife, and some of her relatives, went to the apartment where the unfaithful husband and his lover were staying. The wife broke down the door, surprising her naked husband, and shouted, "I've got you both." The film footage was used in the divorce proceeding and in a reality law show, which portrayed the wife as a heroine in a tale of justifiable revenge.[64]

How the law should respond to adultery has been subject to dispute. The All-China Women's Federation (ACWF)—a Chinese women's rights organization—conducted a survey in which 95 percent of the 4,000 people surveyed favored criminalizing extramarital affairs because of the harm they caused to marriage.[65] Conservative factions of the Communist Party also sought to criminalize adultery. Nevertheless, the National People's Congress (NPC) decided otherwise. Adultery remains legal, although it can constitute grounds for divorce under statutory language referring to "circumstances causing alienation of mutual affection."[66] However, two important exceptions to the decriminalization of adultery involve affairs in the military and in the Communist Party. Individuals having sex with spouses of military officers can be sentenced to three years in prison, even if both parties consented to the encounter. The Communist Party's internal disciplinary codes also outline clear punishments for party officials who commit adultery, ranging from a severe warning to expulsion from the party and loss of the member's political post.[67]

Some evidence suggests that the Communist Party is cracking down on adultery as a result of scandals that caused the Chinese to refer to the party as the "Adultery Party."[68] In one celebrated case, a railway boss had eighteen mistresses.[69] In another case, a senior tax officer was relieved of his duties after disclosure of a contract with his mistress that set out the terms of their affair. The couple had agreed to meet at least once a week, refrain from engaging in sexual activities with any third parties, and pay a fine for reneging on any of the agreement's terms.[70] In the summer of 2012, at least six senior officials were accused of adultery and suspended from their positions. However, not all adulterous politicians appeared to be at risk. According to one official, the enforcement effort was targeted at those who had at least three mistresses.[71]

Among ordinary citizens, one factor that contributes to the frequency of adultery is the large number of rural men who work in the cities and leave their wives behind for long stretches of time. Local Chinese officials became increasingly concerned about the plight of these forty-seven million "left-behind women" in 2014, when one migrant worker went on a shooting spree after learning that his wife was having affairs with two other men.[72]

In India, a heated debate occurred in 2011 after the Bombay High Court rejected a claim that the law against adultery was unconstitutional because it discriminated against men. The petitioner, a Mumbai businessman, had been caught having an affair with a married woman, for which he was subject to penalties of up to five years imprisonment, a fine, or both. The woman was not punishable under the statute.[73]

However, women whose husbands were having affairs were also not entitled to charge their husbands with adultery; that privilege belonged only to the husbands of women who were having affairs. The court declined to hold the law unconstitutional because that "would give free play to extra-marital affairs and affect the stability of marriage." However, the justices added that "it was time that [the statute] was revisited."[74]

Many individuals agreed, but there was no consensus on how the law should be changed. Some argued for decriminalizing adultery. According to one New Delhi lawyer, it would not be "at all progressive" to achieve gender equality by making women equally liable for their extramarital affairs. "It is retrograde. And it's a strange kind of equality that punishes more people for an act that is a totally private matter."[75] "What century are we living in?" asked one women's rights activist. "Having more than one relationship is not a crime."[76] "The government should look at more pressing issues like corruption and terrorism rather than who is sleeping with whom," added a prominent criminal defense lawyer.[77]

By contrast, others argued for making women equally liable and equally entitled to bring charges. As one justice noted, "We need such laws to deter people from committing such acts."[78] The chair of the National Commission for Women agreed: "It's unfair that a wife can't take her husband to court for being unfaithful. Why should she suffer silently? At least the threat of legal action might curb a husband's adulterous activities and save a marriage."[79] One New Delhi accountant would love to charge her husband for his "serial womanising." "But even if I didn't, I resent a man having rights that I don't have. This law is insulting to women."[80] As this book went to press, the insult remained.

Japanese law on adultery traditionally reflected a stark double standard as well. It granted no remedy to the wife of an unfaithful husband, while a husband had the power to charge his wife with adultery, a crime that could be punished by death.[81] The American occupation of Japan following World War II brought a liberalization of sexual norms, and adultery was decriminalized in 1947.[82] According to a 2008 survey by the nation's *Today*, much of the country's adultery now involves sex with prostitutes, who service married businessmen.[83] Politicians' involvement with prostitutes has a well-known history. In 1989, Prime Minister Sousuke Uno was forced to resign after only two months in office when details surfaced about his financial relationship with a geisha.[84] The scandal was compounded by allegations that she was underpaid.

Today, Japan has relatively high rates of infidelity. According to a survey by the Ministry of Health, Labor, and Welfare, more than 20 percent of married men (age sixteen to forty-nine) and 11 percent of married women admitted to having had extramarital sex in the year preceding the survey.[85] In another 2013 poll, almost 15 percent of Japanese housewives admitted that they had committed adultery at some point during their marriage.[86] "Love hotels" and "take-out host" services cater to those with extramarital inclinations, and technology has helped to fulfill those desires. The nation has a host of online encounter sites.[87] Ashley Madison, one of the largest, polled more than 3,500 users in 2014 and found that the top reason for seeking an affair was simple: 51 percent of men and 55 percent of women cited "not enough sex."[88] According to Ashley Madison's CEO, "We're providing the opportunity to have a clandestine affair, and helping millions of people around the world stay in their marriages."[89]

In Taiwan, adultery remains a criminal offense, punishable by up to one year in prison or a fine commensurate with the amount of jail time imposed.[90] Previously, the law prohibited adultery only by women. Although it is now gender neutral on its face, the law is not gender neutral in practice. According to the director of Shih Hsin University's Graduate Institute for Gender Studies,

> If Taiwanese men get caught, they usually apologize, then the wives tend to drop the charge because men are often the economic providers in most families; but if it is the other way around the women are dragged into court.... 50 percent of women who sue their husbands for adultery will eventually drop charges, but only 23 percent of men will do so against their wives, resulting in a higher conviction rate among women.[91]

In 2013, public debate surfaced over whether adultery should be decriminalized. The minister of justice proposed the change on the ground that the law was archaic and an international embarrassment. According to the minister of culture, "It is absurd that marriage should still rely on the support of judges, police officers and detectives."[92] The reform effort failed. Women's groups were divided. Some felt that "criminalization is a weapon against erring husbands that Taiwan's women—often legally disadvantaged in family-related matters—would be loath to lose."[93] The chair of the Modern Women's Foundation disagreed: "It is better to let the spouse go, rather than spending the time intimidating and punishing the parties involved through the criminal justice system. The existence of the crime of adultery does not help promote positive feelings among married couples." Women betrayed by their husbands should "face reality and ... be happy on their own."[94] A former judge agreed. He believed that most women who file adultery charges against their husband do not want to give them a criminal record; they are merely hoping that they will end the affair. But the chances of reconciliation diminish once charges are filed. Many women then regret their initial decision "when they realize the court can't help love to continue."[95] Despite such arguments, support for criminal prohibitions remains high. A Ministry of Justice survey found that 82 percent of the public wanted to retain the current law.[96]

Adultery is also a criminal offense in Korea, punishable by up to two years in jail. Although it is rare for individuals to be imprisoned, that does not stop angry spouses from filing criminal complaints.[97] Each year, more than 1,200 people are indicted under the law, and about half are convicted. Fewer than 50 end up behind bars.[98] The country's Constitutional Court has reviewed the law four times since 1990, upholding it each time. However, the latest decision in 2014 was by the slimmest possible margin, suggesting that the law may be vulnerable if challenges continue.

The latest case attracted national attention because it involved Ok So-Ri, a famous Korean television star. Park Chul, her husband and a famous soap opera actor, accused her of infidelity with a close friend and with an Italian chef who was teaching her how to cook. Ok admitted to having an affair with the friend (but not with the chef), and filed a petition challenging the constitutionality of the adultery statute.[99] Ok claimed that the law "constitutes a serious breach of [an] individual's rights to make decisions concerning sex and privacy under the constitution," and that adultery cases should be handled in civil courts, not criminal courts.[100] According to her lawyer, "The state meddling in which sex partner we should have—that's too much."[101] Ok blamed her infidelity on a loveless marriage to Park, and disclosed at a news conference "that she and her husband had sex only 10 times in their 11 years of marriage."[102] Her husband denied her claims, and said he felt like "an innocent pedestrian hit by a car."[103] Ok's complaint is not rare. One survey by the Korea Institute for Sexology found that nearly 30 percent of married couples said that they are "sexless," defined as having intercourse less than a few times a year.[104]

In Ok's case, five of the court's nine judges found the law unconstitutional, but a two-thirds majority—six of the nine judges—is needed in Korea for the law to be invalidated.[105] Ok received an eight-month suspended sentence. In justifying the lenient treatment, the court noted that her husband's responsibility was "not small" and that she had already suffered "mental pain" from the loss of her privacy.[106]

Although recent surveys suggest that 50 to 70 percent of South Koreans support the adultery law, it has lost some of its staunchest supporters.[107] Two long-standing champions of women's rights, the Korean Women's Association United and the Ministry of Gender Equality and Family, say it is time for South Korea to consider abolishing the prohibition.[108] With their economic status rising, many women no longer fear divorce or believe that they need the law to help them cope with an unfaithful husband. And the growing number of men charging their wives with adultery is causing many women to consider whether the law's protections are worth the risk. According to the chief adviser of the Korean Women Link, "Even though men commit adultery more than women do, men complain about adultery more than women."[109] "Adultery was once considered something only husbands could do," said the president of the Korea Legal Aid Center for Family Relations. "But now women think they can do it too, and some of them actually do it."[110]

Latin America

Relatively little information is available about adultery in Latin America. Many countries traditionally treated unfaithful women more harshly than unfaithful men. Brazil initially criminalized adultery only when committed by a woman; in 1995, it eliminated criminal prohibitions entirely.[111] Now the country addresses infidelity only through civil code provisions, which allow it as a justification for divorce.[112] Traditionally, honor killings for adultery were common. Following a decade of campaigning by women's rights activists, in a 1991 case involving such a killing, the Brazilian Supreme Court condemned the practice. The court declared that "homicide cannot be seen as a normal and legitimate way of reacting to adultery," and that "what is defended is not honor but vanity, exaggerated self-importance."[113] However, a United Nations survey found that honor killings continue to occur, particularly in rural areas.[114] Even after the Supreme Court's 1991 decision reversing the defendant's acquittal, on retrial the lower court again acquitted the defendant of an honor killing.

Argentina also traditionally treated adultery by men and women differently. Until the conduct was decriminalized in 1995, a single act of infidelity was sufficient to convict a wife, while husbands were guilty only if they had a mistress.[115] Adultery is now recognized as grounds for divorce, but Argentinians have a slightly more permissive view of the practice than people in most countries.[116] In performing research for her comparative study, Druckerman found an example of those attitudes: the director of an Argentinean beef company propositioned her directly. When she asked how his wife would feel about the affair, he seemed bewildered by the question. He wanted to know what his wife had to do with it, "since this was between us." Druckerman shouldn't feel offended, he said, because "I am offering you great pleasure."[117]

Mexico decriminalized adultery in 2011.[118] A poll released the same year found that Mexicans were unusually tolerant of sexual affairs by politicians and celebrities; 57 percent were likely to tolerate such conduct.[119] Such attitudes have been on display in the popular support of Mexico's president despite his 2012 admission that he had fathered two children out of wedlock. As a result, he has become the poster boy for a website promoting adultery in Mexico. One billboard showed the president with his index finger over his lips in a hushing gesture and red lipstick on his collar. Next to him are the words, "Unfaithful to his family. Faithful and committed to his country."[120] However, another prominent politician, the leader of the nation's ruling party, resigned in 2014 following reports that his office hired women to have sex with him and placed them on party payrolls.[121]

Islamic Countries

The harshest treatment of marital infidelity occurs in nations governed by Sharia law, a strict legal code derived from the Koran and the teachings of Muhammad, a code that was developed by Muslim scholars in the first three centuries of Islam. Only a minority of Muslim countries are governed solely by Sharia law; they include Afghanistan, Iran, the Maldives, Mauritania, Pakistan, Sudan, Saudi Arabia, Yemen, and the United Arab Emirates.[122] In some other countries, Sharia courts have jurisdiction over family matters, and secular courts have jurisdiction over other matters, including criminal law. Sharia law criminalizes zina, sexual intercourse by individuals who are not married to each other. Stoning as a punishment for the crime can occur legally or illegally in at least fifteen countries.[123] It results in a prolonged and painful death. Flogging is also an option in many countries.[124] Common reasons for the strict punishment of adultery include protection of the family, prevention of disease, and facilitation of rules governing succession and inheritance.[125] Proof of zina requires a confession, testimony by four male eyewitnesses to the act, or an out-of-wedlock pregnancy. Because four eyewitnesses to the crime are extremely rare, but unwed pregnancies are not, women are much more likely than men to be targets of prosecution.[126] In some countries, only women have been convicted of adultery and sentenced to death by stoning.[127] And some nations do not recognize coercion as a defense, so women who are raped can be guilty of zina.[128]

The following is a sample of the kinds of cases that result in prosecution of women for adultery or zina.

- In 2014, a couple convicted of adultery was stoned to death in Pakistan. Six people were arrested in connection with the killing, including the father and brother of the woman and the cleric who ordered the stoning. It was widely expected that no action would be taken against the six men.[129]
- In 2012, a Sudanese woman tried without access to a lawyer or translator was convicted of adultery and sentenced to death by stoning. Her conviction was based on a confession that followed a beating by her brother.[130]
- In 2012, the U.S. State Department's human rights report cited cases of four women who had been stoned for engaging in "illegitimate relationships."[131]
- A 2012 Human Rights Watch report chronicled the case of a husband in Afghanistan who sold his wife to a brothel, where she was forced into prostitution. She was convicted of zina and sentenced to four years in prison.[132]
- In 2011, an adulterous Afghan couple who had eloped to Pakistan were stoned to death in front of hundreds of people. No one who participated in the stoning was charged with a crime, although a graphic film prompted calls for those responsible to be brought to justice.[133]
- The book *The Stoning of Soraya M.* (2011) chronicles the true story of an Iranian woman falsely accused of adultery by her husband

when he could not afford to have two wives. Her father, husband, and sons threw the first stones.[134]

- In 2008, a thirteen-year-old Somalian girl reported a rape to the militia in control of southern Somalia at the time. Instead of prosecuting the rapist, authorities prosecuted her for adultery. A thousand people showed up at a football stadium to watch as fifty men stoned her to death.[135]

- In 2003, Amina Lawal, a Nigerian woman, was sentenced to stoning based on her out-of-wedlock pregnancy. The father of her child was acquitted of zina due to the lack of eyewitness testimony. The case provoked international protest and the judgment was overturned on procedural grounds.[136]

Cases where the husband suspects adultery can also result in honor killings, mutilations, acid attacks, or other brutality.[137] One Indian woman suspected of adultery was set ablaze by her husband and his family while she was sleeping.[138] Sometimes such killings occur when the family cannot meet the burden of proof required for zina.[139] As an Amnesty International statement notes, "The regime of honour is unforgiving; women on whom suspicion has fallen are not given an opportunity to defend themselves, and family members have no socially acceptable alternative but to remove the stain on their honour by attacking the woman."[140] The UN Population Fund estimates that some 5,000 honor killings occur each year, but other estimates vary widely, and few countries collect data systematically.[141] Many families report the incidents as accidents or suicides. The practice is by no means limited to Islamic countries; it also occurs within Islamic immigrant communities across the globe.[142] Although such killings can be triggered by many forms of dishonor, research suggests that suspicion of adultery is the most common cause.[143] The suspicion need not be substantiated to be lethal; the mere perception of infidelity, regardless of its factual basis, is enough to trigger action against the woman.[144]

As a 2010 UN report put it, these are "not isolated incidents," but rather the "extreme manifestation of pre-existing forms of violence" that continue to be "accepted, tolerated or justified."[145] Some countries, including Egypt, Tunisia, Libya, Kuwait, Syria, Lebanon, and Jordan, reduce the penalties for killings prompted by adultery.[146] Although in some regions honor killings spark outrage, in others, they enjoy significant public support. The 2014 hanging of a Palestinian woman suspected of adultery was the culmination of a trend that caused considerable concern.[147] A 2005 survey in Turkey found that 37 percent of respondents believed that a woman who had committed adultery should be killed; 21 percent said her nose or ears should be cut off.[148] In a 2012 incident, an Afghan woman accused of adultery was shot dead, to jeers of jubilation from the 150 men watching. "It is the order of Allah that she be executed," one bystander said.[149]

In some instances, even foreigners have been targeted for prosecution. In 2009, Sally Antia, a British citizen, faced charges of adultery in Dubai after her estranged husband reported her to local police. She was arrested at a hotel in Dubai and sentenced to two months in prison for an adulterous affair. After she served her sentence, she was deported from the UAE, where she had spent the last ten years of her life.[150]

Outrage from the human rights community has had limited results. In some instances, letter-writing campaigns and international protest have brought pressure to bear to prevent executions. But case-by-case activism can at times be counterproductive by provoking resistance from local officials.[151] Much more needs to be done to prevent such cases from arising in the first instance. Sustained pressure from broad coalitions of nations, as well as human rights organizations, might help to reform laws and social practices that impose a sexual double standard and barbaric punishments. The United States would be in a stronger position to lead such efforts if it did not itself criminalize adultery in many jurisdictions.

As this overview suggests, the trend outside Islamic countries is clear. In most societies, adultery is widely condemned, but legal prohibitions are no longer viewed as the appropriate response. Social sanctions are also weaker, and scandals involving extramarital affairs often do not have serious career consequences. In this age of growing sexual permissiveness, only strong traditions, such as those drawing on Sharia law, can make adultery a subject of criminal prosecution and public ostracism. International law strongly condemns such prosecutions. The United States should join the trend and place its moral authority on the side of decriminalization.

8

Conclusion

A time-honored nightclub joke recounts how Moses came down from the mountain and announced, "I have some good news and some bad news. The good news is that I bargained him down to only ten commandments. The bad news is that adultery stays in." For centuries, law has sought to shore up the adultery commandment with criminal and civil penalties. That is now a misdirected effort.

The law governing adultery has an unbecoming history, marked by intrusive inquiries, inconsistent application, and class, racial, and gender bias. Society's double standard was reflected and reinforced by legal prohibitions. Unfaithful wives were treated more harshly than husbands, and expected to overlook their spouses' indiscretions. Where adultery was the primary ground for divorce, fabricated narratives and perjured testimony were widespread.

As sexual attitudes have grown more liberal, laws governing adultery have grown more anachronistic. In the United States, although twenty-one states retain criminal prohibitions, they are almost never enforced, and when they are, the rationales are scarcely compelling. Civil damage awards for criminal conversation and alienation of affection are intermittent and idiosyncratic. Dismissals from employment and discharges from the military are a costly and dubious way to protect legitimate interests. In family matters, marital infidelity bears no necessary relationship to parental fitness or need for alimony. Neither is it a good measure of immigrants' moral fitness for citizenship. In politics, context matters, but fidelity in marriage is generally not a good predictor of effectiveness in office.

In Islamic countries, as Chapter 7 notes, laws against adultery discriminate against women and penalties are sometimes draconian: flogging, stoning, and hanging. Even where laws are gender neutral on their face, their enforcement is directed overwhelmingly against women and girls. In some countries, even rape can constitute adultery.

What would a more defensible legal regime look like? In the United States, legislatures would repeal criminal prohibitions on adultery and abolish civil damages actions for criminal conversation and alienation of affection. Given the political obstacles to reform, courts should be prepared to strike down such statutes in the absence of legislative reform. In light of individuals' strong interests in sexual privacy, and these laws' demonstrated ineffectiveness in deterring adultery, their retention serves no legitimate state interest. For similar reasons, the military should replace sweeping prohibitions on adultery with more targeted bans on conduct that poses a serious threat to unit cohesion, such as sexual relations between individuals in the same chain of command. Existing rules on fraternization may be sufficient to deal with most legitimate concerns.

Adultery should also figure less often in other contexts. Marital infidelity should not affect divorcing couples' financial or custody awards, except in the rare cases in which it demonstrably compromises children's interests. In employment law, dismissals or demotions for adultery should be allowed only where employee job performance or the function of the organization is in fact affected. Vague invocations of reputational concerns or department morale should not be sufficient. Nor should adultery serve to reduce charges of murder; infidelity should not be a license to kill. In political contexts, extramarital affairs should be relevant only when the position involves moral leadership, and the behavior involves gross recklessness, hypocrisy, financial improprieties, prostitution, or other serious misconduct.

"Adultery," said Vladimir Nabokov, "is a most conventional way to rise above the conventional." But it also challenges the conventional and invites us to rethink assumptions about sexual exclusivity. The evils traditionally associated with adultery stem from deceit and betrayal. But adultery practiced openly, with the consent of all concerned, stands on different footing. The limited evidence available on open marriages and polyamorous relationships suggests that they compare favorably with monogamy in terms of party satisfaction and outcomes for children.

Polygamy presents a harder case. Some evidence suggests that children in these families fare worse on average in terms of educational attainment, behavioral problems, and risks of neglect. But the same is true for children in single-mother households, and we do not criminalize those. Given the strong privacy and religious interests at stake, the most sensible strategy would be to end criminal penalties for polygamy, which currently force it into isolated rural areas, where it is harder to detect abuses. Law enforcement should focus on related abuses such as underage marriage, domestic violence, and welfare fraud. Individuals in nontraditional living arrangements should not be forced underground, nor should they fear intervention by child welfare authorities. More education and support structures should be available to help young women make informed choices about marital arrangements and to assist children of polygamous families. Greater respect for individual privacy in sexual matters demands greater tolerance for alternative lifestyles.

How would such a legal regime affect the institution of marriage? If supporters of monogamy are correct, and it is the most fulfilling choice, then marriage has little to fear from legalizing alternatives. These will remain on the fringes of society, and few will choose them. By contrast, if polyamorists are correct, and love need not be exclusive to be the foundation of a stable union, then some couples' lives will be enhanced by expanded opportunities for nontraditional living arrangements.

The law, said Supreme Court justice Oliver Wendell Holmes, is the witness "of our moral life. Its history is the history of the moral development of the race."[1] That development calls for more tolerance for alternative lifestyles and the elimination of legal penalties for adultery.

Notes

I. Introduction

1. Anthony Burgess, quoted in Kate Figes, *Our Cheating Hearts: Love and Loyalty, Lust and Lies* (London: Virago, 2013), 4.

2. Kaeren Harrison and Dennis Marsden, "Preface," in *The State of Affairs: Explorations in Infidelity and Commitment*, ed. Jean Duncombe, Kaeren Harrison, Graham Allan, and Dennis Marsden (Mahwah, NJ: Lawrence Erlbaum Publishers, 2004), xi.

3. "Man Sues Neighbor after Wife Dumps Him," *Chicago Tribune*, November 16, 2004.

4. Judith Treas and Deirdre Giesen, "Sexual Infidelity among Married and Cohabiting Americans," *Journal of Marriage and Family* 62 (February 2000): 48, 59.

5. Frank Pittman, *Private Lies: Infidelity and the Betrayal of Intimacy* (New York: Norton, 1989), 37.

6. J. Lindsey Short, quoted in Nathan Tabor, "Adultery Is Killing the American Family," Renew America, September 22, 2005, http://www.renew america.com/columns/tabor/050922.

7. Figes, *Our Cheating Hearts*, 26, 22.

8. Alfred C. Kinsey, Wardell Baxter Pomeroy, and Clyde E. Martin, *Sexual Behavior in the Human Male* (Philadelphia: W. B. Saunders, 1948); Alfred C. Kinsey, Wardell Baxter Pomeroy, Clyde E. Martin, and Paul A. Gebhard, *Sexual Behavior in the Human Female* (Philadelphia: W. B. Saunders, 1953).

9. Peggy Drexler, "The New Face of Infidelity," *Wall Street Journal*, October 19, 2012.

10. Ibid.; Edward O. Laumann, John H. Gagnon, Robert T. Michael, and Stuart Michaels, *The Social Organization of Sexuality: Sexual Practices in the United States* (Chicago: University of Chicago Press, 1994), 216 (22 percent of husbands and 13 percent of wives admitted to at least one extramarital affair). For other studies, see Helen E. Fisher, *Serial Monogamy and Clandestine Adultery: Evolution and Consequences of the Dual Human Reproductive Strategy* (Oxford Scholarship Online, 2011).

11. Laura Kipnis, "Adultery," *Critical Inquiry* 24 (Winter 1998): 289, 293n4; Mark A. Whisman and Douglas K. Snyder, "Sexual Infidelity in a National Survey of American Women: Differences in Prevalence and Correlates as a Function of Method of Assessment," *Journal of Family Psychology* 21 (2007): 147 (noting that lower prevalence rates are found in face-to-face interviews than on anonymous questionnaires).

12. Michael Norman, "Getting Serious about Adultery: Who Does It and Why They Risk It," *New York Times*, July 4, 1998; Lauren Rosewarne, *Cheating on the Sisterhood: Infidelity and Feminism* (Santa Barbara, CA: Praeger, 2009); Louise De Salvo, *Adultery* (Boston: Beacon Press, 1999), 26.

13. Rosewarne, *Cheating on the Sisterhood*, 10.

14. Norman, "Getting Serious about Adultery." See also Drexler, "The New Face of Infidelity."

15. Tom W. Smith, *American Sexual Behavior: Trends, Socio-demographic Differences, and Risk Behavior* (Chicago: National Opinion Research Center, March 2006), 1.

16. Catherine Johnson, *The New Woman Infidelity Report*, November 1986, 73.

17. See Smith, *American Sexual Behavior*, 1 (citing Hite and other popular studies).

18. Figes, *Our Cheating Hearts*, 1; Anita L. Vangelisti and Mandi Gerstenberger, "Communication and Marital Infidelity," in Duncombe, Harrison, Allan, and Marsden, *The State of Affairs*, 59.

19. Gallup/CNN/*USA Today* Poll, iPOLL Databank, June 10, 1997, http://www.ropercenter.uconn.edu/data_access/ipoll/ipoll.html.

20. John M. Grohol, "How Common Is Cheating and Infidelity Really?" PsychCentral, March 22, 2013, http://psychcentral.com/blog/archives/2013/03/22/how-common-is-cheating-infidelity-really/.

21. Andrew Greeley, "Marital Infidelity," *Society* 31 (May/June 1994): 9, 10. For religion, see Irene Tsapelas, Helen E. Fisher, and Arthur Aron, "Infidelity: When, Where, Why," in *The Dark Side of Close Relationships II*, ed. William R. Cupach and Brian H. Spitzberg (New York: Routledge, 2011), 175–196; and Treas and Giesen, "Sexual Infidelity among Married and Cohabiting Americans," 48, 59.

22. Pamela Druckerman, *Lust in Translation: Infidelity from Tokyo to Tennessee* (New York: Penguin, 2007), 51. For recent evidence, see Tara Parker-Pope, "Love, Sex and the Changing Landscape of Infidelity," *New York Times*, October 27, 2008.

23. Richard Johnson, "The Demography of Adultery," *National Post*, November 16, 2012, http://news.nationalpost.com/news/graphics/graphic-the-demography -of-adultery. See also Adrian J. Blow and Kelley Hartnett, "Infidelity in Committed Relationships II: A Substantive Review," *Journal of Marital and Family Therapy* 31 (2005): 217, 225.

24. Smith, *American Sexual Behavior.*

25. Treas and Giesen, "Sexual Infidelity among Married and Cohabiting Americans," 49; Vangelisti and Gerstenberger, "Communication and Marital Infidelity," 60; Bram P. Buunk and Pieternel Dijkstra, "Men, Women, and Infidelity: Sex Differences in Extradyadic Sex and Jealousy," in Duncombe, Harrison, Allan, and Marsden, *The State of Affairs*, 104; Anthony Peter Thompson, "Emotional and Sexual Components of Extramarital Relations," *Journal of Marriage and the Family* 46 (1984): 35, 36.

26. Drexler, "The New Face of Infidelity"; Kristen P. Mark, Erick Janssen, and Robin R. Milhausen, "Infidelity in Heterosexual Couples: Demographic, Interpersonal, and Personality-Related Predictors of Extradyadic Sex," *Archives of Sexual Behavior*, June 11, 2011.

27. Annette Lawson, *Adultery: An Analysis of Love and Betrayal* (New York: Basic Books, 1988), 28.

28. Lorraine Ali and Lisa Miller, "The Secret Lives of Wives," *Newsweek*, July 12, 2004.

29. Pittman, *Private Lies*, 174.

30. Nicole Perlroth, "Ashley Madison Chief Is Latest to Depart after a Data Breach," *New York Times*, August 29, 2015, B5.

31. Quoted in David Barash, "The Myth of Monogamy," Salon.com, January 23, 2001.

32. David P. Barash and Judith Eve Lipton, *The Myth of Monogamy: Fidelity and Infidelity in Animals and People* (New York: W. H. Freeman, 2001), 10.

33. David M. Buss, *The Dangerous Passion: Why Jealousy Is as Necessary as Love and Sex* (New York: Free Press, 2000), 35; Barash and Lipton, *The Myth of Monogamy*, 19, 59; Helen E. Fisher, *Anatomy of Love: The Natural History of Monogamy, Adultery, and Divorce* (New York: W. W. Norton, 1992); Norman, "Getting Serious about Adultery."

34. Richard A. Friedman, "Infidelity Lurks in Your Genes," *New York Times*, May 22, 2015.

35. Treas and Giesen, "Sexual Infidelity among Married and Cohabiting Americans," 48, 59.

36. Robert Weiss, "Integrity vs. Infidelity: Why Do Men Cheat? (Part I)," *Huffington Post*, November 26, 2012; Robert Weiss, "Why Women Cheat: 5 Reasons for Female Infidelity," *Huffington Post*, February 4, 2013.

37. Figes, *Our Cheating Hearts*, 4–5; Albert Ellis, "Healthy and Disturbed Reasons for Having Extramarital Relations," in *Extramarital Relations*, ed. Gerhard Neubeck (Englewood Cliffs, NJ: Prentice-Hall, 1969), 153, 155–58.

38. Lise VanderVoort and Steve Duck, "Sex, Lies, and Transformation," in Duncombe, Harrison, Allan, and Marsden, *The State of Affairs*, 59; Figes, *Our Cheating Hearts*, 4–5; Kate Figes, "The Infidelity Epidemic: Never Have Marriage Vows Been under So Much Strain," *Daily Mail* (United Kingdom), April 19, 2013.

39. VanderVoort and Duck, "Sex, Lies, and Transformation," 59.

40. Lynn Atwater, "Getting Involved: Women's Transition to First Extramarital Sex," *Alternative Lifestyles* 2 (February 1979): 33, 51, 57.

41. Michael Baisden, *Never Satisfied: How and Why Men Cheat* (Katy, TX: Legacy Publishing, 1995), 115.

42. Druckerman, *Lust in Translation*, 78; Steven M. Ortiz, "Traveling with the Ball Club: A Code of Conduct for Wives Only," *Symbolic Interaction* 20 (1997).

43. Trish Hall, "Infidelity and Women: Shifting Patterns," *New York Times*, June 1, 1987, B8.

44. Michael W. Wiederman, "Extramarital Sex: Prevalence and Correlates in a National Survey," *Journal of Sex Research* 34 (1997): 167, 172.

45. Greeley, "Marital Infidelity," 12; David C. Atkins, Donald H. Baucom, and Neil S. Jacobson, "Understanding Infidelity: Correlates in a National Random Sample," *Journal of Family Psychology* 15 (2001): 735, 745; Treas and Giesen, "Sexual Infidelity among Married and Cohabiting Americans," 59; Anthony Peter Thompson, "Extramarital Sex: A Review of the Research Literature," *Journal of Sex Research* 19 (1983): 1, 10.

46. Atkins, Baucom, and Jacobson, "Understanding Infidelity," 735, 745–746.

47. Alyssa Siegel, "My Cheating Heart: What Causes Infidelity," *Psychology Tomorrow*, September 2013.

48. Ibid.; Chien Liu, "A Theory of Marital Sexual Life," *Journal of Marriage and Family* 62 (2000): 363.

49. Hall, "Infidelity and Women," B8.

50. Treas and Giesen, "Sexual Infidelity among Married and Cohabiting Americans," 48, 59 (studies inconsistent on whether poor relationships led to extramarital sex); Joseph Hooper, "Infidelity Comes Out of the Closet," *New York Times*, April 29, 1999 (citing study finding that men's infidelity was more often the cause for troubled marriages than the effect); Blow and Hartnett, "Infidelity in Committed Relationships II," 217, 222 (citing studies finding little correlation between relationship satisfaction and fidelity); Elizabeth S. Allen and David C. Atkins, "The Association of Divorce and Extramarital Sex in a Representative U.S. Sample," *Journal of Family Issues* 33 (2012): 1477, 1489 (citing study finding that individuals reported that their partner's infidelity was more frequently the cause than the result of marital problems).

51. Tsapelas, Fisher, and Aron, "Infidelity: When, Where, Why."

52. Druckerman, *Lust in Translation*, 99.

53. Blow and Hartnett, "Infidelity in Committed Relationships II," 227, 222.

54. Rosewarne, *Cheating on the Sisterhood*, 78.

55. Druckerman, *Lust in Translation*, 274.

56. Hooper, "Infidelity Comes Out of the Closet."

57. Graham Allan, "Being Unfaithful: His and Her Affairs," in Duncombe, Harrison, Allan, and Marsden, *The State of Affairs*, 134.

58. Hooper, "Infidelity Comes Out of the Closet."

59. Jill Alexander Essbaum, *Hausfrau* (New York: Random House, 2015), 45.

60. Shirley P. Glass and Thomas L. Wright, "Justifications for Extramarital Relationships: The Association between Attitudes, Behaviors and Gender," *Journal of Sex Research* 29 (1992): 361.

61. Weiss, "Why Women Cheat."

62. Rosewarne, *Cheating on the Sisterhood*, 139.

63. Shirley P. Glass and Thomas L. Wright, "Sex Differences in Type of Extramarital Involvement and Marital Dissatisfaction," *Sex Roles* 12 (1985): 1101, 1113.

64. Johnson, *The New Woman Infidelity Report*, 73.

65. Lawson, *Adultery*, 202.

66. Esther Perel, quoted in Hanna Rosin, "Why We Cheat," *Slate*, March 27, 2014, http://www.slate.com/articles/double_x/doublex/2014/03/esther_perel _on_affairs_spouses_in_happy_marriages_cheat_and_americans_don.html.

67. Laurel Richardson, *The New Other Woman: Contemporary Single Women in Affairs with Married Men* (New York: Free Press, 1985), 30.

68. Ibid., 92, 31, 89, 30–31.

69. Ibid., 31, 32, 33.

70. Hall, "Infidelity and Women," B8.

71. Lawson, *Adultery*, 200. Two-thirds of women and half of men reported a sense of being alive as the most important pleasure.

72. Allan, "Being Unfaithful," 129.

73. Figes, *Our Cheating Hearts*, 139.

74. John F. Cuber, "Adultery: Reality versus Stereotype," in Neubeck, *Extramarital Relations*, 191. See also John F. Cuber and Peggy B. Harroff, *The Significant Americans: A Study of Sexual Behavior among the Affluent* (New York: Appleton, 1965), chapter 8.

75. Yoon Hough Kim, "The Kinsey Findings," in Neubeck, *Extramarital Relations*, 71.

76. Rosewarne, *Cheating on the Sisterhood*, 209, 116. See also Richard Tuch, *The Single Woman–Married Man Syndrome* (Northvale, NJ: Jason Aronson Inc., 2000), 11–12, 16–17.

77. Rosewarne, *Cheating on the Sisterhood*, 209; Baisden, *Never Satisfied*.

78. Blow and Hartnett, "Infidelity in Committed Relationships II," 227.

79. Jennifer S. Hirsch et al., *The Secret: Love, Marriage, and HIV* (Nashville, TN: Vanderbilt University Press, 2009), I.

80. Figes, *Our Cheating Hearts*, 194, 257.

81. Hall, "Infidelity and Women," B8.

82. Blow and Hartnett, "Infidelity in Committed Relationships II," 227.

83. Figes, *Our Cheating Hearts*, 195–196.

84. Pittman, *Private Lies*, 37.

85. Druckerman, *Lust in Translation*, 274.

86. Lawson, *Adultery*, 231.

87. Barbara A. Steffens and Robyn L. Rennie, "The Traumatic Nature of Disclosure for Wives of Sexual Addicts," *Sexual Addiction and Compulsivity* 13 (2006): 247.

88. Allan, "Being Unfaithful," 136.

89. Figes, *Our Cheating Hearts*, 162.

90. Kipnis, "Adultery," 293, 323.

91. Lawson, *Adultery*, 168.

92. Figes, *Our Cheating Hearts*, 155; Figes, "The Infidelity Epidemic."

93. Druckerman, *Lust in Translation*, 12.

94. Figes, *Our Cheating Hearts*, 74; Glass and Wright, "Sex Differences," 1101, 1103.

95. Figes, *Our Cheating Hearts*, 9, 19, 176, 169–170.

96. Alfred DeMaris, "Burning the Candle at Both Ends: Extramarital Sex as a Precursor of Marital Disruption," *Journal of Family Issues* 34 (2013): 1475, 1478; Figes, *Our Cheating Hearts*, 133.

97. Allen and Atkins, "The Association of Divorce and Extramarital Sex," 1477, 1488.

98. Figes, *Our Cheating Hearts*, 75.

99. Essbaum, *Hausfrau*, 311.

100. Martin Daly and Margo Wilson, "The Evolutionary Social Psychology of Family Violence," in *Handbook of Evolutionary Psychology: Ideas, Issues and Applications*, ed. Charles B. Crawford and Dennis L. Krebs (Mahwah, NJ: Lawrence Erlbaum Publishers, 1998), 431–456; Vangelisti and Gerstenberger, "Communication and Marital Infidelity," 59; Julianna M. Nemeth, Amy E. Bonomi, Meghan A. Lee, and Jennifer M. Ludwin, "Sexual Infidelity as Trigger for Intimate Partner Violence," *Journal of Women's Health* 21 (2012): 942.

101. Buunk and Dijkstra, "Men, Women, and Infidelity," 108.

102. Figes, *Our Cheating Hearts*, 35.

103. Buunk and Dijkstra, "Men, Women, and Infidelity," 115, 111–112.

104. Jean Duncombe and Dennis Marsden, "'From Here to Epiphany...': Power and Identity in the Narrative of an Affair," in Duncombe, Harrison, Allan, and Marsden, *The State of Affairs*, 143.

105. Lawson, *Adultery*, 136.

106. Figes, *Our Cheating Hearts*, 207, 190.

107. Pittman, *Private Lies*, 261.

108. Figes, *Our Cheating Hearts*, 208–212.

109. Hara Estroff Marano, "From Promise to Promiscuity," *Psychology Today*, July 3, 2012.

110. Johnson, *The New Woman Infidelity Report*, 74.

111. Richardson, *The New Other Woman*, 129, 149.

112. Baisden, *Never Satisfied*, 181, 253.

113. Richardson, *The New Other Woman*, 89, 95, 91, 57.

114. UPI, "U.S. Poll: Adultery Unacceptable to Most," June 25, 2009, http://www.upi.com/Top_News/2009/06/25/US-poll-Adultery-unacceptable -to-most/96431245965385/. The poll reported that 92 percent of those surveyed said extramarital sex was wrong.

115. John Sides, "Americans Have Become More Opposed to Adultery. Why?," *The Monkey Cage*, July 27, 2011, http://themonkeycage.org/2011/07/27/americans -have-become-more-opposed-to-adultery-why/.

116. Lorraine Ali and Lisa Miller, "The Secret Lives of Wives"; Andrew Sullivan, "The Growing Stigma against Adultery," *The Dish*, July 28, 2011, http://dish.andrewsullivan.com/2011/07/28/the-growing-stigma-against -adultry/.

117. Sides, "Americans Have Become More Opposed to Adultery"; Sullivan, "The Growing Stigma against Adultery."

118. Sides, "Americans Have Become More Opposed to Adultery." The logic goes something like this: "If you're in an unhappy marriage, don't cheat. Just get divorced."

119. Treas and Giesen, "Sexual Infidelity among Married and Cohabiting Americans," 48.

120. CBS News Poll, iPOLL Databank, September 18–20, 1997.

121. Bruce Handy, "How We Really Feel about Fidelity," CNN.com, August 31, 1998, http:///www.cnn.com/ALLPOLITICS/1998/08/20/time /fidelity.poll.html.

122. Lawson, *Adultery*, 72.

123. "How Do Americans View Adultery?," CNN.com, August 20, 1998, http://www.cnn.com/ALLPOLITICS/1998/08/20/adultery.poll.

124. Handy, "How We Really Feel about Fidelity."

125. "Political Allegiance Shaped by Stance on Moral Issues in U.S.," CNN/ Opinion Research Corporation Poll, iPOLL Databank, June 26–28, 2009, 148; UPI, "U.S. Poll: Adultery Unacceptable to Most."

126. PRRI/RNS Religion News Survey, iPOLL Databank, June 16–19, 2011, http://publicreligion.org/site/wp-content/uploads/2011/06/Elected-Officials -Scandals-PRRI-RNS.pdf.

127. Pew Research Center, "A Barometer of Modern Morals: Sex, Drugs, and the 1040," Pew Research Center, March 28, 2006, http://www.pewsocialtrends .org/2006/03/28/a-barometer-of-modern-morals. In the poll, researchers read respondents a list of ten behaviors, and respondents said whether the behavior was "morally acceptable, morally wrong, or not a moral issue."

128. "How Do Americans View Adultery?" Eighty-six percent viewed adultery as morally wrong, compared with 79 percent who viewed prostitution as morally wrong.

129. "Political Allegiance Shaped by Stance on Moral Issues in U.S.," Angus Reid Global, October 11, 2010, http://www.angusreidglobal.com/wp-content /uploads/2010/10/2010.10.11_Morality_USA.pdf.

130. "How Do Americans View Adultery?"

131. Pamela Druckerman, "Our Ready Embrace of Those Cheating Pols," *Washington Post*, July 15, 2007; Eric D. Widmer, Judith Treas, and Robert Newcomb, "Attitudes toward Nonmarital Sex in 24 Countries," *Journal of Sex Research* 35 (1988): 349, 351.

132. Associated Press Poll, iPOLL Databank, June 1997 (74 percent); Gallup/ CNN/*USA Today* Poll, iPOLL Databank, May 1997 (61 percent; 55 percent of those with high school education or less and 71 percent of those with a college education).

133. Conservatives were more likely (62 percent) to say that adulterers lacked moral character, with 58 percent of Republicans saying so, and only 47 percent of Democrats. CNN/Opinion Research Corporation Poll, iPOLL Databank, June 26–28, 2009.

134. Druckerman, "Our Ready Embrace of Those Cheating Pols."

135. UPI, "U.S. Poll: Adultery Unacceptable to Most."

136. Fox News/Opinion Dynamics Poll, iPOLL Databank, March 10–11, 1999.

137. "Poll: Clinton's Approval Rating Up in Wake of Impeachment," Allpolitics.com, December 20, 1998, http://www.cnn.com/ALLPOLITICS /stories/1998/12/20/impeachment.poll/.

138. NBC News/Wall Street Journal Poll, iPOLL Databank, February 26–March 1, 1998. Women were more likely (77 percent) than men (69 percent) to think that an adulterous member of the clergy should be dismissed.

139. Gallup/CNN/USA Today Poll, iPOLL Databank, June 10, 1997.

2. Legal History

1. Robert L. Griswold, *Adultery and Divorce in Victorian America, 1800–1900*, Legal History Program Working Papers (Madison: Institute for Legal Studies, University of Wisconsin–Madison Law School, 1986), 14.

2. Daniel E. Murray, "Ancient Laws on Adultery—A Synopsis," *Journal of Family Law* 1 (1961): 89, 91; Claude Hermann Walter Johns, *The Oldest Code of Laws in the World* (Edinburgh: T. and T. Clark, 1911), 24.

3. Murray, "Ancient Laws," 92; John Merlin Powis Smith, *The Origin and History of Hebrew Law* (Chicago: University of Chicago Press, 1931), 225–226.

4. Marvin M. Moore, "The Diverse Definitions of Criminal Adultery," *University of Kansas City Law Review* 30 (1962): 219; John Gardner Wilkinson, *The Manners and Customs of the Ancient Egyptians* (New York: Scribner and Welford, 1879), 303.

5. Murray, "Ancient Laws," 95; Arthur Coke Burnell and Edward W. Hopkins, *The Ordinances of Manu, VII–XIVII* (London: Trubner and Co., 1884), 234–237.

6. For the Bible, see Deuteronomy 5:18; Exodus 20:14; and Leviticus 20:10. For Roman law, see Stephanie Coontz, *Marriage, a History: From Obedience to Intimacy,*

or How Love Conquered Marriage (New York: Viking, 2005), 84; Annette Lawson, *Adultery: An Analysis of Love and Betrayal* (New York: Basic Books, 1988), 42; Murray, "Ancient Laws," 96; Percy Ellwood Corbett, *The Roman Law of Marriage* (Oxford: Clarendon Press, 1930), 128; Susan Treggiari, *Roman Marriage* (Oxford: Clarendon Press, 1991), 285, 461; B. Boaz Cohen, *Jewish and Roman Law, A Comparative Study* (New York: Jewish Theological Seminary Press, 1966), 635.

7. Moore, "Diverse Definitions," 219.

8. Charles E. Torcia, *Wharton's Criminal Law*, 15th ed. (New York: Thomson Reuters, 1994), section 210 at 528; Frederick Pollack and Frederic William Maitland, *The History of English Law Before the Time of Edward I*, 2nd ed. (1898; New York: Cambridge University Press, 1952), 543.

9. Laura Hanft Korobkin, *Criminal Conversations: Sentimentality and Nineteenth-Century Legal Stories of Adultery* (New York: Columbia University Press, 1998).

10. Kate Figes, *Our Cheating Hearts: Love and Loyalty, Lust and Lies* (London: Virago, 2013), 47.

11. David M. Turner, *Fashioning Adultery: Gender, Sex and Civility in England, 1660–1740* (Cambridge, UK: Cambridge University Press, 2002), 184.

12. Moore, "Diverse Definitions," 221.

13. *Law Magazine*, quoted in ibid.

14. Geoffrey May, "Experiments in the Legal Control of Sex Expression," *Yale Law Journal* 39 (1929): 219; Thomas Eustace Smith, *A Summary of the Law and Practice in the Ecclesiastical Courts*, 7th ed. (London: Steven and Haynes, 1920), 124; Johanna Rickman, *Love, Lust, and License in Early Modern England: Illicit Sex and the Nobility* (Burlington, VT: Ashgate Publishing, 2008), 19.

15. Turner, *Fashioning Adultery*, 156, 157.

16. May, "Experiments in the Legal Control of Sex Expression," 227; Turner, *Fashioning Adultery*, 4.

17. Turner, *Fashioning Adultery*, 5–6.

18. Lawrence Stone, *Road to Divorce: England, 1530–1987* (Oxford: Oxford University Press, 1990), 280, 251, 252.

19. Val Horsler, *All for Love: Seven Centuries of Illicit Liaison* (London: Bloomsbury Academic, 2006), 85.

20. Stone, *Road to Divorce*, 141.

21. Ginger S. Frost, *Living in Sin: Cohabiting as Husband and Wife in Nineteenth-Century England* (Manchester: Manchester University Press, 2008), 72–73; Caroline Dunn, *Stolen Women in Medieval England: Rape, Abduction and Adultery, 1100–1500* (Cambridge, UK: Cambridge University Press, 2013), 134.

22. Frost, *Living in Sin*, 91.

23. Stone, *Road to Divorce*, 171, 7.

24. Frost, *Living in Sin*, 99.

25. Laura Gowing, *Domestic Dangers: Women, Words, and Sex in Early Modern London* (Oxford: Oxford University Press, 1996), 219–231; Rickman, *Love, Lust and License in Early Modern England*, 14.

26. Fiona McDonald, *Other Women: The History of the Mistress* (Stroud, U.K.: History Press, 2013), 18, 40; Horsler, *All for Love.*

27. Horsler, *All for Love*, 133, 102, 76–78.

28. Ibid., 117.

29. Keith Thomas, "The Double Standard," *Journal of the History of Ideas* 20 (1959): 195; Horsler, *All for Love*, 19, 27; Turner, *Fashioning Adultery*, 14.

30. Horsler, *All for Love*, 29.

31. Stone, *Road to Divorce*, 369.

32. Linda R. Hirshman and Jane E. Larson, *Hard Bargains: The Politics of Sex* (New York: Oxford University Press, 1998), 106.

33. Barbara Leckie, *Culture and Adultery: The Novel, the Newspaper and the Law, 1857–1914* (Philadelphia: University of Pennsylvania Press, 1999).

34. Stone, *Road to Divorce*, 397; Horsler, *All for Love*, 174.

35. Turner, *Fashioning Adultery*, 127; William Blackstone, *Commentaries on the Laws of England, Book the Fourth* (Oxford: Clarendon Press, 1770), 191–192; Jeremy Horder, *Provocation and Responsibility* (London: Oxford University Press, 1992), 87–88. For the defense in other nations, see, for example, Georgina Black, *Perfect Wives, Other Women: Adultery and Inquisition in Early Modern Spain* (Durham, NC: Duke University Press, 2001), 114.

36. Leckie, *Culture and Adultery*, 85; Robert Pearsall, *The Worm in the Bud: The World of Victorian Sexuality* (London: Weidenfeld and Nicolson, 1969), 220.

37. Turner, *Fashioning Adultery*, 181.

38. Leckie, *Culture and Adultery*, 101; Allen Horstman, *Victorian Divorce* (New York: St. Martin's Press, 1985), 99.

39. Turner, *Fashioning Adultery*, 198.

40. Jeremy D. Weinstein, "Adultery, Law, and the State: A History," *Hastings Law Journal* 38 (1986): 195, 225.

41. Lawrence M. Friedman, *Crime and Punishment in America* (New York: Basic Books, 1994), 34.

42. John D'Emilio and Estelle B. Freedman, *Intimate Matters: A History of Sexuality in America*, 3rd ed. (Chicago: University of Chicago Press, 2012), 12, 28, 29, 30.

43. Ibid., 28; Mary Beth Norton, *Founding Mothers and Fathers: Gendered Power and the Forming of American Society* (New York: Alfred A. Knopf, 1996), 74 (noting that four New England colonies prescribed the death penalty).

44. Natalie E. H. Hull, *Female Felons: Women and Serious Crime in Colonial Massachusetts* (Urbana: University of Illinois Press, 1987), 31; Jonathan Turley, "Adultery, in Many States, Is Still a Crime," *USA Today*, April 25, 2010.

45. Hull, *Female Felons*, 31. See also Hirshman and Larson, *Hard Bargains*, 63 (noting that adultery was a capital offense in colonial Virginia but that the death sentence was never imposed).

46. Norton, *Founding Mothers and Fathers*, 343, 342.

47. Moore, *Diverse Definitions*, 229.

48. Ibid., 226. See also Torcia, *Wharton's Criminal Law*, 530, 530n10.

49. Gabrielle Viator, "The Validity of Criminal Adultery Prohibitions after Lawrence v. Texas," *Suffolk University Law Review* 39 (2006): 837.

50. See Cropsey v. Ogden, 11 N.Y. 228, 230 (N.Y. 1854); Chlystek v. Califano, 599 F.2d 1270, 1271 (3d Cir. 1979).

51. Simpson v. Simpson, 162 Va. 621, 175 S.E. 320, 326 (Va. 1934); In re Estate of Lenherr, 314 A.2d 255, 258 (Pa. 1974), vi (provision designed to protect sensibilities of injured spouse).

52. Norton, *Founding Mothers and Fathers*, 264; Evans v. Murff, 135 F. Supp. 907, 910–911 (D. Md. 1955) (quoting laws of 1715); Winfield Owen, "Adultery: A Review," *Boston University Law Review* 17 (1937): 328.

53. D'Emilio and Freedman, *Intimate Matters*, 28.

54. Ibid.

55. Nathaniel Hawthorne, *The Scarlet Letter*, ed. Ross C. Murfin (New York: Bedford / St Martin's, 2006), 241; Norton, *Founding Mothers and Fathers*, 264.

56. D'Emilio and Freedman, *Intimate Matters*, 12.

57. Norton, *Founding Mothers and Fathers*, 344.

58. Hendrik Hartog, "The Public Law of a County Court: Judicial Government in Eighteenth Century Massachusetts," *American Journal of Legal History* 20 (1976): 282, 299–308.

59. Edward M. Steel, "Criminality in Jeffersonian America—A Sample," *Crime and Delinquency* 18 (1983): 154.

60. David J. Bodenhamer, *The Pursuit of Justice: Crime and Law in Antebellum Indiana* (New York: Garland, 1986), 140.

61. Friedman, *Crime and Punishment*, 140

62. Ibid., 130; emphasis in the original.

63. Cal. Penal Code section 2661 (1872).

64. Friedman, *Crime and Punishment*, 130, 131.

65. Collins v. State, 14 Ala. 608 (1848).

66. Lawrence M. Friedman and Robert V. Percival, *The Roots of Justice: Crime and Punishment in Alameda County, California, 1870–1910* (Chapel Hill: University of North Carolina Press, 1981), 144–145.

67. D'Emilio and Freedman, *Intimate Matters*, 5.

68. William Corbett, *Advice to Young Men and (Incidentally) to Young Women in the Middle and Higher Ranks of Life* (New York: John Doyle, 1831), 156–157.

69. D'Emilio and Freedman, *Intimate Matters*, 96; Bertram Wyatt-Brown, *Southern Honor: Ethics and Behavior in the Old South* (New York: Oxford University Press, 2007), 299, 315–316.

70. State v. Sanders, 30 Iowa 582 (1870).

71. Robert E. Rodes, "On Law and Chastity," *Notre Dame Law Review* 76 (2001): 643, 649; Commonwealth v. Brown, 136 A.2d 138, 140 (Pa. Super. Ct. 1957); Byrd v. State, 222 N.W.2d 696, 700 (Wis. 1974).

72. State v. Trachsel, 150 Iowa 135, 136, 137 (1911).

73. Annual Report, Police Commissioner of the City of New York (1911; year ending December 31, 1910), 12, 14.

74. Annual Report, Police Department of the City of Chicago (1927; year ending December 31, 1926), 19.

75. George Worthington and Ruth Topping, "The Second Sessions of the Municipal Court of the City of Boston," *The American Social Hygiene Association* 191 (1922).

76. Friedman, *Crime and Punishment*, 345.

77. Alfred C. Kinsey, Wardell B. Pomeroy, and Clyde E. Martin, *Sexual Behavior in the Human Male* (Philadelphia: W. B. Saunders, 1948); Alfred C. Kinsey, Wardell B. Pomeroy, Clyde E. Martin, and Paul A. Gebhard, *Sexual Behavior in the Human Female* (Philadelphia: W. B. Saunders, 1953).

78. Model Penal Code Section 213.6 (Proposed Official Draft 1962), 434 n.17.

79. Friedman, *Crime and Punishment*, 345.

80. Loren Schweninger, *Families in Crisis in the Old South: Divorce, Slavery, and the Law* (Chapel Hill: University of North Carolina Press, 2012), 2.

81. Viator, "The Validity of Criminal Adultery Prohibitions," 842.

82. Griswold, *Adultery and Divorce in Victorian America*, 1–2.

83. Schweninger, *Families in Crisis in the Old South*, 23, 25.

84. Ibid., 27, 69, 70.

85. Griswold, *Adultery and Divorce in Victorian America*, 42, 3, 25, 26.

86. O'Bryan v. O'Bryan, 13 Missouri Reports 17 (1850).

87. D'Emilio and Freedman, *Intimate Matters*, 96.

88. Inskeep v. Inskeep, 5 Iowa Reports 208 (1857).

89. Auld v. Auld, 16 New York Supplement 804, 806 (1891).

90. Griswold, *Adultery and Divorce in Victorian America*, 22, 24.

91. Ibid., 31.

92. Thomas v. Thomas, 51 Illinois Reports 164 (1869).

93. Osborn v. Osborn, 44 New Jersey Equity Reports, 258–260, 261 (1888).

94. Graft v. Graft, 76 Indiana Reports 138 (1881).

95. Coble v. Coble, 55 North Carolina Reports 392, 395 (1856).

96. Hild v. Hild, 157 A.2d 442, 447 (Md. 1960); Swoyer v. Swoyer, 145 A. 190 (Md. 1929); Hill v. Hill, 49 Md. 450 (1878); McCabe v. McCabe, 146 A.2d 768 (Md. 1958).

97. *Hild*, 157 A.2d 448. See also Christian v. Christian, 275 P.2d 422 (1954).

98. Bunim v. Bunim, 83 N.E.2d 848, 850 (N.Y. 1949) (Fuld, J., dissenting).

99. Ibid., 849.

100. *Swoyer*, 145 A. 190.

101. *McCabe*, 146 A.2d 768, 770–771.

102. *Christian*, 275 P.2d 422, 425.

103. Wilcox v. Wilcox, 287 S.W.2d 622, 624 (Ky. Ct. App. 1955).

104. Joanna L. Grossman and Lawrence M. Friedman, *Inside the Castle: Law and the Family in 20th Century America* (Princeton, NJ: Princeton University Press, 2011), 161.

105. Walter Gellhorn, *Children and Families in the Courts of New York City: A Report* (New York: Dodd, Mead, 1954), 285–288.

106. Grossman and Friedman, *Inside the Castle*, 167–168; Reed v. Littleton, 289 N.Y. Supp. 798 (Sup. Ct. 1936).

107. *New York Sunday Mirror*, 1934, cited in "Collusive and Consensual Divorce and the New York Anomaly," *Columbia Law Review* 36 (1936): 1121, 1131.

108. Leon C. Marshall and Geoffrey May, *The Divorce Court*, vol. 1 (Baltimore: Johns Hopkins University Press, 1932), 231.

109. Clarence E. Martin, quoted in Dorothy Dunbar Bromley, "Divorce by Collusion Stirs a Tempest; Bench and Bar Awaken to Conditions That Tend to Make a Mockery of the Proceedings in American Courts," *New York Times*, December 10, 1933.

110. Bromly, "Divorce by Collusion."

111. Deborah L. Rhode, *Justice and Gender: Sex Discrimination and the Law* (Cambridge, MA: Harvard University Press, 1989), 147; Andrew J. Cherlin, *The Marriage-Go-Round: The State of Marriage and the Family in America Today* (New York: Knopf, 2009), 96.

112. Doe v. Roe 20 Atl. 83, 84 (Me. 1890); Accord, Kroessin v. Keller, 62 N.W. 438 (Minn. 1895).

113. Oppenheim v. Kridel, 140 N.E. 227, 231 (1923).

114. Ibid., 230.

115. Yundt v. Hartrunft, 41 Ill. 9, 12 (1866); Accord, Botwinick v. Annenberg, 204 App. Div. 436, 198 N.Y.S. 151 (1923).

116. Nathan P. Feinsinger, "Legislative Attack on 'Heart Balm,'" *Michigan Law Review* 33 (1935): 996.

117. Eclov v. Birdsong, 166 F.2d 960 (D.C. Cir. 1948).

118. Lewis v. Roby, 65 A. 524 (Vt. 1907); Browning v. Jones, 52 Ill. App. 597 (1893); Rea v. Tucker, 51 Ill. 110 (1868).

119. Feinsinger, "Legislative Attack on 'Heart Balm,'" 995.

120. Grievance Committee of Hartford County Bar v. Broder, 152 A. 292, 294, 295 (1930).

121. In re Titus, 50 N.Y. St. Reports 636, 21 N.Y. Supp. 724 (1892).

122. State v. Byrkett, 4 Ohio Dec. 89 (1894).

123. Cerceo v. Darby, quoted in Faust v. Police Civil Service Commission of Borough of State College, 347 A.2d 765, 769 (1975).

124. *Faust,* 347 A.2d 765, 769. Three years later, another Pennsylvania court upheld a dismissal of an officer who had procured an apartment under the pretext that it would be used for surveillance, when in fact it was used for adulterous liaisons. Oswald v. City of Allentown, 388 A.2d 1128 (1978).

125. Suddarth v. Slane, 539 F. Supp. 612 (W.D. Va. 1982).

126. Shuman v. City of Philadelphia, 470 F. Supp. 449, 461 (E.D. Pa. 1979).

127. Briggs v. North Muskegon Police Department, 563 F. Supp. 585, 590, 592 (W.D. Mich. 1983).

128. Naturalization Act of 1790, chapter 3, section 1, 1 Stat. 103.

129. Petition of Axelrod, 25 F. Supp. 415 (E.D. N.Y. 1938).

130. Petition of Binitez, 113 F. Supp. 105 (S.D. N.Y. 1953).

131. Petitions of Rudder, 159 F.2d 695, 698, 697 (2d Cir. 1947).

132. 8 U.S.C. Section 1101(f) (1964).

133. Senate Report No. 1515, 812st Cong. 2d Sess. 700–701, 712 (1950).

134. For the lack of legislative history, see Dickhoff v. Shaugnessy, 142 F. Supp. 535, 538 (1956). For varying decisions, see Michael T. Hertz, "State Adultery Law and the 'Good Moral Character' Naturalization Requirement," *Harvard Journal on Legislation* 7 (1969): 294, 295.

135. Wadman v. Immigration and Naturalization Service, 329 F.2d 812 (9th Cir. 1964) (applying California law and allowing petition); Estrin v. United States, 80 F.2d 105 (2d Cir. 1935) (single act of adultery was enough to prevent naturalization); Flumerfelt v. United States 230 F.2d 870 (9th Cir. 1956) (single act of sexual "indiscretion" was sufficient to show a lack of good moral character).

136. *Dickhoff,* 142 F. Supp. 541.

137. Petition for Naturalization of O___N, 233 F. Supp. 504, 510 (S.D. N.Y. 1964).

138. Texas Penal Code art. 1220 (Vernon 1925). For other state laws, see Jeremy D. Weinstein, "Adultery, Law, and the State: A History," *Hastings Law Journal* 38 (1986): 195, 232–236.

139. Price v. State, 18 Tex. App. 474 (1885).

140. Sensobaugh v. State, 92 Tex. Crim. 417, 244 S.W. 379 (1922).

141. State v. Greenlee, 33 N.M. 449, 455, 269 P. 331, 333 (1928).

142. William Andrew Swanberg, *Sickles the Incredible* (Baltimore: Butternut and Blue, 1956), 46.

143. Nat Brandt, *The Congressman Who Got Away with Murder* (Syracuse, NY: Syracuse University Press, 1991), 90–91.

144. Swanberg, *Sickles the Incredible*, 54.

145. "The Cole-Hiscock Case—Argument for a Postponement of the Trial—The Cause to Be Tried at a Special Term of the Oyer and Terminer," *New York Times*, February 3, 1868, 1, discussed in Lawrence M. Friedman and William E. Havemann, "The Rise and Fall of the Unwritten Law: Sex, Patriarchy and Vigilante Justice in the American Courts," *Buffalo Law Review* 61 (2013): 997.

146. "The Cole-Hiscock Murder," *New York Times*, December 9, 1868, 6.

147. "'Unwritten Law' Made to Let Man Preserve Home," *Atlanta Constitution*, March 9, 1924, C3, discussed in Friedman and Havemann, "The Rise and Fall of the Unwritten Law," 1019.

148. Friedman and Havemann, "The Rise and Fall of the Unwritten Law," 1020.

149. Ibid., 1029.

150. "Pardon for Murderess," *New York Times*, July 8, 1904, 1.

151. "Unwritten Law Plea Made in Wallis Trial," *Los Angeles Times*, March 7, 1946, A2; "Wallis Murder Case Dismissed," *Los Angeles Times*, March 12, 1946, 112.

152. Scroggs v. State, 93 S.E.2d 583 (Ga. App. 1956).

153. Friedman and Havemann, "The Rise and Fall of the Unwritten Law," 1047.

3. The American Legal Landscape

1. Glenn Williamson, quoted in Michelle Boorstein, "Va. Adultery Case Goes from Notable to a Nonevent," *Washington Post*, August 25, 2004, B4.

2. Andrew D. Cohen, "How the Establishment Clause Can Influence Substantive Due Process: Adultery Bans after Lawrence," *Fordham Law Review* 79

(2011): 605, 613. Since that article, Colorado and New Hampshire have repealed their adultery laws. See http://www.denverpost.com/politics/ci_22850726/bill -repeal-colo-adutlerty-law-signed; http://legiscan.com/NH/bill?HB1125/2014.

3. On the ten-dollar fine in Maryland, see Md. Criminal Law Code Ann. Section 10–501. On Michigan law, see Jenny Jarvie, "Footnote on Adultery Turns into a Spotlighted Affair," *Los Angeles Times*, January 22, 2007.

4. Cohen, "How the Establishment Clause Can Influence Substantive Due Process," 614n55; Gabrielle Viator, Note, "The Validity of Criminal Adultery Prohibitions after Lawrence v. Texas," *Suffolk University Law Review* 39 (2006): 837, 845.

5. Lawrence Friedman, quoted in Michael Sheridan, "Woman Caught Having Sex in Park, Charged with Adultery—In New York," *New York Daily News*, June 9, 2010.

6. Prevatte v. Prevatte, 377 S. Ed. 114 (S.C. 1989).

7. "Judge Rules State Adultery Law Unconstitutional," *Bismarck Tribune*, February 28, 2005.

8. Don Smith, "Adultery Charge Filed," *Newsday*, March 3, 1991, 18.

9. Carolyn Donahoe, "Adultery: It's Not Just a Sin, It's a Crime," *Washington Times*, June 29, 1990, E1.

10. Alyssa Newcomb, "Police Investigating Woman for Violating Adultery Law," ABC News, January 13, 2012, http://abcnews.go.com/blogs/headlines /2012/01/police-investigating-woman-for-violating-adultery-law.

11. Barry Leibowitz, "Ariz. Man Wants Wife Prosecuted for Adultery," CBS News, January 18, 2012, http://www.cbsnews.com/news/ariz-man-wants-wife -prosecuted-for-adultery/.

12. Robert E. Eaton, quoted in William E. Schmidt, "Adultery as a Crime: Old Laws Dusted Off in a Wisconsin Case," *New York Times*, April 30, 1990.

13. Sewell Chan, "Is Adultery a Crime in New York?," *New York Times*, March 21, 2008.

14. Jonathan Turley, "Adultery, in Many States, Is Still a Crime," *USA Today*, April 25, 2010.

15. On Virginia, see Jonathan Turley, "Of Lust and the Law," *Washington Post*, September 5, 2004, B1. On Illinois and Minnesota, see Turley, "Adultery." On Wisconsin, New York, and Maryland, see Schmidt, "Adultery as a Crime."

16. Thurman W. Arnold, *The Symbols of Government* (New Haven, CT: Yale University Press, 1935), 160.

17. Tom Prichard, quoted in Turley, "Adultery."

18. Timothy Horrigan, quoted in Norma Love, "Adultery Still a Crime in New Hampshire after 200 Years," *Huffington Post*, March 18, 2010, http://www .huffingtonpost.com/2009/12/13/adultery-still-a-crime-in_n_390366.html.

19. Love, "Adultery Still a Crime."

20. Robert Preston, quoted in Alberta I. Cook, "Adultery Statute Survives Debate in New Hampshire," *National Law Journal* 4 (1987): 14; Preston, quoted in Donahoe, "Adultery," E1.

21. John Chandler, quoted in Cook, "Adultery Statute Survives Debate."

22. William Doino, of the *Wanderer*, a Catholic weekly, quoted in Martin J. Siegel, "For Better or For Worse: Adultery, Crime and the Constitution," *Journal of Family Law* 30 (1991): 45, 50.

23. "Bill to Repeal of Colorado Adultery Law Signed," *Denver Post*, March 22, 2013.

24. Scott C. Fergus, quoted in Schmidt, "Adultery as a Crime."

25. Walter Wadlington, quoted in Donahoe, "Adultery," E1.

26. Paul Rothstein, quoted in ibid.

27. Carey v. Population Services International, 431 U.S. 678, 687n5 (1977).

28. Hollenbaugh v. Carnegie Free Library, 436 F. Supp. 1328, 1331 (1977), 545 F.2d 382, cert. den. 439 U.S. 1052 (1978).

29. Hollenbaugh v. Carnegie Free Library, 436 F. Supp. 1331, 1333, 545 F.2d 382, cert. den. 439 U.S. 1052 (1978).

30. Hollenbaugh v. Carnegie Free Library, cert den. 439 U.S. 1052, 1054, 1057 (Marshall, J., dissenting).

31. Griswold v. Connecticut, 381 U.S. 479, 498 (1965) (Goldberg, J., concurring), and Poe v. Ullman, 367 U.S. 497, 546 (1961) (Harlan, J., dissenting).

32. Commonwealth v. Stowell, 449 N.E.2d 357, 360 (Ma. 1983).

33. Kraus v. Village of Barrington Hills, 571 F. Supp. 538, 542–543 (N.D. Ill. 1982).

34. Lawrence v. Texas, 539 U.S. 558, 572, 578 (2003).

35. Cass R. Sunstein, "What Did Lawrence Hold? Of Autonomy, Desuetude, Sexuality, and Marriage," *Supreme Court Review* 2003, 27, 46.

36. *Lawrence*, 539 U.S. 599 (Scalia, J., dissenting).

37. Sunstein, "What Did Lawrence Hold?," 65.

38. Viator, "The Validity of Criminal Adultery Prohibitions after Lawrence v. Texas," 853.

39. *Griswold*, 381 U.S. 485–486. The Court held that prohibition on contraceptives violates the constitution.

40. Ibid., 486.

41. Loving v. Virginia, 388 U.S. 1, 11 (1967).

42. The decision is unpublished. See "Judge Rules State Adultery Law Unconstitutional," *Bismarck Tribune*, February 28, 2005.

43. Thong v. Andre Chreky Salon, 634 F. Supp. 2d 40, 47 (D. D.C. 2009). The Virginia decision was Martin v. Ziherl, 607 S.E.2d 367 (Va. 2005).

44. Johnson v. San Jacinto Junior College, 498 F. Supp. 555 (S.D. Texas 1980). The court held that the plaintiff's summary dismissal without an opportunity to be heard violated due process.

45. Ibid., 577.

46. Fugate v. Phoenix Civil Service Board, 791 F.2d 736, 742 (9th Cir. 1986).

47. Wilson v. Swing, 463 F. Supp. 555, 563 (M.D. N.C. 1978).

48. Suddarth v. Slane, 539 F. Supp. 612, 615, 616 (W.D. Va. 1982).

49. Ibid., 616.

50. Mercure v. Van Buren Township, 81 F. Supp. 2d 814 (E.D. Mich. 2000).

51. Marcum v. McWhorter, 308 F.3d 635, 643 (6th Cir. 2002); Caruso v. City of Cocoa, Florida, 260 F. Supp. 2d 1191 (M.D. Fla. 2003).

52. *Marcum*, 308 F.3d 643.

53. Beecham v. Henderson County, Tennessee, 422 F.3d 372, 378 (6th Cir. 2005).

54. Starling v. Board of County Commissioners, 602 F.3d 1257, 1261 (11th Cir. 2010).

55. Seegmiller v. Laverkin City, 528 F.3d 762, 772 (10th Cir. 2008).

56. Stevens v. Holder, 966 F. Supp. 2d 622, 638 (E.D. Va. 2013).

57. Compare In the Matter of the Petition for Naturalization of C-C-J-P, 299 F. Supp. 767 (N.D. Ill. 1969) (state law governed), and Brea-Garcia v. Immigration and Naturalization Service, 531 F.2d 693 (3d Cir. 1976) (state law governed) with Petition for Naturalization of Rolf Richard Schroers, 336 F. Supp. 1348 (S.D. N.Y. 1971) (federal law governed).

58. Schroers, 336 F. Supp. 1348.

59. In re Edgar, 253 F. Supp. 151 (E.D. Mich. 1966).

60. PL 97–116 (HR 4327), December 29, 1981, 95 Stat. 1611.

61. Etape v. Napolitano, 664 F. Supp. 2d 498 (D. Md. 2009). The petition was denied on other grounds.

62. Hutelmyer v. Cox, 514 S.E.2d 554, 557 (N.C. App. 1999).

63. Ibid., 560.

64. Caroline L. Batchelor, Comment, "Falling Out of Love with an Outdated Tort: An Argument for the Abolition of Criminal Conversation in North Carolina," *North Carolina Law Review* 87 (2010): 1910, 1915n35; Sheri Stritof, "Alienation of Affection State Laws," About.com, December 2009, http://marriage.about.com/od/legalities/a/alienation.htm. Since these sources were published, North Carolina has disallowed both criminal conversation and alienation of affection and West Virginia has eliminated the tort of criminal conversation. Joanna L. Grossman and Lawrence M. Friedman, "The Legal Price of Adultery Goes Down: North Carolina and West Virginia Abandon Heartbalm Actions," Justia.com, June 24, 2014, http://verdict.justia.com/2014/06/24/legal-price-adultery-goes. For questions about the continued viability of New Mexico's law, see Alan M. Malott, "Alienation of Affections Tort Mostly Inapplicable in N.M.," *Albuquerque Journal*, April 5, 2010.

65. Jacob M. Appel, "Hate the Husband? Sue the Mistress!," *Huffington Post*, March 18, 2010, citing awards of $1.4 million and $2 million.

66. Oddo v. Presser, 581 S.E.2d 123 (N.C. App. 2003). Joanna L. Grossman and Lawrence M. Friedman, *Inside the Castle: Law and the Family in 20th Century America* (Princeton, NJ: Princeton University Press, 2011), 102.

67. Misenheimer v. Burris, 637 S.E.2d 173, 176 (N.C. 2006).

68. Grossman and Friedman, *Inside the Castle*, 102; Alice Gomstyn and Lee Ferran, "Wife's $9M Message to Mistresses: 'Lay Off,'" ABC News, March 23, 2010, http://www.ABCnews.go.com/GMA/Business/wife-wins-million-husbands-alleged-mistress/story?id=10177637.

69. Saunders v. Alford, 607 So. 2d 1214 (Miss. 1992).

70. Golden v. Kaufman, 760 S.E.2d 883 (W. VA. 2014); Grossman and Friedman, "The Legal Price of Adultery Goes Down."

71. *Saunders*, 607 So. 2d 1216. See also Wyman v. Wallace, 615 P.2d 452, 455 (Wash. 1980); Hunt v. Hunt, 309 N.W.2d 818, 822 (S.D. 1981); Norton v. MacFarlane, 818 P.2d 8 (Utah 1991).

72. *Saunders*, 607 So. 2d 1214.

73. *Norton*, 818 P.2d 17.

74. Neal v. Neal, 873 P.2d 871, 875 (Id. 1994).

75. Karchner v. Mumie, 156 A.2d 537, 539 (Penn. 1959); Vaughn v. Blackburn, 431 S.W.2d 887, 889 (Ky. 1968); Sebastian v. Kluttz, 170 S.E.2d 104, 115–116 (N.C. App. 1969).

76. William M. Kelly, "The Case for Retention of Causes of Action for Intentional Interference with the Marital Relationship," *Notre Dame Law Review* 48 (1972): 426, 433.

77. Bearbower v. Merry, 266 N.W.2d 128 (Iowa 1978). See also Fadgen v. Lenkner, 365 A.2d 147, 149 (Penn. 1976). Even if the parties have signed a separation agreement, that will not bar an action for criminal conversation. Nunn v. Allen, 574 S.E.2d 35, 43 (N.C. App. 2002).

78. Feldman v. Feldman, 480 A.2d 34, 35, 36 (N.H. 1984).

79. Fitch v. Valentine, 959 So. 2d 1012 (Miss. 2007).

80. *Hunt*, 309 N.W.2d 823 (Dunn, J. concurring).

81. Several unsuccessful efforts to ban the law have been placed before legislatures. Keren Rivas, "Alienation Cases Are All Too Common," *Burlington Times*, February 19, 2006.

82. Note, "Constitutional Barriers to Civil and Criminal Restrictions on Pre- and Extra-marital Sex," *Harvard Law Review* 104 (1991): 1660, 1672. On property and alimony, see Matthew Butler, "Grounds for Divorce: A Survey," *Journal of Contemporary Legal Issues* 11 (2000): 164, 166. On custody and support, see Lorraine Ali, "The Secret Lives of Wives," *Newsweek*, July 11, 2004. On the Texas requirement that the affair must be shown to cause marital breakup, see Kelly McClure and Chris Meuse, "Adultery and Its Impact on Divorce," *Dallas Bar Association*, September, 2011, http://www.dallasbar.org/sites/default/files/headnotes_09_final-web.pdf; Peter Nash Swisher, "Marriage and Some Troubling Issues with No-Fault Divorce," *Regent University Law Review* 17 (2004): 243. On custody, see Farris v. Farris, 532 So. 2d 1041, 1043 (1988). For statutes providing for relevance of adultery in determining spousal support, see Fla. Stat.

Section 61.08(1) (2010); Ga. Code Ann. Section 19–6–1(b) (2010); S.C. Code Ann. Section 20–3–130(A) (2009); Va. Code Ann. Section 20–107.1(E) (2010); W.V. Code Ann. Section 48–8–104 (2010). For adultery as an entitlement to alimony, see Adams v. Adams, 374 S.E.2d 450 (1988); N.C. General Statutes Section 50–16.2(1) (1989). For adultery as a bar to alimony, see Doe v. Doe, 634 S.E.2d 51 (S.C. App. 2006).

83. Hand v. Hand, 257 S.E.2d 507 (Ga. 1979).

84. Menge v. Menge, 491 So. 2d 700 (La. App. 1986).

85. Nemeth v. Nemeth, 481 S.E.2d 181, 184 (S.C. App. 1997).

86. In the Matter of David G. Blanchflower, 834 A.2d 1010, 1011 (N.H. 2003).

87. Patin v. Patin, 371 So. 2d 682, 683 (Fla. App. 1979); see also RGM v. DEM, 410 S.E.2d 564, 566–567 (S.C. 1991).

88. *Blanchflower*, 834 A.2d 1015 (Brock, C H., dissenting).

89. For twelve factors, see Elliott v. Elliott, 11 So. 3d 784 (Miss. App. 2009); Armstrong v. Armstrong, 618 So. 2d 1278, 1280 (Miss. App. 1993). For fifteen factors, see Wooten v. Wooten, 615 S.E.2d 98 (S.C. 2005). For failure to mention fault in allocating property, see Tatum v. Tatum, 54 So. 3d 855 (Miss. App. 2010); Kay v. Kay, 12 So. 3d 622 (Miss. App. 2009); Elliott v. Elliott, 11 So. 3d 784.

90. Doe v. Doe, 634 S.E.2d 51 (S.C. App. 2006). See also Simpson v. Simpson, 660 S.E.2d 278 (S.C. App. 2008).

91. In re Marriage of J-H-M and E-C-M, 544 S.W.2d 582, 585 (Mo. Ct. App. 1976).

92. Compare Brown v. Brown, 237 S.E.2d 89, 91 (Va. 1977) (citing relevance of moral values) with Brinkley v. Brinkley, 336 S.E.2d 901 (Va. App. 1985) (affirming award of custody to adulterous mother) and Monk v. Monk, 386 So. 2d 753, 755 (Ala. App. 1980) (awarding custody to adulterous mother where no adverse effect on child).

93. Woodham v. Woodham, 17 So. 3d 153 (Miss. App. 2009); Collins v. Collins, 98 So. 3d 506 (Miss. App. 2012). See also Franks v. Franks, 873 So. 2d 135 (Miss. App. 2004).

94. Brekeen v. Brekeen, 880 So. 2d 280 (Miss. App. 2004).

95. Chastain v. Chastain, 672 S.E.2d 108 (S.C. App. 2009).

96. Wayne R. LaFave, *Criminal Law*, 4th ed. (St. Paul, MN: Thomson/West, 2003), 780; Joel E. Smith, "Spouse's Confession of Adultery as Affecting Degree of Homicide Involved in Killing Spouse or His or Her Paramour," 93 A.L.R.3d 925 (1979 and Supp. 1990).

97. LaFave, *Criminal Law*, 780.

98. Model Penal Code Section 210.3(1)(b) (1962).

99. Commonwealth v. Schnopps, 417 N.E.2d 1213 (Mass. 1981).

100. Raines v. State, 277 S.E.2d 47 (Ga. 1981).

101. For jurisdictions that allow being told about adultery as provocation, see LaFave, *Criminal Law*, 779–781.

102. Commonwealth v. Bermudez, 348 N.E.2d 802 (1976). See also Biggs v. State, 441 So.2d 989 (Ga. App. 1983).

103. State v. Shane, 590 N.E.2d 272, 279 (Ohio 1992).

104. People v. Chevalier, 544 N.E.2d 942 (Ill. 1989).

105. Commonwealth v. LeClair, 708 N.E.2d 107 (Mass. 1999). For other cases finding that a wife's confession was insufficient provocation, see People v. Bradley, 581 N.E.2d 310 (Ill. 1991); Biggs v. State, 441 So. 2d 989. See also *Bermudez*, 348 N.E.2d 802.

106. People v. Sutton, 818 N.E.2d 793 (Ill. App. 2004); Speake v. State, 610 So. 2d 1238 (Ala. App. 1992); State v. Cooley, 536 S.E.2d 666 (S.C. 2000).

107. *Cooley*, 536 S.E.2d 666.

108. Susan D. Rozelle, "Controlling Passion: Adultery and the Provocation Defense," *Rutgers Law Journal* 37 (2005): 197, 226.

109. People v. Berk, 629 N.Y.S.2d 588 (1995). See also Burger v. State, 231 S.E.2d 769, 770, 771 (Ga. 1977).

110. *Burger*, 231 S.E.2d 769, 771.

111. See Emily L. Miller, "(Wo)manslaughter: Voluntary Manslaughter, Gender, and the Model Penal Code," *Emory Law Journal* 50 (2001): 665, 692–693.

112. Kimberly Wilmot-Weidman, "After a 3-Year Fight, Murder Is Finally Murder in Maryland," *Chicago Tribune*, November 23, 1997, C1.

113. Robert E. Cahill, quoted in "She Strays, He Shoots, Judge Winks," *New York Times*, October 22, 1994, A22.

114. Wilmot-Weidman, "After a 3-Year Fight," C1.

4. Sex in the Military

1. Gregory L. Vistica and Evan Thomas, "Sex and Lies," *Newsweek*, June 2, 1997, 26.

2. Nancy Gibbs and John F. Dickerson, "Wings of Desire," *TIME International* (South Pacific Edition), June 2, 1997, 32.

3. Vistica and Thomas, "Sex and Lies," 29.

4. *All Things Considered*, NPR radio broadcast, June 16, 1997.

5. Carolyn Maloney, quoted in Gibbs and Dickerson, "Wings of Desire."

6. Kelly Flinn, *Proud to Be: My Life, the Air Force, the Controversy* (New York: Random House, 1997), 213.

7. "Poll: Many Believe Air Force Treated Flinn Unfairly," CNN, May 23, 1997, http://www.cnn.com/US/9705/23/flinn.poll/index.html.

8. Gallup/CNN/*USA Today* Poll, iPOLL Databank, June 1997, http://www.ropercenter.uconn.edu/data_access/ipoll/ipoll.html.

9. NBC News/*Wall Street Journal* Poll, iPOLL Databank, June 19–23, 1997.

10. On regulations, see Gibbs and Dickerson, "Wings of Desire."

11. Rowan Scarborough, "Challenge to Adultery Ban Unlikely," *Washington Times*, June 2, 1997, A4. For the frequency of administrative actions, see C. Quince Hopkins, "Rank Matters but Should Marriage? Adultery, Fraternization, and Honor in the Military," *UCLA Women's Law Journal* 9 (1999): 177, 248.

12. Hopkins, "Rank Matters," 234, 250.

13. Stephen Deakin, "British Military Ethos and Christianity," *British Army Review*, no. 138, (Winter 2005): 97, 101.

14. Edward M. Byrne, *Military Law*, 2nd ed. (Annapolis, MD: Naval Institute Press, 1977), 7–8.

15. Christopher Scott Maravilla, "The Other Don't Ask Don't Tell: Adultery under the Uniform Code of Military Justice after *Lawrence v. Texas*," *Capital University Law Review* 37 (2009): 659, 661–662.

16. Manual for Courts-Martial United States (2008 ed.), Paragraph 62(e).

17. Hopkins, "Rank Matters," 234–248; Maravilla, "The Other Don't Ask Don't Tell," 660; Katherine Moon, *Sex among Allies: Military Prostitution in US-Korea Relations* (New York: Columbia University Press, 1997); Ian Fisher, "Army's Adultery Rule Is Don't Get Caught," *New York Times*, May 17, 1997, A1.

18. Hopkins, "Rank Matters," 249; David Van Biema and Sally B. Donnelly, "The Rules of Engagement," *TIME International* (South Pacific Edition), June 2, 1997; Cynthia Enloe, *Bananas, Beaches, and Bases: Making Feminist Sense of International Politics* (Berkeley: University of California Press, 1990), 81–92.

19. Van Biema and Donnelly, "Rules of Engagement."

20. Fisher, "Army's Adultery Rule," A1.

21. Wesley O. Hagood, *Presidential Sex: From the Founding Fathers to Bill Clinton* (Secaucus, NJ: Citadel Press, 1998), 134; Kay Summersby Morgan and Barbara Wyden, *Past Forgetting: My Love Affair with Dwight D. Eisenhower* (New York: Simon and Schuster, 1976).

22. Merle Miller, *Plain Speaking: An Oral Biography of Harry S. Truman* (New York: Berkeley, 1974), 340; Hagood, *Presidential Sex*, 133.

23. Summersby, *Past Forgetting*; John Kifner, "Eisenhower Letters Hint at Affair with Aide," *New York Times*, June 6, 1991.

24. Lolita C. Baldor, "Sex Is Major Reason Military Commanders Are Fired," Associated Press, January 21, 2013.

25. Barbara Wilson, quoted in Hopkins, "Rank Matters," 202–203.

26. MCM, Paragraph 62(b)(1)–(3).

27. Ibid., Paragraph 62(c).

28. Ibid., Paragraph 59(c)(2) and (3).

29. Ibid., Paragraph 1(d)(2); Katherine Annuschat, "An Affair to Remember: The State of the Crime of Adultery in the Military," *San Diego Law Review* 47 (2010): 1161, 1175n94.

30. Michael Kilian, "Military Adultery Regulation Eased," *Chicago Tribune*, July 30, 1998.

31. Chappell v. Wallace, 462 U.S. 296, 300 (1983).

32. James M. Winner, "Beds with Sheets but No Covers: The Right to Privacy and the Military's Regulation of Adultery," *Loyola of Los Angeles Law Review* 31 (1998): 1073, 1103.

33. William Henry Peerenboom, quoted in Scarborough, "Challenge to Adultery Ban Unlikely," A4.

34. United States v. Green, 39 M.J. 606, 609 (A.C.M.R. 1994).

35. United States v. Orellana, 62 N.J. 595, 598, 599, 601 (N.M. Ct. Crim App. 2005).

36. Frank Bruni, "Adultery Alone Often Fails to Prompt a Military Prosecution," *New York Times,* December 13, 1998; Hopkins, "Rank Matters," 247–248.

37. Bruni, "Adultery Alone Often Fails to Prompt a Military Prosecution."

38. Penland v. Mabus, 643 F. Supp. 2d 14, (D.D.C. 2009); Annuschat, "An Affair to Remember," 1162.

39. Annuschat, "An Affair to Remember," 1190; Chris Amos, "0–4 Sentenced to 60 Days in Adultery Case," *Navy Times,* May 25, 2008.

40. Chris Amos, "Reprisal Allegations in Adultery Case Disputed," *Navy Times,* June 14, 2008; Annuschat, "An Affair to Remember," 1190n191.

41. "Court-Martialed Navy Officer Alleges Sex, Lies, Corruption," 10 News, KGTV San Diego, July 22, 2009, http://www.10news.com/nes/court-martialed -navy-officer-alleges-sex-lies-corruption.

42. Gary Solis, former military prosecutor and Georgetown adjunct professor, quoted in Annuschat, "An Affair to Remember," 1163.

43. Ed O'Keefe, "Could Congress Have Changed the Outcome of Two High Profile Cases of Military Sexual Assault? Maybe," *Washington Post,* March 24, 2014.

44. Neil A. Lewis, "Case against Ex-chaplain Opens Focusing on Affair," *New York Times,* December 9, 2003, A20.

45. "Army Rebukes Muslim Chaplain over Adultery and Pornography," *New York Times,* March 23, 2004, A20.

46. Sarah Kershaw, "Guantánamo Chaplain and His Wife Speak Out," *New York Times,* December 5, 2003, A24.

47. Van Biema and Donnelly, "Rules of Engagement."

48. "Sex and the Military, Cont'd," *Washington Post,* June 6, 1997, A26.

49. Van Biema and Donnelly, "Rules of Engagement."

50. Mark Thompson, "Sex, the Army, and a Double Standard," *TIME,* May 4, 1998.

51. Bradley Graham, "Hale Case Spurs Tighter Army Retirement Process," *Washington Post,* July 8, 1998, A4.

52. Elizabeth Becker, "Army Demotes Retired NATO Commander Who Admitted Affairs with Wives of Subordinates," *New York Times,* September 3, 1999, 12.

53. Ibid., 1.

54. Michael O'Hanlan, quoted in Josh White, "4-Star General Relieved of Duty; Rare Move Follows Allegations of an Extramarital Affair," *Washington Post*, August 10, 2005.

55. Neal Puckett, quoted in ibid.

56. William Cohen, quoted in "Defense Chief Denies Adultery 'Witch Hunt,'" *Chicago Tribune*, June 4, 1997.

57. Cohen, quoted in Andrea Stone, "General's Affair Re-ignites Debate over Policy," *USA Today*, June 6, 1997, A3.

58. Stone, "General's Affair," A1.

59. John McCain, quoted in ibid.

60. Britt Minzer, quoted in ibid.

61. Gallup/CNN/*USA Today* Poll, iPOLL Databank, June 10, 1997. This discrepancy could also be traced to the different circumstances of each case, especially given the fact that Flinn lied about her affair and disregarded direct orders, and the fact that Ralston's affair had occurred in the past.

62. Ibid. Of respondents, women were more likely (65 percent) than men (50 percent) to think that adultery that happened in the past should give rise to an exception.

63. NBC News/*Wall Street Journal* Poll, iPOLL Databank, June 19–23, 1997.

64. Gallup/CNN/*USA Today* Poll, iPOLL Databank, June 10, 1997.

65. Frank Bruni, "The Siren and the Spook," *New York Times*, November 12, 2012.

66. Michael D. Shear, "Petraeus Quits; Evidence of Affair Was Found by F.B.I.," *New York Times*, November 9, 2012.

67. "Opinion Roundup: Does the Petraeus Affair Matter?," NPR, November 13, 2012, http://www.npr.org/2012/11/13/165046181/opinion-roundup-does -the-petraeus-affair-matter.

68. Roger Simon, "Gen. David Petraeus Is Dumb, She's Dumber," *Politico*, November 13, 2012, http://www.politico.com/news/stories/1112/83733.html.

69. William Galston, "The Military's Laws on Adultery Make No Sense," *New Republic*, November 15, 2012.

70. Richard Cohen, "Get Petraeus Back to Work," *Washington Post*, November 12, 2012.

71. Katie Roiphe, "Stop Judging, You Prudes," *Slate*, November 13, 2012, http://www.slate.com/articles/double_x/roiphe/2012/11/david_petraeus_and _paula_broadwell_the_real_reasons_we_care_about_the_affair.html.

72. On resignation, see Quinnipiac University Poll, iPOLL Databank, December 5, 2012, http://www.quinnipiac.edu/institutes-centers/polling -institute/national/release-detail?ReleaseID=1820. On crime, see CNN/ORC International Poll, iPOLL Databank, November 27, 2012, http://politicalticker .blogs.cnn.com/2012/11/27/cnn-poll-thumbs-down-on-w-h-reaction-to-benghazi -attack-and-petraeus-resignation/.

73. Cox Commission, *Report of the Commission on the 50th Anniversary of the Uniform Code of Military Justice* (Washington, DC: National Institute of Military Justice, 2001), 11.

74. MCM, Part IV, Paragraph 83.

75. Martha Chamallas, "The New Gender Panic: Reflections on Sex Scandals and the Military," *Minnesota Law Review* 83 (1998): 305, 360.

76. Hopkins, "Rank Matters," 260.

77. *Green*, 39 M.J. 606, 610.

78. United States v. Kroop, 34 M.J. 628 (A.F. Ct. Crim. App. 1992), affirmed, 38 M.J. 470 (C.M.A. 1993).

79. "Army General Loses 2 Stars, Must Retire in Sex Scandal," *Chicago Tribune*, November 17, 1999, 16.

80. "General in Assault Case Will Retire with Demotion," *New York Times*, June 21, 2014, A15.

81. Kirby Dick, "Don't Trust the Pentagon to End Rape," *New York Times*, June 3, 2013, A23.

82. Helene Cooper, "Pentagon Study Finds 50% Increase in Reports of Military Sexual Assaults," *New York Times*, May 1, 2014; Helene Cooper, "Reports of Sexual Assaults in Military on Rise," *New York Times*, December 3, 2014; Department of Defense, *Report to the President of the United States on Sexual Assault Prevention and Responses* (Washington, DC: Department of Defense, 2014), 15. Rates were also up in a 2013 study; Jennifer Steinhauer, "Reports of Military Sexual Assault Rise Sharply," *New York Times*, November 7, 2013, A2.

83. Department of Defense, *Report to the President*, 15.

84. Cooper, "Pentagon Study."

85. Jackie Speier, "Why Rapists in Military Get Away with It," CNN, June 21, 2012, http://www.cnn.com/2012/06/21/opinion/speier-military -rape.

86. Sabrina Rubin Erdely, "The Rape of Petty Officer Bumer," *Rolling Stone*, February 14, 2013, 59.

5. Alternative Lifestyles

1. George Peter Murdock, *Social Structure* (New York: Macmillan, 1949), 265.

2. Murdoch found only 43 of 193 societies to be characterized by monogamy and only 2 by polyandry. Ibid., 28. For more recent research, see Miriam K. Zeitzen, *Polygamy: A Cross-cultural Analysis* (London: Bloomsbury Academic Press, 2008).

3. Roger H. Rubin, "Alternative Lifestyles Revisited, or Whatever Happened to Swingers, Group Marriages, and Communes?," *Journal of Family Issues* 22 (2001): 711, 723.

4. Ibid.

5. Meg Barker and Darren Langdridge, "Introduction," in *Understanding Non-monogamies*, ed. Meg Barker and Darren Langdridge (New York: Routledge, 2010). See the Loving More website, http://www.lovemore.com; Peter. J. Benson, *The Polyamory Handbook: A User's Guide* (Bloomington: AuthorHouse, 2008); Kaye Bellemeade, *Swinging for Beginners: An Introduction to the Lifestyle* (New Tradition Books, 2008); Dossie Easton and Catherine A. Liszt, *The Ethical Slut: A Guide to Infinite Sexual Possibilities* (San Francisco: Greenery Press, 1997).

6. Elisabeth Sheff cites 1.5 million to 9.8 million: Elisabeth Sheff, *The Polyamorists Next Door: Inside Multiple-Partner Relationships and Families* (Lanham, MD: Rowman and Littlefield, 2014), 3. Jessica Bennett cites half a million: Jessica Bennett, "Polyamory: The Next Sexual Revolution?," *Newsweek*, July 28, 2009. Brian G. Gilmartin cites 900,000: Brian G. Gilmartin, *The Gilmartin Report* (Secaucus, NJ: Citadel, 1978), 11. One survey of some 3,574 couples found that 15 to 26 percent had an understanding that allowed nonmonogamy under some circumstances, a figure that most find implausibly high. Philip Blumstein and Pepper Schwartz, *American Couples: Money, Work, Sex* (New York: William Morrow and Co., 1983), 585.

7. Richard J. Jenks, "Swinging: A Review of the Literature," *Archives of Sexual Behavior* 27 (1998): 507; Jane Tucker, "Taming the Green-Eyed Monster: On the Need to Rethink Our Cultural Conception of Jealousy," *Yale Journal of Law and Feminism* 25 (2013): 217, 237.

8. Hadar Aviram, "Make Love, Not Law: Perceptions of the Marriage Equality Struggle among Polyamorous Activists," *Journal of Bisexuality* 7 (2008): 261, 264; Hadar Aviram and Gwendolyn M. Leachman, "The Future of Polyamorous Marriage: Lessons from the Marriage Equality Struggle," *Harvard Journal of Law and Gender* 38 (2015): 268, 297.

9. Arline M. Rubin and James R. Adams, "Outcomes of Sexually Open Marriages," *Journal of Sex Research* 22 (1986): 311. The term was popularized by Nena O'Neill and George O'Neill, *Open Marriage: A New Life Style for Couples* (New York: M. Evans, 1972).

10. Celia Morris Eckhardt, *Fanny Wright: Rebel in America* (Cambridge, MA: Harvard University Press, 1984); Linda R. Hirshman and Jane E. Larson, *Hard Bargains: The Politics of Sex* (New York: Oxford University Press, 1999), 137.

11. Lori D. Ginzberg, "'The Hearts of Your Readers Will Shudder': Fanny Wright, Infidelity, and American Freethought," *American Quarterly* 46 (June 1994): 195, 199, 205.

12. Taylor Stoehr, *Free Love in America: A Documentary History* (New York: AMS Press, 1979).

13. William L. Smith, *Families and Communes: An Examination of Nontraditional Lifestyles* (Thousand Oaks, CA: Sage, 1999), 61.

14. William Alfred Hinds, *American Communities and Co-operative Colonies* (Chicago: Charles H. Kerr, 2011); Deborah Anapol, *Polyamory in the Twenty-First Century: Love and Intimacy with Multiple Partners* (Lanham, MD: Rowman and Littlefield, 2012), 45–46; Gerald Gutek and Patricia Gutek, *Visiting Utopian Communities: A Guide to the Shakers, Moravians, and Others* (Columbia: University of South Carolina Press, 1998), 130–137.

15. Raymond Lee Muncy, *Sex and Marriage in Utopian Communities* (Bloomington: Indiana University Press, 1973).

16. John C. Spurlock, *Free Love: Marriage and Middle-Class Radicalism in America, 1825–1860* (New York: New York University Press, 1988), 102, 226.

17. Stephen Pearl Andrews, quoted in Stoehr, *Free Love in America*, 76.

18. Stoehr, *Free Love in America*, 103–105.

19. Madeleine B. Stern, ed., *The Victoria Woodhull Reader* (Weston, MA: M&S Press, 1974), 23.

20. Hirshman and Larson, *Hard Bargains*, 138; John D'Emilio and Estelle B. Freedman, *Intimate Matters: A History of Sexuality in America*, 2nd ed. (Chicago: University of Chicago Press, 1998), 162.

21. Spurlock, *Free Love*, 227.

22. D'Emilio and Freedman, *Intimate Matters*, 163.

23. Anapol, *Polyamory*, 49n4; Emma Goldman, *Living My Life* (New York: Knopf, 1931).

24. Arland Thornton, "The International Fight against Barbarism: Historical and Comparative Perspectives on Marriage Timing, Consent, and Polygamy," in *Modern Polygamy in the United States: Historical, Cultural, and Legal Issues*, ed. Cardell K. Jacobson with Lara Burton (New York: Oxford University Press, 2011); Richard S. Van Wagoner, *Mormon Polygamy: A History* (Salt Lake City: Signature Books, 1989); Orma Linford, "The Mormons and the Law: The Polygamy Cases," *Utah Law Review* 9 (1964): 308; B. Carmon Hardy, *Doing the Works of Abraham—Mormon Polygamy: Its Origin, Practice, and Demise* (Norman, OK: The Arthur H. Clark Company, 2007).

25. See Utah, Admission as a State, ch. 138, 28 Stat. 107 (1894); Irwin Altman and Joseph Ginat, *Polygamous Families in Contemporary Society* (New York: Cambridge University Press, 1996), 26; Adrienne D. Davis, "Regulating Polygamy: Intimacy, Default Rules, and Bargaining for Equality," *Columbia Law Review* 110 (2010): 1955, 1969.

26. James Brooke, "Utah Struggles with a Revival of Polygamy," *New York Times*, August 23, 1998.

27. Smith, *Families and Communes*, 95–100.

28. Ulla Anobile and Richard J. Anobile, *Beyond Open Marriage* (New York: A&W Publishers, 1979), 42, 44, 46.

29. Anapol, *Polyamory*, 57–58.

30. Maura Strassberg, "The Challenge of Post-modern Polygamy: Considering Polyamory," *Capital Law Review* 31 (2003): 439, 499, 502.

31. Jenks, "Swinging," 509–510; Curtis Bergstrand and Jennifer Blevins Williams, "Today's Alternative Marriage Styles: The Case of Swingers," *Electronic*

Journal of Human Sexuality 3 (2000), http://www.ejhs.org/volume3/swing/body.htm.

32. Terry Gould, "The Other Swing Revival," *Saturday Night* 113 (1998): 48; Rubin, "Alternative Lifestyles," 721.

33. Jessica Bennett, "Only You. And You. And You: Polyamory—Relationships with Multiple, Mutually Consenting Partners—Has a Coming-Out Party," *Newsweek*, July 29, 2009.

34. Anapol, *Polyamory*, 61.

35. Sheff, *The Polyamorists Next Door*, 175–176.

36. For the role of nonmonogamy among nonmarried gay couples, see Michael Shernoff, "Negotiated Nonmonogamy and Male Couples," *Family Process* 45 (2006): 407.

37. For popular perceptions, see Jenks, "Swinging," 510.

38. Tucker, "Taming the Green-Eyed Monster," 237; Eugene E. Levitt, "Alternative Life Style and Marital Satisfaction: A Brief Report," *Annals of Sex Research* 1 (1988): 455, 459; Jenks, "Swinging," 517.

39. Bergstrand and Williams, "Today's Alternative Marriage Styles."

40. Richard Rayner, "The Way We Live Now: 4–9–00: Phenomenon; Back in the Swing," *New York Times*, April 9, 2000.

41. Anobile and Anobile, *Beyond Open Marriage*, 117–118.

42. Sheff, *The Polyamorists Next Door*, 33–34, 35.

43. Jenks, "Swinging," 515.

44. Anobile and Anobile, *Beyond Open Marriage*, 87.

45. Ibid., 88.

46. Some bigamy statutes, however, encompass cohabitation. For a decision finding Utah's prohibition on cohabitation unconstitutional, see Brown v. Buhman, 947 F. Supp. 2d 1170 (D. Utah 2013), discussed infra.

47. Larry L. Constantine and Joan M. Constantine, *Group Marriage: A Study of Contemporary Multilateral Marriage* (New York: Macmillan, 1973), 191.

48. Tammy Nelson, "The New Monogamy: How Far Should We Go?," *Psychotherapy Networker* 34 (July/August, 2010).

49. Sheff, *The Polyamorists Next Door*, 128.

50. Constantine and Constantine, *Group Marriage*, 191.

51. Anapol, *Polyamory*, 189.

52. Constantine and Constantine, *Group Marriage*, 147.

53. Elizabeth F. Emens, "Monogamy's Law: Compulsory Monogamy and Polyamorous Existence," *New York University Review of Law and Social Change* 29 (2004): 277, 311–312.

54. Bennett, "Polyamory: The Next Sexual Revolution?" For one of the most celebrated custody battles, see In the Matter of A.M., No. K1719 (Juv. Ct., Memphis and Shelby County, TN, April 16, 1999), discussed in Emens, "Monogamy's Law," 310.

55. Anapol, *Polyamory*, 20.

56. Anobile and Anobile, *Beyond Open Marriage*, 97.

57. Katherine Frank and John DeLamater, "Deconstructing Monogamy: Boundaries, Identities, and Fluidities across Relationships," in Barker and Langdridge, *Understanding Non-monogamies*, 19.

58. Anapol, *Polyamory*, 18.

59. Ibid., 13.

60. Frank and DeLamater, "Deconstructing Monogamy," 16, 19.

61. Sheff, *The Polyamorists Next Door*, 54, 59, 60.

62. For equal satisfaction, see Rubin and Adams, "Outcomes of Sexually Open Marriages," 311; Gilmartin, *The Gilmartin Report*. For higher levels of satisfaction, see Bergstrand and Williams, "Today's Alternative Marriage Styles"; Constantine and Constantine, *Group Marriage*, 100.

63. Sheff, *The Polyamorists Next Door*, 197; Anapol, *Polyamory*, 43; Jacquelyn J. Knapp and Robert N. Whitehurst, "Sexually Open Marriage and Relationships: Issues and Prospects," in *Marriage and Alternatives: Exploring Intimate Relationships*, ed. Roger W. Libby and Robert N. Whitehurst (Glenview, IL: Scott Foresman, 1977), 147, 154–155.

64. Constantine and Constantine, *Group Marriage*, 169; Sheff, *The Polyamorists Next Door*, 40.

65. Constantine and Constantine, *Group Marriage*, 164.

66. Elisabeth Sheff, "Strategies in Polyamorous Parenting," in Barker and Langdridge, *Understanding Non-monogamies*, 171, 174, 172.

67. Strassberg, "The Challenge of Post-modern Polygamy," 524, 464n172.

68. Anopol, *Polyamory*, 131; Ryan Nearing, "But What about the Kids?," *Loving More Magazine*, Winter 2001, 10–13.

69. Sheff, *The Polyamorists Next Door*, 224–225, 143, 269.

70. Constantine and Constantine, *Group Marriage*. On the benefits for children in polyamorous families, also see Mark Goldfeder and Elisabeth Sheff, "Children of Polyamorous Families: A First Empirical Look," *Journal of Law and Social Deviance* 5 (2013): 150.

71. James W. Ramey, "Intimate Groups and Networks: Frequent Consequence of Sexually Open Marriage," *The Family Coordinator* 24 (1975): 515; Bram Buunk, "Jealousy in Sexually Open Marriages," *Alternative Lifestyles* 4 (1981): 357.

72. Samuel S. Janus and Cynthia L. Janus, *The Janus Report on Sexual Behavior* (New York: John Wiley and Sons, 1993).

73. Rubin and Adams, "Outcomes of Sexually Open Marriages," 314.

74. Martin S. Weinberg, Colin J. Williams, and Douglas W. Pryor, *Dual Attraction: Understanding Bisexuality* (New York: Oxford University Press, 1995), 262.

75. Timothy Egan, "The Persistence of Polygamy," *New York Times*, February 28, 1999; Zeitzen, *Polygamy*, 94; Ronald C. Den Otter, "Three May Not Be a Crowd: The Case for a Constitutional Right to Plural Marriage," *Emory Law Journal* 64 (2015): 1977, 1983.

76. Van Wagoner, *Mormon Polygamy*, 180–181.

77. Janet Bennion, "The Many Faces of Polygamy: An Analysis of the Variability in Modern Mormon Fundamentalism in the Intermountain West," in Jacobson and Burton, *Modern Polygamy in the United States*, 165; John Pomfret, "Polygamists Fight to Be Seen as Part of Mainstream Society," *Washington Post*, November 21, 2006; Brooke, "Utah Struggles with a Revival of Polygamy."

78. Anapol, *Polyamory*, 179.

79. Paul Van Dam, quoted in Dirk Johnson, "Polygamists Emerge from Secrecy, Seeking Not Just Peace but Respect," *New York Times*, April 9, 1991.

80. John Witte Jr., "Why Two in One Flesh: The Western Case for Monogamy over Polygamy," *Emory Law Journal* 64 (2015): 1675, 1686.

81. Katilin R. McGinnis, "Sister Wives: A New Beginning for United States Polygamist Families on the Eve of Polygamy Prosecution," *Jeffrey S. Moorad Sports Law Journal* 19 (2012): 249, 261; Clayton Sandell and Christina Caron, "Polyga-

mist Warren Jeffs Guilty of Child Rape," ABC News, August 4, 2011, http://abcnews.go.com/story?id=14228198.

82. "What's New with the Sister Wives," TLC, quoted in Thomas Buck Jr., "From Big Love to the Big House: Justifying Anti-polygamy Laws in an Age of Expanding Rights," *Emory International Law Review* 26 (2012): 939, 942.

83. William Baude, "Is Polygamy Next?," *New York Times,* July 21, 2015.

84. Sean Loughlin, "Santorum Under Fire for Comments on Homosexuality," CNN, April 22, 2003, http://www.cnn.com/2003/ALLPOLITICS/04/22/santorum.gays/.

85. Stephen Largent, quoted in David L. Chambers, "Polygamy and Same-Sex Marriage," *Hofstra Law Review* 26 (1997): 53, 58.

86. Reynolds v. United States, 98 U.S. 145 (1878).

87. Cleveland v. United States, 329 U.S.14, 19 (1946).

88. Harms are discussed in State v. Green, 99 P.3d 820 (Utah, 2004). See also State v. Holm, 137 P.3d 726 (Utah 2006).

89. *Brown,* 947 F. Supp. 2d at 1225.

90. *Reynolds,* 98 U.S. at 164–165.

91. *Green,* 99 P.3d at 830.

92. Reference re: Section 293 of the Criminal Code of Canada, 2011 BCSC 1588 (2011) BCLR (5th) 96.

93. Julia Chamberlin and Amos N. Guiora, "Polygamy: Not 'Big Love' but Significant Harm," *Women's Rights Law Reporter* 35 (2014): 144, 176. For the harms to children generally, see Martin Guggenheim, "Texas Polygamy and Child Welfare," *Houston Law Review* 46 (2009): 759; Rose McDermott and Jonathan Cowden, "Polygyny and Violence against Women," *Emory Law Journal* 64 (2015): 1767; Witte, "Why Two in One Flesh," 1763.

94. Zeitzen, *Polygamy,* 172; Richard A. Vazquez, "The Practice of Polygamy: Legitimate Free Exercise of Religion or Legitimate Public Menace? Revisiting Reynolds in Light of Modern Constitutional Jurisprudence," *New York University Journal of Legislation and Public Policy* 5 (2001): 225, 241–242.

95. Rose McDermott, "Polygamy, More Common than You Think," *Wall Street Journal,* April 1, 2011. For abuses connected with polygamy, see Stephen Macedo, *Just Married: Same-Sex Couples, Monogamy, and the Future of Marriage* (Princeton, NJ: Princeton University Press, 2015), 187, 201.

96. Shayna M. Sigman, "Everything Lawyers Know about Polygamy Is Wrong," *Cornell Journal of Law and Public Policy* 16 (2006): 101, 172–173. See generally McDermott and Cowden, "Polygyny and Violence against Women."

97. Chamberlin and Guiora, "Polygamy: Not 'Big Love,'" 182–183; Zeitzen, *Polygamy*, 174; Pamela Manson, "'Lost Boys' File Suit against FLDS Church," *Salt Lake Tribune*, August 28, 2004.

98. Adrienne D. Davis, "Regulating Polygamy: Intimacy, Default Rules, and Bargaining for Equality," *Columbia Law Review* 110 (2010): 1955, 1975; Vazquez, "The Practice of Polygamy," 244.

99. Zeitzen, *Polygamy*, 104; Altman and Ginat, *Polygamous Families in Contemporary Society*, 99; Sigman, "Everything Lawyers Know," 101, 172–173; Philip L. Kilbride, *Plural Marriage for Our Times: A Reinvented Option?* (London: Bergin and Garvey, 1994).

100. Chamberlin and Guiora, "Polygamy: Not 'Big Love,'" 182.

101. Elizabeth Joseph, "My Husband's Nine Wives," *New York Times*, May 23, 1991, A31.

102. Chambers, "Polygamy and Same-Sex Marriage," 73; Janet Bennion, "History, Culture, and Variability of Mormon Schismatic Groups," in Jacobson and Burton, *Modern Polygamy in the United States*, 116.

103. Bennion, "The Many Faces of Polygamy," 172.

104. Zeitzen, *Polygamy*, 180. See also Adrienne Katherine Wing, "Polygamy from Southern Africa to Black Britannia to Black America: Global Critical Race Feminism as Legal Reform for the Twenty-First Century," *Journal of Contemporary Legal Issues* 11 (2001): 811, 858.

105. Tyson Gibbs and Judith Campbell, "Practicing Polygyny in Black America: Challenging Definition, Legal and Social Considerations for the African American Community," *Western Journal of Black Studies* 23 (1999): 144, 150–151.

106. Zeitzen, *Polygamy*, 180; Kilbride, *Plural Marriage for Our Times*.

107. Stevi Jackson and Sue Scott, "The Personal Is Still Political: Heterosexuality, Feminism and Monogamy," *Feminism and Psychology* 14 (2004): 151, 155.

108. Buck, "From Big Love to the Big House," 962–963.

109. Jonathan Turley, "Polygamy Laws Expose Our Own Hypocrisy," *USA Today*, October 3, 2004.

110. Drucilla Cornell, *At the Heart of Freedom: Feminism, Sex, and Equality* (Princeton, NJ: Princeton University Press, 1998), 124–125.

111. Sheff, *The Polyamorists Next Door,* 285–286.

112. Strassberg, "The Challenge of Post-modern Polygamy," 549.

113. Buck, "From Big Love to the Big House," 972.

114. Frank Newport and Igor Himelfarb, "In U.S., Record-High Say Gay, Lesbian Relations Morally OK," Gallup, May 20, 2013, http://www.gallup.com /poll/162689/record-high-say-gay-lesbian-relations-morally.aspx.

115. Thornton, "The International Fight against Barbarism," 283, 285.

116. Constantine and Constantine, *Group Marriage,* 195, 196.

117. Hadar Aviram, "Make Love, Not Law: Perceptions of the Marriage Equality Struggle among Polyamorous Activists," in *Bisexuality and Same-Sex Marriage,* ed. M. Paz Galupo (Binghamton, NY: Haworth Press, 2007), 277, 281.

118. Aviram, "Make Love, Not Law," *Journal of Bisexuality,* 278.

119. Valerie White, "Polyamory and the Law," *Loving More Magazine* 28 (2002): 7.

120. Bennion, "The Many Faces of Polygamy," 166, 177–179.

6. Sex and Politics

1. Robert P. Watson, *Affairs of State: The Untold History of Presidential Love, Sex, and Scandal, 1789–1900* (Lanham, MD: Rowman and Littlefield, 2012), 39.

2. Joseph E. Persico, *Franklin and Lucy: President Roosevelt, Mrs. Rutherford, and the Other Remarkable Women in His Life* (New York: Random House, 2008), 125; Resa Willis, *FDR and Lucy: Lovers and Friends* (New York: Routledge, 2006), 41; Blanche Wiesen Cook, *Eleanor Roosevelt,* vol. 1, *1884–1933* (New York: Penguin Books, 1992), 228.

3. Doris Kearns Goodwin, *No Ordinary Time: Franklin and Eleanor Roosevelt—The Home Front in World War II* (New York: Simon and Schuster, 1994), 20.

4. Willis, *FDR and Lucy,* 41; Cook, *Eleanor Roosevelt,* 228.

5. Persico, *Franklin and Lucy,* 126–127.

6. Goodwin, *No Ordinary Time,* 517, 529, 561, 591–592, 602.

7. Joseph P. Lash, *Eleanor and Franklin* (New York: W. W. Norton, 1971), 220; Goodwin, *No Ordinary Time,* 19, 227.

8. Persico, *Franklin and Lucy*, 127: Goodwin, *No Ordinary Time*, 19.

9. Goodwin, *No Ordinary Time*, 20, 98.

10. Wesley O. Hagood, *Presidential Sex: From the Founding Fathers to Bill Clinton* (Secaucus, NJ: Citadel Press, 1998), 105, 116.

11. Goodwin, *No Ordinary Time*, 121.

12. Persico, *Franklin and Lucy*, 165.

13. Ibid., 186.

14. Goodwin, *No Ordinary Time*, 120.

15. Persico, *Franklin and Lucy*, 195, 226.

16. Eleanor Roosevelt, *This I Remember* (New York: Praeger, 1975), 348–349.

17. Alice Roosevelt Longworth, quoted in Willis, *FDR and Lucy*, 30.

18. Hagood, *Presidential Sex*, 116.

19. Ibid., 117; Persico, *Franklin and Lucy*.

20. Goodwin, *No Ordinary Time*, 221, 222.

21. Robbie Brown and Shaila Dewan, "Mysteries Remain after Governor Admits an Affair," *New York Times*, June 24, 2009.

22. Brown and Dewan, "Mysteries Remain"; Tamara Lush and Evan Berland, "SC Gov 'Crossed Lines' with Women," Associated Press, June 30, 2009. See also Alex Roth and Valerie Bauerlein, "Sanford Says He Had Extramarital Affair," *Wall Street Journal*, June 24, 2009; Cliff LeBlanc and John O'Connor, "Sanford Admits Affair: 'I've Let Down a Lot of People,'" *The State*, June 25, 2009.

23. Brown and Dewan, "Mysteries Remain."

24. Ibid.

25. CNN/Opinion Research Corporation Poll, iPOLL Databank, June 26–28, 2009, http://www.ropercenter.uconn.edu/data_access/ipoll/ipoll.html.

26. "Leadership in South Carolina," *New York Times*, June 26, 2009.

27. Shaila Dewan, "S.C. Panel Kills Measure to Impeach Governor," *New York Times*, December 16, 2009.

28. Robbie Brown, "Sanford's Wife Files for Divorce," *New York Times*, December 11, 2009; Jenny Sanford, *Staying True* (New York: Ballantine, 2010).

29. Ashley Parker, "On Capitol Hill, Sanford Picks Up Where He Left Off," *New York Times*, May 15, 2013.

30. Jonah Goldberg, quoted in Ross Douthat, "Mark Sanford's God," NewYorkTimes.com, May 9, 2013, http://douthat.blogs.nytimes.com/2013/05/09/mark-sanfords-god/.

31. Kim Severson, "Looking Past Sex Scandal, South Carolina Returns Ex-governor to Congress," *New York Times*, May 7, 2013.

32. Nate Silver, "Sanford and the Electoral Effect of Sex Scandals," *New York Times*, May 8, 2013.

33. Garry Wills, *The Kennedy Imprisonment: A Meditation on Power* (Boston: Little, Brown, 1982), 17.

34. Tony Sciacca, *Kennedy and His Women* (New York: Manor Books, 1976), 140.

35. Wills, *The Kennedy Imprisonment*, 29–30; Hagood, *Presidential Sex*, 171.

36. Hagood, *Presidential Sex*, 138, 149.

37. Nigel Cawthorne, *Sex Lives of the Presidents: An Irreverent Expose of the Chief Executive from George Washington to the Present Day* (New York: St. Martin's Press, 1998), 219.

38. Hagood, *Presidential Sex*, 170.

39. Ibid., 144, 151.

40. Pamela Druckerman, "Our Ready Embrace of Those Cheating Pols," *Washington Post*, July 15, 2007, B1.

41. Cawthorne, *Sex Lives of the Presidents*, 226–227.

42. Hagood, *Presidential Sex*, 178; Cawthorne, *Sex Lives of the Presidents*, 229.

43. Angie Dickinson, quoted in Hagood, *Presidential Sex*, 168.

44. Robert A. Caro, *The Years of Lyndon Johnson: The Path to Power* (New York: Knopf, 1982), 485.

45. Robert Dallek, *Lone Star Rising: Lyndon Johnson and His Times, 1908–1960* (New York: Oxford University Press, 1991), 189; Druckerman, "Our Ready Embrace of Those Cheating Pols," B1.

46. Hagood, *Presidential Sex*, 187, 194, 195.

47. Shelley Ross, *Fall From Grace: Sex, Scandal, and Corruption in American Politics from 1702 to the Present* (New York: Ballantine, 1988), 209; Carl Rowan, "Move Over, This Is Your President," *Buffalo News*, January 28, 1998, B7.

48. Matt Bai, *All the Truth Is Out: The Week Politics Went Tabloid* (New York: Knopf, 2014), 29.

49. Jim McGee, Tom Fielder, and James Savage, "The Gary Hart Scandal: How It Happened," *Miami Herald*, May 10, 1987.

50. Gail Sheehy, "The Road to Bimini: Rebellious Gary Hart Caught Wrong Wave," *Vanity Fair*, September 1987.

51. McGee, Fielder, and Savage, "The Gary Hart Scandal."

52. Tom Morganthau, with Margaret Garrard Warner, Howard Fineman, and Erik Calonius, "The Sudden Fall of Gary Hart," *Newsweek*, May 18, 1987.

53. Paul Taylor, "Playing with Fire: When Gary Hart Destroyed His Own Candidacy, He Also Destroyed the Hopes and Dreams of His Loyal Staff," *Washington Post*, July 12, 1987.

54. E. J. Dionne Jr., David Johnston, Wayne King, and Jon Nordheimer, "Courting Danger: The Fall of Gary Hart," *New York Times*, May 9, 1987.

55. Matt Bai, "How Gary Hart's Downfall Forever Changed American Politics," *New York Times Magazine*, September 18, 2014.

56. McGee, Fielder, and Savage, "The Gary Hart Scandal."

57. "Gary Hart's Judgment," *New York Times*, May 5, 1987, A34.

58. Bai, "How Gary Hart's Downfall."

59. Sheehy, "The Road to Bimini."

60. Morganthau et al., "The Sudden Fall of Gary Hart."

61. Bai, *All the Truth Is Out*, 154–155.

62. Morganthau et al., "The Sudden Fall of Gary Hart."

63. William Raspberry, "Victimized ... by Himself," *Washington Post*, May 6, 1987. See also Laura Stoker, "Judging Presidential Character: The Demise of Gary Hart," *Political Behavior* 15 (1993): 193.

64. Bai, *All the Truth Is Out*, 7, 12–13.

65. Cawthorne, *Sex Lives of the Presidents*, 257.

66. Ken Gormley, *The Death of American Virtue: Clinton vs. Starr* (New York: Crown Publishing, 2010), 10.

67. Peter Baker, *The Breach: Inside the Impeachment and Trial of William Jefferson Clinton* (New York: Scribner, 2000), 34.

68. Robert Busby, *Defending the American Presidency: Clinton and the Lewinsky Scandal* (New York: Palgrave, 2001), 42.

69. Hagood, *Presidential Sex*, 216–217.

70. Busby, *Defending the American Presidency*, 43; Hagood, *Presidential Sex*, 209; David Brock, "His Cheatin' Heart," *American Spectator*, January 1994, 21.

71. For the interview, see www.youtube.com/watch?v=lwXE52e9IFg.

72. Jim Moore, *Clinton: Young Man in a Hurry* (Fort Worth, TX: Summit Group, 1992), 190; Deborah Orr, "Don't Stand by Him, Hillary," *Independent*, March 12, 1999.

73. "Clinton Hires Attorney to Fend Off Sex Suit," *Capital*, May 5, 1994, A2. See also Richard Lacayo, "Jones v. the President," *TIME*, May 16, 1994, 45.

74. Hagood, *Presidential Sex*, 231.

75. Andrew Morton, *Monica's Story* (New York: St. Martin's Press, 1999), 63.

76. Jeffrey Toobin, *A Vast Conspiracy* (New York: Random House, 1999), 85.

77. Morton, *Monica's Story*, 64, 66.

78. Busby, *Defending the American Presidency*, 53.

79. Morton, *Monica's Story*, 80–81.

80. Gormley, *The Death of American Virtue*, 535.

81. Morton, *Monica's Story*, 84.

82. Toobin, *A Vast Conspiracy*, 180.

83. William Jefferson Clinton, *My Life* (New York: Knopf, 2005), 774.

84. Morton, *Monica's Story*, 151–52.

85. Joseph R. Blaney and William L. Benoit, *The Clinton Scandals and the Politics of Image Restoration* (Westport, CT: Praeger, 2001), 85.

86. Toobin, *A Vast Conspiracy*, 244.

87. Deborah L. Rhode, "Conflicts of Commitment: Legal Ethics in the Impeachment Context," *Stanford Law Review* 52 (2000): 269, 317, 318.

88. Don Van Natta Jr., "The Nation: The New Scandalisms; It Depends on What Your Definition of Linguistic Trend Is," *New York Times*, October 17, 1999, A27.

89. Maureen Dowd, "Liberties; The Wizard of Is," *New York Times*, September 16, 1998, 24.

90. Elizabeth Drew, *The Corruption of American Politics: What Went Wrong and Why* (Secaucus, NJ: Carol Publishing Group, 1999), 323–325.

91. For excerpts, see Baker, *The Breach*, 34; James Bennet, "Testing of a President: The Overview: Clinton Admits Lewinsky Liaison to Jury; Tells Nation 'It Was Wrong,' but Private," *New York Times*, August 18, 1998, A1.

92. Blaney and Benoit, *The Clinton Scandals*, 99; CNN/*USA Today*/Gallup Poll, August 17, 1998.

93. Gormley, *The Death of American Virtue*, 559.

94. Hillary Rodham Clinton, *Living History* (New York: Scribner, 2003), 466, 468, 471, 474.

95. House of Representatives, Document Number 105–3111, 393 (E.D. Ark. 1998) (Deposition of William Jefferson Clinton in Jones v. Clinton).

96. Jerry Seper and Paul Bedard, "Friend Jordan Denies Telling Lewinsky to Lie Under Oath," *Washington Times*, January 23, 1998, A12.

97. Gormley, *The Death of American Virtue*, 614–646; Richard A. Posner, *An Affair of State: The Investigation, Impeachment, and Trial of President Clinton* (Cambridge, MA: Harvard University Press, 2009).

98. Molly W. Sonner and Clyde Wilcox, "Forgiving and Forgetting: Public Support for Bill Clinton during the Lewinsky Scandal," *PS: Political Science and Politics* 32 (1999): 557, 554, 556.

99. *Wall Street Journal*/NBC News/Annenberg Center poll, cited in Maureen Dowd, "A Popular President," *New York Times*, July 19, 2014.

100. Busby, *Defending the American Presidency*, 176.

101. Frank Rich, "Journal; Monicagate Year Two," *New York Times*, December 16, 1998.

102. Clinton, *Living History*, 475.

103. Todd Gitlin, "The Clinton-Lewinsky Obsession: How the Press Made a Scandal of Itself," *Washington Monthly*, December 1998.

104. Busby, *Defending the American Presidency*, 182.

105. Gitlin, "The Clinton-Lewinsky Obsession"; Arthur H. Miller, "Sex, Politics, and Public Opinion: What Political Scientists Really Learned from the Clinton-Lewinsky Scandal," *PS: Political Science and Politics* 32 (1999): 721, 724 (noting that even 73 percent of Republican Midwesterners said there was too much coverage).

106. Busby, *Defending the American Presidency*, 210.

107. Blaney and Benoit, *The Clinton Scandals*, 97.

108. Timothy M. Gray, " 'The Clinton Show': 2,406 Days Running," *Variety*, August 24, 1998.

109. Busby, *Defending the American Presidency*, 176.

110. Ibid., 175, 176; Jeremy Varon, "It Was the Spectacle, Stupid: The Clinton-Lewinsky-Starr Affair and the Politics of the Gaze," in *Public Affairs: Politics in the Age of Sex Scandals,* ed. Paul Apostolidis and Juliet A. Williams (Durham, NC: Duke University Press, 2004), 240–241.

111. Gitlin, "The Clinton-Lewinsky Obsession."

112. Sam Howe Verhovek, "Testing of a President: The Critic; Clinton Foe Admits Affair with Married Man," *New York Times,* September 11, 1998, A20.

113. "Second Lawmaker Who Criticized Clinton Admits Affair," *St. Louis Post-Dispatch* (Missouri), September 11, 1998, A8.

114. Verhovek, "Testing of a President," A20.

115. "Second Lawmaker Who Criticized Clinton Admits Affair," A8; "Lives of the Republicans, Part Two," Salon.com, September 16, 1998, http://www.salon.com/news/1998/09/016news.html.

116. Verhovek, "Testing of a President," A20.

117. John Heilemann and Mark Halperin, "Saint Elizabeth and the Ego Monster," *New York Magazine,* January 9, 2010.

118. Andrew Young, *The Politician* (New York: St. Martin's Press, 2010), 167.

119. Ibid., 221.

120. Heilemann and Halperin, "Saint Elizabeth."

121. Howard Kurtz and Lois Romano, "Edwards Admits He Had an Affair: Ex-candidate Says He Didn't Father Baby with Campaign Worker," *Washington Post,* August 9, 2008.

122. Howard Kurtz, "Tabloid Takedown: That No One Else Would Touch, Altered a Presidential Election and Earned Journalistic Credibility Overnight," *Playboy,* March 1, 2011.

123. Katherine A. Seelye, "Edwards Admits to Affair in 2006," *New York Times,* August 8, 2008.

124. Young, *The Politician,* 288–289. In an accompanying statement, he similarly confessed that he had become "increasingly egocentric and narcissistic." Kurtz and Romano, "Edwards Admits He Had an Affair."

125. Heilemann and Halperin, "Saint Elizabeth."

126. Maureen Dowd, "Keeping It Rielle," *New York Times,* August 9, 2008.

127. Gabriel Sherman, "After the Fall," *New Republic,* June 30, 2010.

128. Kim Severson, "Justice Dept. Will Not Retry Edwards in Corruption Case," *New York Times*, June 14, 2012.

129. Peter Lattman and Kim Severson, "John Edwards Revisits His Past, Hanging Out Law Shingle Again," *New York Times*, November 18, 2013.

130. Sherman, "After the Fall."

131. "The Vitter Affair: As It Stands Now," *Your Right Hand Thief*, July 16, 2007, http://righthandthief.blogspot.com/2007/07/laffaire-vitter-as-it-stands-now.html.

132. Adam Nossiter, "A Senator's Moral High Ground Gets a Little Shaky," *New York Times*, July 11, 2007.

133. E. J. Dionne Jr., "Give Him a Break: Sen. Vitter Has Sinned, but It's Time to Stop Nosing into Our Politicians' Private Lives," *Pittsburgh Post Gazette*, July 13, 2007, B7.

134. Jan Moller, "David Vitter Sex Scandal Gets Spotlight Again in Debate with Charlie Melancon," *Times-Picayune*, October 28, 2010.

135. "Poll: Vitter's 'Serious Sin' Apparently Not Seriously Damaging," *Politico*, August 20, 2007, http://www.politico.com/blogs/thecrypt/0807/Poll_Vitters_serious_sin_apparently_not_seriously_damaging.html.

136. Bruce Eggler, "Wendy Vitter Has Never Been Shy about Standing Her Ground," *Times-Picayune*, July 23, 2007.

137. David Kocieniewski and Danny Hakim, "Felled by Scandal, Spitzer Says Focus Is on His Family," *New York Times*, March 13, 2008.

138. Laura Kipnis, *How to Become a Scandal: Adventures in Bad Behavior* (New York: Metropolitan Books, 2010), 5.

139. Don Van Natta Jr. and Jo Becker, "Spitzer Fall Began with Bank Reports," *New York Times*, March 13, 2008.

140. Danny Hakim and William K. Rashbaum, "Spitzer, Linked to a Sex Ring as a Client, Gives an Apology," *New York Times*, March 11, 2008, A1.

141. Alan Feuer and Ian Urbina, "Client 9 in Room 871: Notes on a Rendezvous," *New York Times*, March 11, 2008, B1.

142. William K. Rashbaum, "18 Arrested in Lucrative Prostitution Ring out of Staten Island," *New York Times*, April 8, 2004; Nina Bernstein, "Foes of Sex Are Stung by the Fall of an Ally," *New York Times*, March 12, 2008.

143. Bernstein, "Foes of Sex Are Stung by the Fall of an Ally."

144. Evan Thomas, "His Dark Journey," *Newsweek*, March 15, 2008.

145. Martha Nussbaum, "Trading on America's Puritanical Streak," *Atlanta Journal-Constitution*, March 14, 2008.

146. Jane Ridley, "Pain of Eliot Spitzer Scandal for Ex-governor's Wife Silda Recalled on New CBS Show 'Good Wife,'" *New York Daily News*, September 2, 2009.

147. Barbara Ross, "Eliot Spitzer and Longtime Wife Silda Wall File Divorce Papers," *New York Daily News*, January 16, 2014.

148. Kipnis, *How to Become a Scandal*, 8. The discussion in this section draws on Deborah L. Rhode, *Lawyers as Leaders* (New York: Oxford University Press, 2013), 109.

149. Laura Kipnis, *Against Love: A Polemic* (New York: Pantheon, 2003).

150. G. R. Goethals, David W. Messick, and S. T. Allison, "The Uniqueness Bias: Studies of Constructive Social Comparison," in *Social Comparison: Contemporary Theory and Research*, ed. Jerry M. Suls and Thomas Ashby Wills (Hillsdale, NJ: Lawrence Erlbaum, 1991), 149, 161–162.

151. Eric Dezenhall, quoted in John Schwartz, "Résumés Made for Fibbing," *New York Times*, May 22, 2010.

152. Piercarlo Valdesolo and David DeSteno, "The Duality of Virtue: Deconstructing the Moral Hypocrite," *Journal of Experimental Social Psychology* 44 (2008): 1334.

153. Joris Lammers, Diederick A. Stapel, and Adam D. Galinsky, "Power Increases Hypocrisy: Moralizing in Reasoning, Immorality in Behavior," *Psychological Science* 21 (2010): 737.

154. See surveys cited in ibid., 738; Adam D. Galinsky, Joe C. Magee, Deborah H. Gruenfeld, Jennifer A. Whitson, and Katie A. Liljenquist, "Power Reduces the Press of the Situation: Implications for Creativity, Conformity, and Dissonance," *Journal of Personality and Social Psychology* 95 (2008): 1450.

155. Roy F. Baumeister and John Tierney, *Willpower: Rediscovering the Greatest Human Strength* (New York: Penguin, 2011); Stephanie Rosenbloom, "Ambition + Desire = Trouble," *New York Times*, June 17, 2011.

156. For Democratic strategist Celinda Lake on the public's tendency to be more judgmental about women than men, see Sheryl Gay Stolberg, "Naked

Hubris: When It Comes to Scandal, Girls Won't Be Boys," *New York Times,* June 11, 2011. For Northwestern professor Gunnbjorg Lavoll's explanation of the harsher social consequences for women, see Julia Baird, Newsweek, Girls Will Be Girls. Or Not," *Newsweek,* March 22, 2008, http://www.newsweek.com/girls-will -be-girls-or-not-84327. On the higher frequency of infidelity in men and its social acceptance, see Ronald F. Levant and Gary R. Brooks, *Men and Sex: New Psychological Perspectives* (New York: John Wiley, 1997), 84, 87.

157. Lionel Tiger, quoted in Rebecca Dana, "Why Women Don't Have Sex Scandals," *Daily Beast,* December 10, 2009.

158. Stolberg, "Naked Hubris," WKI.

159. CNN/Opinion Research Corporation Poll, iPOLL Databank, June 26–28, 2009. Those with some high school education were the least likely to think voters should know about politicians' adultery (57 percent), and those with some college education were the most likely to think voters should know (67 percent). Men were more likely (66 percent) than women (56 percent) to think voters should know about politicians' adultery, and Republicans were more likely (66 percent) than Democrats (59 percent).

160. Druckerman, "Our Ready Embrace of Those Cheating Pols."

161. Campbell Robertson, "Politicians Are Slowed by Scandal, but Many Still Win the Race," *New York Times,* July 17, 2013; Druckerman, "Our Ready Embrace of Those Cheating Pols."

162. William Bennett, quoted in Gerard Baker, "Sex Americana," *Wall Street Journal,* July 8, 2009.

163. Shelly Russ, *Fall from Grace: Sex, Scandal, and Corruption in American Politics from 1702 to the Present* (Boston: Ballantine Books, 1988), 241.

164. Danny Hakim and Trymaine Lee, "New Governor and Wife Talk of Past Affairs," *New York Times,* March 19, 2008, A1; Ben Lesser, Joe Mahoney, and Greg Smith, "Gov. Paterson Says He May Have Used Campaign Cash for Hotel Hookup," *New York Daily News,* March 20, 2008; see also Mike McIntire, "Paterson Says He Would Have Repaid Any Personal Use of His Campaign Funds," *New York Times,* March 19, 2008.

165. David L. Rosenhan, "Moral Character," *Stanford Law Review* 27 (1975): 925, 926. See also Walter Mischel, *Personality and Assessment* (New York: Wiley, 1968), 21–26.

166. Hugh Hartshorne and Mark A. May, *Studies in the Nature of Character: Studies in Deceit,* (New York: Macmillan, 1928), bk. 1, 377–390, 407–412; bk. 2, 211–221. See also Mischel, *Personality and Assessment,* 250–326; Daryl J. Bem and Andrea Allen, "On Predicting Some of the People Some of the Time: The Search for Cross-situational Consistencies in Behavior," *Psychological Review* 81 (1974): 506; Walter Mishel and Yuichi Shoda, "A Cognitive Affective System Theory of Personality: Reconceptualizing Situations, Dispositions, Dynamics and Invariance in Personality Structure," *Psychological Review* 102 (1995): 246.

167. Hartshorne and May, *Studies in Deceit,* bk. 2, 211–221.

168. Samuel D. Warren and Louis Brandeis, "The Right to Privacy," *Harvard Law Review* 4 (1890): 196.

169. Bai, *All the Truth Is Out,* 23.

7. International Perspectives

1. Maïa de la Baume, "State Secret Revealed: Mitterrand as a Doting Father," *New York Times,* November 30, 2012.

2. Robert Herriman, "Poll: ~75% of Muslims in Egypt, Pakistan Favor Stoning People for Adultery," Examiner.com, December 6, 2010, http://www .examiner.com/article/poll-75-of-muslims-egypt-pakistan-favor-stoning-people -for-adultery; "Stoning Adulterers," Pew Research Center, January 18, 2011, http://www.pewresearch.org/daily-number/stoning-adulterers/ (82 percent).

3. David P. Schmitt, "Patterns and Universals of Mate Poaching across 53 Nations: The Effects of Sex, Culture, and Personality on Romantically Attracting Another Person's Partner," *Journal of Personality and Social Psychology* 86 (2004): 560, 561 (10 to 25 percent); Pamela Druckerman, *Lust in Translation: Infidelity from Tokyo to Tennessee* (New York: Penguin, 2007), 58 (rates as low as 2 percent).

4. Druckerman, *Lust in Translation,* 58.

5. "Global Sex Survey 2005," Durex, 2005, http://www.comodo.it/global _survey/global_sex_survey_2005.pdf; "Sexual Wellbeing Survey," Durex, 2011, http://www.durex.com/EN-CA/SEXUALWELLBEINGSURVEY/pages /default.aspx.

6. Saksith Saiyasombut and Siam Voices, "Are Thais Really the Most Adulterous Couples in the World?," *Asian Correspondent,* August 29, 2012,

http://asiancorrespondent.com/88503/are-thais-really-the-most-adulterous
-couples-in-the-world/.

7. Eric D. Widmer, Judith Treas, and Robert Newcomb, "Attitudes toward Nonmarital Sex in 24 Countries," *Journal of Sex Research* 35 (1998): 349, 351.

8. Susan Sachs, "Adultery a Crime? The Turks Think Again and Say No," *New York Times*, September 15, 2004, http://www.nytimes.com/2004/09/15 /international/europe/15turkey.html; Nora Fisher Onar and Meltem Müftüler-Baç, "The Adultery and Headscarf Debates in Turkey: Fusing 'EU-niversal' and 'Alternative' Modernities," *Women's Studies International Forum* 34 (2011): 378, 384–385.

9. Sachs, "Adultery a Crime?"

10. International Models Project on Women's Rights, "Current Legal Framework: Adultery in Romania," impowr.org, April 30, 2013, http://www .impowr.org/content/current-legal-framework-adultery-romania.

11. The crime of adultery was abolished in England in 1857, in Ireland in 1976, and in Germany in 1969. Frances Raday, "Background Information on Statements Issued by the Working Group," paper presented by the UN Working Group on the Issue of Discrimination against Women in Law and in Practice, Geneva, Switzerland, October 18, 2012; International Models Project on Women's Rights, "Summary: Adultery in Germany," impowr.org, June 5, 2013, http://www .impowr.org/content/summary-adultery-germany.

12. "No one shall be subjected to arbitrary or unlawful interference with his privacy, family, home or correspondence, nor to unlawful attacks on his honour and reputation." International Covenant on Civil and Political Rights, Article 17(1).

13. Raday, "Background Information."

14. Convention on the Elimination of All Forms of Discrimination against Women, Article 16.

15. Raday, "Background Information."

16. Office of the High Commissioner for Human Rights, "Statement by the United Nations Working Group on the Issue of Discrimination against Women in Law and in Practice," UNHR, October 18, 2012, http://www.ohchr.org/EN /NewsEvents/Pages/DisplayNews.aspx?NewsID=12672&.

17. Raday, "Background Information."

18. Widmer, Treas, and Newcomb, "Attitudes toward Nonmarital Sex in 24 Countries," 352.

19. Richard Wike, "French More Accepting of Infidelity than People in Other Countries," Pew Research Center, January 14, 2014, http://www.pewresearch.org /fact-tank/2014/01/14/french-more-accepting-of-infidelity-than-people-in -other-countries/.

20. Forty-seven percent of respondents in France believed that married people having an affair was "morally unacceptable," while "12% say it is actually morally acceptable." Ibid.

21. Ibid.

22. Elaine Sciolino, "A Tell-All's Tale: French Politicians Stray Early and Often," *New York Times,* October 17, 2006.

23. "Ex-IMF Chief Strauss-Kahn Takes Job as Bank Boss," *France 24,* September 25, 2013, http://www.france24.com/en/20130925-france-strauss -kahn-takes-job-head-investment-firm/.

24. Kim Willsher, "Dominique Strauss-Kahn Fails to Have Kiss-and-Tell Book Banned," *Guardian,* February 26, 2013, http://www.theguardian.com/world /2013/feb/26/dominique-strauss-kahn-fails-book-banned.

25. Doreen Carvajal and Maïa de la Baume, "Sex Life Was 'Out of Step,' Strauss-Kahn Says, but Not Illegal," *New York Times,* October 13, 2012.

26. "Ex-IMF Chief Strauss-Kahn Takes Job as Bank Boss."

27. Druckerman, *Lust in Translation,* 115, 116, 126, 143.

28. Associated Press, "Prince Charles to Marry Camilla Parker Bowles," FOX News, February 10, 2005, http://www.foxnews.com/story/2005/02/10/prince -charles-to-marry-camilla-parker-bowles/.

29. "The Camillagate Transcript," Gossip/News, recorded December 31, 1989, http://www.geocities.ws/rickanddarvagossip/camillagate.html.

30. Associated Press, "Prince Charles to Marry Camilla Parker Bowles."

31. "The Big Story: It's Just the Robinson's Family Affair," Independent.ie, August 18, 2014, http://www.independent.ie/irish-news/politics/the-big-story -its-just-the-robinsons-family-affair-30505733.html.

32. "The Many Trials of Silvio Berlusconi Explained," BBC, May 9, 2014, http://www.bbc.com/news/world-europe-12403119.

33. Ariel Levy, "Basta Bunga Bunga," *New Yorker,* June 6, 2011; Alexander Stille, *The Sack of Rome: Media + Money + Celebrity = Power = Silvio Berlusconi* (New York: Penguin, 2007).

34. CNN Staff, "Italy's Silvio Berlusconi, 76, Reveals Plans to Marry 27-Year-Old," CNN World, December 19, 2012, http://www.cnn.com/2012/12 /18/world/europe/italy-berlusconi-engaged/.

35. "Silvio Berlusconi Sex Conviction Overturned," BBC, July 18, 2014, http://www.bbc.com/news/world-europe-28369408.

36. Article 7 of the EU Charter contains a right to respect for private and family life. European Union Agency for Fundamental Rights, "Information Society, Privacy and Data Protection," FRA (January 2014), http://fra.europa.eu /en/theme/information-society-privacy-and-data-protection. In *Metropolitan Church of Bessarabia v. Moldova,* the European Court of Human Rights outlined an associational right for religious groups, which included protection against state interference. Jim Murdoch, "Protecting the Right to Freedom of Thought, Conscience and Religion under the European Convention on Human Rights," *Council of Europe,* 2012, 23.

37. Schüth v. Germany, unreported, Application No. 1620/03 (ECHR Sept. 23, 2010).

38. Obst v. Germany, unreported, Application No. 425/03 (ECHR Sept. 23, 2010).

39. Josep Ferrer Riba, "Domestic Relations," *InDret,* 2001, 4, http://www .indret.com/pdf/065_en.pdf.

40. International Models Project on Women's Rights, "Summary: Adultery in Germany"; Brigitte Ecolivet-Herzog, "The New French Divorce Law," *The International Lawyer* 11 (1977): 201, 202; International Models Project on Women's Rights, "Current Legal Framework: Adultery in Russian Federation," impowr.org, January 16, 2013, http://www.impowr.org/content/current-legal -framework-adultery-russian-federation.

41. Ecolivet-Herzog, "The New French Divorce Law," 209–210, 213, 206, 207, 208.

42. Erin Iungerich, "Provocation Excuse: Using International Laws and Norms to Give Perspective in the Domestic Sphere," *Law Journal for Social Justice* 4 (2013): 43, http://ljsj.files.wordpress.com/2014/01/iungerich-provocation-excuse.pdf.

43. James Slack, "Judges Sink Harriet Harman's 'Obnoxious' Plan to Strip Men of Infidelity Murder Defence," *Daily Mail*, October 28, 2009, http://www .dailymail.co.uk/news/article-1223367/Judges-sink-Harriet-Harmans-obnoxious -plan-to-strip-men-of-infidelity-murder-defence.

44. R. v. Clinton, [2012]EWCA Crim. 2, [2012]I Cr. App. R. 26 (Jan. 17, 2012); Vera Baird, "'Infidelity Plus'—The New Defense against Murder," *Guardian*, January 23, 2012, http://www.theguardian.com/commentisfree/2012 /jan/23/infidelity-plus-defence-murder.

45. "Poll Reveals Face of Russian Adulterer," *Russia Today*, May 25, 2010, http://rt.com/news/poll-face-russian-adulterer/.

46. Widmer, Treas, and Newcomb, "Attitudes toward Nonmarital Sex in 24 Countries."

47. International Models Project on Women's Rights, "Current Legal Framework: Adultery in Russian Federation."

48. Julia Ioffe, "The Cheating Cheaters of Moscow: How Infidelity Has Become Accepted and Even Expected in Russia," *Slate*, December 1, 2010, http://www.slate.com/articles/d.ouble_x/doublex/2010/12/the_cheating _cheaters_of_moscow.single.html.

49. Irina Tartakovskaya, quoted in ibid.

50. "Those Cheating Hearts," *Australian*, September 8, 2007, http://www .theaustralian.com.au/arts/those-cheating-hearts/story -e6frg8n6-1111114340479?nk=7db37b8ace7d2f9d3bb3a7d6d3e6d49d.

51. "Kremlin Sex, Lies and Videotape," CBS News, March 18, 1999, http://www.cbsnews.com/news/kremlin-sex-lies-and-videotape/.

52. Natalya Shulyakovskaya, "Skuratov Campaigns to Reveal Real Putin," *Moscow Times*, January 27, 2000, http://www.themoscowtimes.com/news/article /skuratov-campaigns-to-reveal-real-putin/267483.html.

53. Thomas Grove and Timothy Heritage, "Russian Defence Chief Crossed Putin's Political 'Family,'" Reuters, *Chicago Tribune*, November 8, 2012, http:// articles.chicagotribune.com/2012-11-08/news/sns-rt-russia-defencescandal -pixl5e8m7jam-20121108_1_russian-defence-serdyukov-viktor-zubkov.

54. Masha Lipman, "Putin's Circle: Corruption, Connections, and Adultery?," *New Yorker*, November 24, 2012, http://www.newyorker.com/news/news-desk /putins-circle-corruption-connections-and-adultery.

55. Jason Bush, "Russia Grants Amnesty to Former Defence Minister Anatoly Serdyukov—Report," Reuters, March 6, 2014, http://uk.reuters.com/article /2014/03/06/uk-russia-amnesty-serdyukov-idUKBREA250GY20140306.

56. Lipman, "Putin's Circle."

57. Scott Neuman, "Putin Divorce Final; Ex-wife Expunged from Kremlin Bio," NPR, April 2, 2014, http://www.npr.org/blogs/thetwo-way/2014/04/02 /298367559/putin-divorce-final-ex-wife-expunged-from-kremlin-bio.

58. Masha Lipman, "The Putin Divorce: What Russia's Rulers Hide," *New Yorker*, June 8, 2013, http://www.newyorker.com/news/news-desk/the-putin -divorce-what-russias-rulers-hide.

59. Will Englund, "Hardly a Ripple in Russia Adultery: Allegations Like Those against Clinton Have Been Everyday Life in Russia since the Czars' Days," *Baltimore Sun*, February 1, 1998, http://articles.baltimoresun.com/1998–02–01 /news/1998032036_1_adultery-sexual-harassment-scandal.

60. Li Zhisui, *The Private Life of Chairman Mao*, trans. Tai Hung-Chao (London: Random House, 1996); Emily Honig, "Socialist Sex: The Cultural Revolution Revisited," *Modern China* 29 (April 2003): 143.

61. Druckerman, *Lust in Translation*, 254.

62. Cameron Frecklington, "China: The Next Market for the World's Top Adultery Site," *Atlantic*, May 28, 2014.

63. James Farrer, quoted in Frecklington, "China."

64. Elaine Jeffreys, "Regulating Private Affairs in Contemporary China: Private Investigators and the Policing of Spousal Infidelity," *China Information* 24 (2010): 149, 151, 159–160.

65. Ronald C. Keith and Zhiqiu Lin, *New Crime in China: Public Order and Human Rights* (New York: Routledge, 2006), 73.

66. Marriage Law of the People's Republic of China, Chapter 4, Article 32, http://newyork.china-consulate.org/eng/lsqz/laws/t42222.htm#M.

67. Liu Minghui, "Adultery Is More of a Moral than Legal Crime," *China Daily*, July 3, 2014, http://www.chinadaily.com.cn/opinion/2014–07/03/content _17639210.htm.

68. "Chinese Communist Party Satirized as 'The Adultery Party,'" *New Tang Dynasty Television*, July 5, 2014, http://www.ntd.tv/en/programs/news-politics /china-forbidden-news/20140705/168291-chinese-communist-party-satirized

-as-39the-adultery-party39-.html; Adam Taylor, "It's Official: The Chinese Government Is at War with Adultery," *Washington Post*, July 16, 2014.

69. Taylor, "It's Official."

70. Tom Phillips, "Chinese Official Shamed over Adultery 'Contract' that Fines Bad Behaviour," *Telegraph*, November 18, 2013.

71. Taylor, "It's Official."

72. "'Jealous Husband' Sentenced to Death for China Killings," BBC, August 12, 2014, http://www.bbc.com/news/world-asia-28751231.

73. Indian Penal Code Section 497. See also "Thou Shalt Not Covet Thy Neighbour's Wife," *Telegraph* (India), July 20, 2011.

74. "Thou Shalt Not Covet Thy Neighbour's Wife."

75. Sadhana Ramachandran, quoted in Armit Dhillon, "Court Could Punish Errant Wives," *Gulf News*, January 7, 2009.

76. Sandhya Gokhale, quoted in Mini Pant Zachariah, "From Bed to Worse," *Hindustan Times*, December 22, 2008.

77. Satish Maneshinde, quoted in ibid.

78. V. S. Malimath, quoted in "Thou Shalt Not Covet Thy Neighbour's Wife."

79. Girja Vyas, quoted in Dhillon, "Court Could Punish Errant Wives."

80. Amrit Dhillon, "Activists Target Adultery Law," *South China Morning Post*, April 17, 2007.

81. Lynn Berat, "The Role of Conciliation in the Japanese Legal System," *American University International Law Review* 8 (1992): 125, 131.

82. Mark McLelland, *Love, Sex, and Democracy in Japan during the American Occupation* (New York: Palgrave Macmillan, 2012), 49.

83. Druckerman, *Lust in Translation*.

84. Steven R. Weisman, "Ex-geisha Accuses Uno of a Dangerous Liaison," *New York Times*, June 10, 1989; "Japanese Party Starts Searching for Uno Successor," philly.com, July 25, 1989, philly.com/1989-07-25/news/26133051_1_japanese-party-Idp-prime-minister-sosuke-uno.o.

85. Jake Adelstein, "Equal-Opportunity Infidelity Comes to Japan," *Japan Times*, July 6, 2013, http://www.japantimes.co.jp/news/2013/07/06/national/media-national/equal-opportunity-infidelity-comes-to-japan/#.VAOI5TJdWSo.

86. Andrew Miller, "14.8% of Japanese Housewives Claim to Have Committed Adultery," *Japan Today*, January 12, 2013, http://www.japantoday.com/category /lifestyle/view/14-8-of-japanese-housewives-claim-to-have-committed-adultery.

87. Yuri Kageyama, "Adultery Site Is Big in Japan," *USA Today*, April 2, 2014, http://www.usatoday.com/story/tech/2014/04/02/adultery-site-japan/7192969/.

88. "Japanese Have Taste for Infidelity," Stuff.co.nz, March 4, 2014, http://www.stuff.co.nz/world/asia/9898314/Japanese-have-taste-for-infidelity.

89. Sofia Mitra-Thakur, "Adultery Website Signs Up 12,000 Hongkongers in Just One Week," *South China Morning Post*, August 29, 2013, http://www.scmp .com/news/hong-kong/article/1300381/adultery-dating-website-founder-im -not-devil.

90. Taiwan's Criminal Code, Article 239, quoted in "Taiwan's Archaic Adultery Law," *Asia Sentinel*, June 19, 2013, http://www.asiasentinel.com/society /taiwans-archaic-adultery-law/; Irene Lin, "Decriminalization of Adultery Discussed," *Taipei Times*, January 3, 2000, http://www.taipeitimes.com/News /local/archives/2000/01/03/18080.

91. "Taiwan's Archaic Adultery Law."

92. "Adultery Law Debate Reignited," *Taiwan Insights*, March 27, 2013, http://toddywang.pixnet.net/blog/pst/50214362-%5B2013-07-31-shane%5D -adultery-law-debate-reognited.

93. Lin, "Decriminalization of Adultery Discussed."

94. Yao Shu-wen, quoted in "Adultery Law Debate Reignited."

95. Huang Ja-lei, quoted in Lin, "Decriminalization of Adultery Discussed."

96. "Taiwan's Archaic Adultery Law."

97. Jeremy D. Morley, "Korean Adultery Law," Law Offices of Jeremy D. Morley, International Family Law, http://www.international-divorce.com /adultery-law-korea.htm; "Adultery Law Upheld by Slimmest Margin," *Chosunilbo*, October 31, 2008.

98. Choe Sang-Hun, "Koreans Agog as Off-Screen Soap Becomes Court-room Drama," *New York Times*, May 19, 2008, http://www.nytimes.com/2008/05 /19/world/asia/19adultery.html?pagewanted=all&_r=0.

99. Ibid.

100. Morley, "Korean Adultery Law."

101. Choe, "Koreans Agog."

102. "Korean Adulterer Faces Jail Term," BBC, November 26, 2008, http://news.bbc.co.uk/2/hi/asia-pacific/7750538.stm; Joohee Cho, "Why Is Adultery So Popular in South Korea?," ABC News, December 19, 2008, http://blogs.abcnews.com/worldview/2008/12/why-is-adultery.html.

103. Choe, "Koreans Agog."

104. "Why Is Adultery So Popular in South Korea?"

105. For general descriptions of the reasoning of the court's nine judges for holding the law constitutional or unconstitutional, see "Adultery Law Upheld by Slimmest Margin."

106. "Ok So-ri: South Korean Actress Found Guilty of Adultery," *Huffington Post*, January 17, 2009, http://www.huffingtonpost.com/2008/12/17/ok-sori-south-korean-actr_n_151671.html.

107. "Why Is Adultery So Popular in South Korea?" (50 percent); Choe, "Koreans Agog" (70 percent); Kim Myun Joong, "Should Adultery Be a Crime?," Law Offices of Jeremy D. Morley, International Family Law, http://www.international-divorce.com/korea;should-adultery-be-a-crime (69 percent).

108. Choe, "Koreans Agog."

109. Yang Hai Kyoung, quoted in Joong, "Should Adultery Be a Crime?"

110. Choe, "Koreans Agog."

111. Leila Linhares Barsted and Jacqueline Hermann, "Legal Doctrine and the Gender Issue in Brazil," *Journal of Gender, Social Policy, and the Law* 7 (1999): 235, 243, http://www.wcl.american.edu/journal/genderlaw/07/barsted.pdf.

112. International Models Project on Women's Rights, "Current Legal Framework: Adultery in Brazil," impowr.org, October 29, 2013, http://www.impowr.org/content/current-legal-framework-adultery-brazil#footnote1_35k5wx3.

113. "Headliners: On Their Honor," *New York Times*, March 31, 1991, http://www.nytimes.com/1991/03/31/weekinreview/headliners-on-their-honor.html.

114. "Decriminalization of Adultery and Defenses," United Nations Entity for Gender Equality and the Empowerment of Women, 2012, http://www.endvawnow.org/en/articles/738-decriminalization-of-adultery-and-defenses.html.

115. "Convention on the Elimination of All Forms of Discrimination against Women," CEDAW/C/ARG/2/Add.2 (English translation), CEDAW, United Nations, August 18, 1994, http://www.un.org/esa/documents/ga/cedaw/17

/country/Argentina/cedawc-arg2add2en.HTM; International Models Project on Women's Rights, "Current Legal Framework: Adultery in Argentina," impowr .org, August 27, 2012, http://www.impowr.org/content/current-legal-framework -adultery-argentina.

116. Wike, "French More Accepting of Infidelity."

117. Pamela Druckerman, quoted in Emma Bovary, "Those Cheating Hearts," *Australian*, September 8, 2007, http://www.theaustralian.com.au/arts/those -cheating-hearts/story-e6frg8n6–1111114340479?nk=7db37b8ace7d2f9d3bb3a7 d6d3e6d49d.

118. Elena Arteaga, "Mexico Votes to Take Adultery Off of Its List of Criminal Offenses," KTSM News, March 26, 2011, http://www.ktsm.com /global/mexico-votes-to-take-adultery-off-of-its-list-of-criminal-offense.

119. Bob Tourtellotte, "Mexico Is Most Tolerant Nation for Sex Scandals: Poll," Reuters, September 8, 2011, http://www.reuters.com/article/2011/09/08 /us-sexscandals-poll-idUSTRE7872PG20110908; Megan Gibson, "When It Comes to Sex Scandals, Mexico Is the Most Tolerant Country," *TIME*, September 9, 2011, http://newsfeed.time.com/2011/09/09/when-it-comes-to-sex-scandals -mexico-is-the-most-tolerant-country/.

120. Cyntia Barrera, "Mexican Presidency Front-Runner's Image Used to Promote Adultery," Reuters, June 6, 2012, http://www.reuters.com/article/2012 /06/06/us-mexico-election-penanieto-idUSBRE85512K20120606.

121. "Mexican Politician at Center of Sex Scandal Says He's Victim of 'Media Campaign,'" *Latin American Herald Tribune*, October 10, 2014, http://www.laht.com /article.asp?ArticleId=1895859&CategoryId=14091; "Sex, Politics, and a Headache for Mexico's PRI," Business Insider, *Economist*, April 8, 2014, http://www .businessinsider.com/sex-politics-and-a-headache-for-mexicos-pri-2014-4.

122. Omar Sacirbey, "Shariah 101: What Is It and Why Do States Want to Ban It?," *Washington Post*, July 25, 2013.

123. Emma Batha, "Factbox: Stoning—Where Does It Happen?," Thompson Reuters Foundation, September 29, 2013, http://www.trust.org/item/2013 0927165059-w9g0i. See also "Stoning: Legal or Practised in 16 Countries and Showing No Signs of Abating," WLUML's Submission to the UN Secretary General on the Question of the Death Penalty to the 27th Session of the Human Rights Council, Women Living under Muslim Laws, March, 2014.

124. See, for example, U.S. Department of State, *United Arab Emirates 2013 Human Rights Report,* Bureau of Democracy, Human Rights, and Labor (2013); "Qatar—Cleric Says Adultery Not Punishable by Stoning Death under Sharia Law," *A Big Message,* May 12, 2013, http://www.abigmessage.com/qatar-cleric-says -adultery-not-punishable-by-stoning-death-under-sharia-law.html.

125. Gamil Muhammed Hussein, "Basic Guarantees in the Islamic Criminal Justice System," in *Criminal Justice in Islam: Judicial Procedure in the* Shari'a, ed. Muhammad Abdel Haleem, Adel Omar Sherif, and Kate Daniels (New York: I. B. Taurus and Co., 2003), 37–38.

126. Sarah Crutcher, "Stoning Single Nigerian Mothers for Adultery: Applying Feminist Theory to an Analysis of Gender Discrimination in International Law," *Hastings Women's Law Journal* 15 (2004): 239, 248; David Smith, "Sudanese Woman Sentenced to Stoning Death over Adultery Claims," *Guardian,* May 31, 2012.

127. Crutcher, "Stoning Single Nigerian Mothers," 239–240.

128. Raday, "Background Information."

129. Gul Yousafzai, "Pakistani Couple Stoned to Death for Adultery; Six Arrested," Reuters, February 17, 2014, http://www.reuters.com/article/2014/02 /17/us-pakistan-couple-stoned-idUSBREAIGI8F20140217; Annabel Symington, "'Adulterous' Couple Illegally Stoned to Death in Remote Pakistan," *Times* (London), February 17, 2014.

130. Smith, "Sudanese Woman Sentenced to Stoning Death."

131. Benjamin Weinthal, "Embracing the Stone Age: Iran Retains Medieval Penalty for Adultery," FOX News, June 5, 2013, http://www.foxnews.com/world /2013/06/05/embracing-stone-age-iran-retains-medieval-penalty-for-adultery/.

132. Human Rights Watch, *"I Had to Run Away": The Imprisonment of Women and Girls for "Moral Crimes" in Afghanistan* (New York: Human Rights Watch, 2012), 75.

133. Quentin Sommerville, "Woman Stoned to Death in North Afghanistan," RAWA News, January 27, 2011.

134. Freidoune Sahebjam, *The Stoning of Soraya M.,* trans. Richard Seaver (New York: Arcade Publishing, 2011).

135. Daniel Howden, "'Don't Kill Me,' She Screamed. Then They Stoned Her to Death," *Independent,* November 9, 2008, http://www.independent.co.uk/news /world/africa/dont-kill-me-she-screamed-then-they-stoned-her-to-death

-1003462.html; "Somalia: Girl Stoned Was a Child of 13," Amnesty International UK, press release, November 1, 2008, http://www.amnesty.org.uk/press-releases/somalia-girl-stoned-was-child-13; Raday, "Background Information."

136. Lawal did not confess four times as required by Sharia law. Kia N. Roberts, "Constitutionality of Shari'a Law in Nigeria and the Higher Conviction Rate of Muslim Women under Shari'a Fornication and Adultery Laws," *Southern California Review of Law and Women's Studies* 14 (2005): 315, 322; Somini Sengupta, "Facing Death for Adultery, Nigerian Woman Is Acquitted," *New York Times,* September 26, 2003. For a history of the case, see Crutcher, Stoning Single Nigerian Mothers.

137. See, for example, Sara Hossain and Lynn Welchman, *"Honour": Crimes, Paradigms, and Violence against Women* (New York: Zed Books, 2005); Ziba Mir-Hosseini and Vanja Hamzić, *Control and Sexuality: The Revival of* Zina *Laws in Muslim Contexts* (London: Women Living under Muslim Laws, 2010).

138. "Pregnant Woman Set Afire," *Hindustan Times,* October 24, 2005.

139. Hakim Almasmari, "Yemen: Honor Crimes—Injustice for Women," Women Living under Muslim Laws, October 3, 2006, http://www.wluml.org/node/3229.

140. "Broken Bodies, Shattered Minds: Torture and Ill-treatment of Women," Amnesty International, March 6, 2001, http://www.amnesty.org/en/documents/ACT40/001/2001/en.

141. John Alan Cohan, "Honor Killings and the Cultural Defense," *California Western International Law Journal* 40 (2010): 177, 192.

142. Hillary Mayell, "Thousands of Women Killed for Family 'Honor,'" *National Geographic,* February 12, 2002, http://news.nationalgeographic.com/news/2002/02/0212_020212_honorkilling.html; Cohan, "Honor Killings," 199.

143. Ahmed Ali Brohi, "A Sociological Analysis of Honor Killing in Pakistan: A Case of Sindh Province," *New Horizons* 4 (2010): 13.

144. Cohan, "Honor Killings," 196.

145. "Killings of Women in Pakistan and Afghanistan 'Tragic Reminder of an Increasing Global Concern,'" Targeted News Service, July 18, 2012.

146. Lama Abu Odeh, "Honor Killings and the Construction of Gender in Arab Societies," *American Journal of Comparative Law* 58 (2010): 911, 915.

147. Anne-Marie O'Connor, "Anger among Palestinians as Honor Killings Spike," *Washington Post,* March 4, 2014.

148. Sarah Rainsford, "'Honour' Crime Defiance in Turkey," BBC, October 19, 2005, http://news.bbc.co.uk/2/hi/europe/4357158.stm.

149. Hamid Shalizi and Amie Ferris-Rotman, "Taliban Publicly Execute Woman Near Kabul: Officials," Reuters, July 7, 2012.

150. Barbara Surk, "Sally Antia, Mark Hawkins Sentenced 2 Months for Adultery in Dubai," *Huffington Post*, July 3, 2009, http://www.huffingtonpost.com/2009/06/02/sally-antia-mark-hawkins_n_210338.html.

151. Somini Sengupta, "The World; When Do-Gooders Don't Know What They're Doing," *New York Times*, May 11, 2003; Ayesha Iman and Sindi Medar-Gould, "How Not to Help Amina Lawal: The Hidden Dangers of Letter Campaigns," *CounterPunch*, May 15, 2003.

8. Conclusion

1. Oliver Wendell Holmes, "The Path of the Law," *Harvard Law Review* 10 (1897): 457, 459.

Acknowledgments

This book owes many debts. I am deeply grateful to Thomas LeBien at Harvard University Press, who supported and improved this project from the outset and shepherded it through publication. I am also indebted to Gagan Gupta, Brittany Marie Jones, and Lisa Valenti-Jordan for their excellent research, and Eun Sze and Ashley Moore for their superb help in preparing the manuscript for publication. The staff of the Stanford Law library provided invaluable reference assistance: Sean Kaneshiro, Marion Miller, Sonia Moss, Rich Porter, Rachael Samberg, Sergio Stone, George Vizvary, Erika Wayne, Beth Williams, and George Wilson. This book is dedicated to Lawrence Friedman, in gratitude for his insightful comments and mentorship over three decades. Finally, I owe my greatest debt to my husband, Ralph Cavanagh, whose support and editorial guidance made this book possible.

Index